Ageing

Perspectival Explorations
towards Theo-gerontology

Ageing

Perspectival Explorations towards Theo-gerontology

Editor

Songram Basumatary

Gurukul Lutheran Theological College & Research Institute

Christian World Imprints

First Published in 2020 by

Gurukul Publications
Gurukul Lutheran Theological College & Research Institute
94 Purasawalkam High Road, Kilpauk, Chennai-600010
gltc.principal@gmail.com
www.gltc.edu
Phone: +91 44 42651072

&

Christian World Imprints
Christian Publishing & Books from India
C-3, Wazirpur Industrial Area
Delhi-110052
cwidelhi2017@gmail.com
www.ChristianWorldImprints.com
Phone: +91 11 41526079

ISBN: 978-93-5148-520-9 (HB)
ISBN: 978-93-5148-521-6 (PB)

Printed in India.

Dedicated to
all vulnerable and dependent Aged Women
and Men of contemporary society

Contents

Introduction

A rose is not a rose if it lives for long! The beauty of rose lies not in its charming look and its fragrance, but it is in the ugliness of thorny plant! Life is beautiful, if only it comes out of the thorns! There lies deep philosophical questions on worth of Ageing life: Do anyone love a fading rose? Is Ageing beautiful? Do anyone love greying hair, charmless wrinkling skin, mumbling mouth and voice? Do anyone not afraid of losing the charming and beautiful look and the energetic vigour of body and mind? Do anyone miss to cherish independence, freedom, pleasure, happiness, comfort and other beauties of young age? Do anyone wants the loneliness, pain, dependency, disappointment, displeasure, frustration and the whole host of unpleasant experiences of old age?

It is doubtless truth that 'Ageing' or 'growing old' is a reality in all things and in all living beings. As all things move and change by passing day, human life too moves and changes. And the beauty of reality as a whole and the reality of our life, perhaps is the change. As change occurs, the beauty unfolds. But who can see it and embrace it? The reality check of the contemporary human society shows that the large number of Aged population undergo life on the thorny bush. In the growing individualistic and materialistic world, they are increasingly becoming one of the most vulnerable section of peoples within their own homes and communities. The beauty of their life is outshined with ugliness of their fading life. Their achievements, their knowledge and talents appear worthless and in large cases, they become underserving recipients of care from the young as their condition of being physically weak, fragile, inactive is economically seen as unproductive. In other words, since their worth of human person is measured by physical strength, they are counted as valueless. This, in many societies in large scale, force the Aged people to feel themselves as worthless and useless, if not a burden; and they prefer to be confined themselves to old Aged home or in retirement villages.

The Bible, in number of occasions presents both romantic as well as tragic view of Ageing. Glorious and splendor on the one hand, and troublesome on the other. The long life is a blessing of God and old age is full of experience, treasure of wisdom, discernment and understanding (Prov. 20:29; Job. 12:12; 32:7; Job 32:9). Contrarily, Bible also presents, in number of occasions, old age as curse that needs concern from someone. The very promise and concern of the Lord for the elderly (Isaiah 46:4), prayer for not casting away or forsaking due to lack of strength (Ps. 71:9, 18), and the expression of troublesome life during age of 70 and 80 (Ps. 90:10) suggests the tragic life of Aged people.

We also see similar views in the history of human society at large and the history of the people of faiths in particular. The human reality and history are filled with both glorification and dehumanization of Aged ones. While, in many of the societies and communities of faith and cultures, the Aged ones are honoured and respected; they are also ignored, abandoned and dehumanized because of their burdensome physical condition and psycho-emotional health. In our times now too, we see increasing number of Aged ones living as destitute in shelter homes as well as in their own homes with no one to care for.

Considering such images and realities of Aged people in the past, and more so, in present times, Gurukul Lutheran Theological College and Research Institute has taken yet another bold theological step to make a fresh adventure to address the grave issues facing Aged people in our homes, Church and society at large by organizing Gurukul Summer Institute-2020 with following four key objectives:

- To discover the concept of Ageing in various traditions.
- To analyze the reality of Ageing in the contemporary Church and society.
- To undertake deep reflection on the issue of Ageing from diverse perspectives.
- To develop theological and practical resources to address the issue of Ageing.

In nutshell, the institute envisages to provide viable conceptual reflections and practical responses to the issue that may enhance community care, social security and graceful Ageing. Towards that end, this volume of Gurukul Publications, as an outcome of the institute, is critical theological explorations on the issue of Ageing, not from a mere sympathetic solidarity perspective, i.e., what is to be done for, but from an active participatory perspective, i.e., what they can contribute.

For conceptual clarity and understanding the reality of Ageing as well as for easy access to data available for analysis, the persons over 65 years of age is taken here as 'Ageing' or 'Aged', 'old', 'elderly' person/people. And in order to understand the graveness of the issue and the pressing demand for concern for the Ageing, the data presented in the highlights of "2019 Revision World Population Prospects" of United Nations, Department of Economic and Social Affairs Population Dynamics is used in various essays.[1] This data for the first time in history reveals that persons Aged 65 or above outnumbered children under five years of age globally in 2018. One in 11 (9%) of the world

1 Available at: https://population.un.org/wpp/Publications/Files/WPP2019_Highlights.pdf

population are Aged. It makes an alarming prediction that by 2050 it will be one in six will be over age 65 (16%) and the number of persons Aged 80 years or over is projected to triple, from 143 million in 2019 to 426 million by 2050. And it is more alarming for Europe and Northern America that by 2050, one in four persons could be Aged 65 or over.

This volume contains seventeen essays from multi-disciplinary dimensions. The *first* one in the row is "Problematizing the Epistemological and Practical Issues of Ageing: Blessing or Curse…!" by **M. Peter Singh** in which the author makes conceptual clarifications of the philosophical notions and its trends in Ageing by divesting deep into various philosophical concepts and epistemological constructs on issues relating to Ageing with a brief overview on the contemporary World scenario, and finally makes an ciritical judgement – whether Ageing is a Blessing or a Curse! The author begins with an assumption that though there are certain theoretical and theological constructs available providing some knowledge on the issue, there is no sufficient constructive epistemology which may promote well-being of elders in the families, society and Church. By trying to understand Heidegger's idea of "happy elderly paradox", the author systematically diagnoses the available concepts and theoretical constructs, explores the issues, and confront the existential realities of Ageing. One of the strong challenges posed in this essay is theological reflection-action and ethical choice we need to take in order to make relevant response to the growing trends of indifference towards Aged people. For "Life is an affirmation and is intrinsically valuable" and calls for a moral responsibility of not only bearing the responsibility of care, but also valuing the human value of Aged people.

The *second*, *third* and *fourth* essays in this volume are from Old Testament Perspective. The first one is "'Ageing' in Jewish Interpretations" by **John Samuel** which is a deep rhetorical-analytic narratives of how the Rabbinic Literatures present a joyful and healthy image of Aged people. The author begins with visualization of Jacob, a ninety-seven years old man engaging in a wrestle with an angelic being for several hours and overcoming the mysterious robust person (Genesis 32:25), and then narrates number of other figures in the Bible, and finally concludes with a strong affirmation that "Ageing' is a blessing from God! The author beautifully presents the Biblical view of Ageing in sharp contrast with the view of the utilitarian philosophers. In succinct way, it is argued that the Biblical view of human life is based on creation theology – human beings are created in the image of God. So, all people have intrinsic worth, and the Old age is precious and honourable. The more they grow older, the more they are to be praised. This is why, a revolutionary commandment was introduced by God through Moses: 'Honour your father and mother.' This commandment demands not only a mere honour, but an 'act of human rights.'

Secondly, **Aravind Jeyakumar Moniraj** in his essay presents a complex understanding of Ageing in the Hebrew Bible due to indistinguishability between theological intention and what is sociologically taken for granted. Number of examples show that growing older is not only blessing, but also 'definite testing.' This fact is proved with a critical analysis of Ecclesiastes 12:2-5. The author unravels from various imageries that the old age is a time of affliction, sadness, the fading capacity of joy and so on. There are agony the elderly people undergo different levels in their respective social contexts. As they grow older, feeble, dependent and economically non-productive, their space and voice gradually shrinks and their significance gets diminished. Nevertheless, there is also positive gerontological imageries which present the life of all human persons as precious and sacred. Ageing provides opportunity for increased growth toward maturity and wisdom and the journey of the faith life enables the Aged-people to face difficulties and death with confidence. After making a comparison and contrast, the author concludes that there is a call for a social responsibility to revere the Aged and create a space where they can live a life with all its fullness. Not as mere recipients of care, but active agents of enriching lives of all.

Thirdly, in his essay – "Growing Old in the Ancestral Narratives: A Theological Perspective", **Nagaiyasamy N. S. Samuel** investigates how Ageing is viewed and portrayed in Ancestral Narratives. The author also reveals a fact that the older adult spirituality has a unique place in Jewish tradition. The ear of the older people can distinctly hear and follow the commandment. Citing examples of ancestors, the author concludes that Ageing is an indispensable human condition. Human beings are rare mixture of physique and spiritual elements. Human Beings are part of nature as they come from matter; they are spiritual beings as they are breathed by very breath of God. Therefore, accepting the fact of Ageing is psychological preparation. For the psyche does not let it down, although the physique feels Aged.

The *fifth* and *sixth* essays are from New Testament perspective. **Shanthi S. Monica** in her essay – "Re-reading Lukan "Birth Narratives" with the Optics of Ageing" unravels how the Messianic significance of role played by well-Aged – Elizabeth, Zachariah, Anna and Simeon are undermined in the traditional interpretations of Birth Narratives. The author critically engages in hermeneutical exploration and brings out the fact that Luke's inclusion of the four older people into the Birth Narratives transcends both traditional and contemporary labelling of the Ageing population as inadequate, unproductive and burdensome. The author makes a strong challenge that the re-reading Luke's Birth Narratives with the optics of Ageing would truly help us to be cognisant of a fact that life is a gift of God and transcend our limited pseudo perceptions about Aged population.

Using the conflict approach as sociological hermeneutic tool, **Edwin Jebaraj** in his essay – "Ageing and Intergenerational Conflict in the New Testament: Towards Age-Friendly Communities" makes an attempt to analyse the theme of Ageing from the book of Acts through the book of Revelation. He brings out four pertinent points very clearly: Ageing is a social construct, there is always conflict between the old and the young as fund in the book of Acts; there is power play between the two as it is seen in the Pauline letters; and Jesus is elder-friendly as it is portrayed in book of Revelation. One of the finest insights in the essay is the vision of intergenerational friendly communities based on Lamb model over against the inter-generational conflict based on Lion model. The graceful Ageing is possible only if there is intergenerational friendly communities bound with the love of elder-friendly Jesus.

The *seventh* and *eight* essays in the volume is from historical perspective. In "Issue of Ageing in the Early Writings of History of Christianity: A Response" **Babu. C.** makes an exhaustive survey and critically analyses how Aged people are viewed and presented in the early writings as well as how the Church as a whole made social engagement towards the Aged people. Tracing the influences of Jewish and Greco-Roman society, the author makes a point that though the Christian social action fostered a new vigour of human and spiritual values in Aged people of all genders, the early Christian writings paid little attention to Ageing related "problems stemmed from social, economic, religious, cultural and political aspects." Instead the focus was more on life, death and judgment that followed old age. The references made on old age are mostly spiritualization of old age associated with spirituality and otherworldly transition of life. The old age was greatly upheld as final stage of life to enter the eternal life rather than addressing the issues facing Aged people in their real existential life.

In yet another essay from historical perspective, **S. David Joseph Raj** in his essay – "Ageing in World History: An Overview of Programmes and Policies" presents a brief survey of Ageing in the world history and an overview on various programmes and policies; and shows a fact that Ageing has been an age old problem in every society. Ageing was seen very positively in various societies in the past with high respect and honour because of their experience, knowledge and understanding. They are considered not only as treasure of a family, but entire community or society. Unfortunately, the history also shows that with the advancement of society, the status of elderly people steadily degrading. Due to economic pressers, they are steadily seen as undue burden for the family members. The author argues that even various Programmes and Policies on Ageing appears ineffective to combat the problems facing Aged people in contemporary society. The only measures to address the problem, the author proposes is 'Home-based Care' which is the need of the hour. This will lead to the creation of 'Elderly Friendly Communities' and build a better future for elderly people.

The *ninth* and *tenth* essays in the volume are from Mission perspective. In "Ageing: Awakening the Mission Mandate of the Church", **Rebecca Azariah** investigates how the Church, in fulfilling her mission mandate, is doing enough for the growing population of older adults, especially the Aged women. With special focus on the plight of Aged women, the author brings a resilient challenge to the mission of the Church to counter the emerging culture against older adults with a message of God's comforting presence and purpose in their lives. The church must awaken in her mission to accept and embrace Aged women as "image of God" and their potentialities as valuable asset for God's mission. The church must stand for encouraging and inspiring Aged women in the process of Ageing and take them along as equal agents of God's mission.

K. Vijayan in his essay – "A Postmodern Missiological Response to the Issue of Ageing" makes attempt to bring about turn around in mission by introducing "mission to and from the Aged." The author by using the Reconstructive Postmodern Mission approach which enables people to imagine, dream or share a vision of new alternative relationships where *both* centre *and* periphery, male *and* female, young *and* old, liberation *and* salvation, physical *and* spiritual, reflection *and* praxis etc. are recognised and integrated for relevant patterns of Christian witness in today's postmodern context. For Reign of God can be reconstructed through the lives and witness of the Aged people. There is therefore a great challenge to bring in older people from the fringes of the human community, periphery to the center, from vulnerable to venerable, from exclusion to inclusion, and from minimal to full participation in God's mission.

The *eleventh* and *twelfth* essays on the row are from the perspective of Hindu religious traditions by **Giri Krishnan** and **Wilson Paluri.** In his essay – "*Vānapratha-sannyāsa* Schemes of Life as Gerotranscendence: An Appraisal of a Hindu Perspective of Ageing" **Giri Krishnan** brings out how Ageing is an opportunity for spiritual development to fulfill the ultimate goal of life according to Hindu view of life, and how Aged people are offered *seva* by the society by exploring one ancient religious views of the Aged in the Indian context – the *vānaprastha-sannyāsāśrama* Schemes of Life as Gerotranscendant. The author investigates various aspects of Ageing in *āśrama* scheme of life, and analyzes if the notion of positive Ageing is present in it in view of gerotranscendence. After exploration and critical appraisal of Ageing in *āśrama* scheme the author delineates implications for or possible Christian adaptation to addres the issue of Ageing. The author strongly feels that the spirituality of Ageing as seen in *āśrama* scheme and in gerotranscendence can be taken into account to deal with the issues of the Aged. As India is known for its richness of religiosity and spirituality, utilizing the spiritual resources like *vānaprastha-sannyāsa* scheme of life may be a viable option for a purposeful or graceful Ageing approach in the Indian context.

In another essay, **Wilson Paluri** comes up with yet another alternative to address the issue of Ageing. With a details exploration of Socio-religious *Jarā-śāstra* in Classical Hinduism, the author makes a conclusion that the common Hindu people understand *vṛddhāvastha* and *jarā* as associated with the expectation of suffering and the negative feelings of fear and unpleasantness, rather than the expectation of joy and positive feeling of comfort and blessedness. Whereas, whether he/she deserves it or not, Christian feels assured of the place in heaven after death. For in and through Christ, death is made transient and not permanent. Such hope gives new meaning to life, especially to the older people. The biblical understanding of renewed form of maturity, restoration to community life, honouring elders, and a capacity to challenge anxiety with trust in God would help the elderly end their life journey with comfort and joy. Yet, the author is of the opinion that revisit of the Socio-religious *Jarā-śāstra* of Classical Hinduism and other social-religious principles such as *puruṣārtha*, *saṁskāras*, *pitṛ yajña*, *varṇa* and *āśrama* can also provide constructive insights for families that have become more modernized and lost the value of familial and community care, particularly the care for the elders.

The *thirteenth* essay in the volume is from a communication perspective. Focusing on the methodological process of user-centered system design, **D. Samuel Sounderaraj Singh** in his essay – "New Media: A Caregiver for the Aged" makes an exploration of ways the new media can help to prevent feeling of isolation and loneliness among Aged people in their daily lives, as well as how it can create an interest to develop and remain socially-connected to live their best. The author is of the opinion that isolation is one of the thwarts for the Aged people. Therefore, it is the responsibilities of the caretakers to help the Aged to get acquainted with the new media facilities available to socially stay connected.

The *last four* essays in the volumes are from ethical and theological perspective through which the authors try to explore towards *theo-gerontology*. First, **Mervin Shinoj Boas** proposes for a gerontological hermeneutics from theo-epistemological perspective that would help towards ethical deconstruction of negative images of Aged people. Dwelling deep into theoretical frameworks of knowledge constructions, the author strongly argues that Ageing cannot be reduced to the realm of being purely scientific or theoretical construct, but a practical experiential realities. The author envisions that Ageing is liberated from the captivity of theories based on subjectivity into the ground of praxis depended upon objectivity. The redressal of the issue of Ageing requires different interdisciplinary as well as multidisciplinary academic discourses not only theoretically but practically also by considering Ageing as a reality of all living beings. The ethical understandings of Ageing should therefore be a combination of theory and praxis. There is a need of theory as well as praxis on Ageing for a holistic approach. The author also proposes that the gerontological hermeneutics go beyond the borders of anthropocentrism. Transcend anthropocentism and bio-centrism in order to reach out to the realm of Eco-centrism.

Secondly, **Nelavala Gnana Prasuna** in her essay – "Indian Feminist Theo-gerontology: Towards Growing Positively" shows that though Ageing is often looked upon as a disaster by many, it is possible to "growing positively." The secret for this is positive thinking and positive outlook of life. As an alternative theological response to multiple questions relating to negative experience and image of Aged women, the author explores an Indian Feminist Theo-gerontology from within older women's perspectives and their own agencies that would deconstruct the socially created stereotyped understanding and myths about old age in general and Aged women in particular. Through this theology the author envisions to challenge not only the social structures that dehumanize the older women, but to recover the biblical images of older people in reaffirming God's image in them.

Thirdly, the essay – "Theological Culture of Ageing Together" by **Daniel Kirubaraj** envisions a theology embedded cultural practices of Ageing together over against technologically promoted virtual culture. The author makes challenge that there is a need of an organic relationship of Theology, Culture and Community Life, and a participatory 'Ageing Together' as theological culture inbuilt in the very life of community. Based on the theological construct of holistic and participatory God-Nature-Human-Culture or the culture of equal and independent interaction of God, Nature and the Humans, the author searches for a viable Theological Culture of Ageing Together as alternative framework to address the issue of Ageing.

Finally, considering the negative image and space of Aged people in society, **Songram Basumatary**, in his highly critical and reflective essay – "Theo-critical Exploration of *Ageing*: Towards a *Theo-gerontology*" makes a strong thesis that *Ageing* and issues around *Ageing* are not mere bio-physical processes or a social phenomenon, but a deep theological mystery and *theo-spiritual* reality. Based on the Biblical accounts on Ageing as blessed moments and a satisfying experience of life, challenges the socially constructed negative images and terrifying and burdensome stage of life. The author, through a proposed *Theo-gerontology*, makes a bold theological vision towards liberating *Ageing* from de-humanizing and dreadful negative images with a conviction that *Ageing* is a crucible – a point where communities can transcend the limits of *Ageing* and provide not just a better space for *Aged* people to experience

"Graceful Ageing" but also to recognise their agency towards building a community of justice peace and harmony through their *geron-theo-spirituality*.

This volume is certainly a new contribution to the discourses on Ageing related issues and theologies in terms of perspectives. The distinctiveness of this volume is the radical counter against the negative images of Ageing and the ill treatment against the Aged people. It is hoped and believed that this volume will offer some conceptual tools and epistemological resources to bring revolution in thinking and transformation in attitude by which agency of Aged people are recognised and their human existence as image of God is re-located in the right space.

With this concluding note, I, as editor of the volume, congratulate and thank all the contributors of intellectual pieces and practical insights for addressing the issue of Ageing in Church and society at large. I also extend my sincere gratitude to the responsible governing officials of the Gurukul Lutheran Theological College & Research Institute, particularly the Chairperson, Rt. Rev. O. Michael Benhur; Rev. Joshuva Peter, the Treasurer of GCC and the Executive Secretary of UELCI, and Rev. Dr. John Samuel, the Principal for all their supports in organising the *Gurukul Summer Institute-2020* and bringing out yet another volume towards fulfilling the bold theological vision of Gurukul. I also thank *Christian World Imprints* for giving us the platform to share our theological concerns and new intellectual endeavours to the wider academia and common public readers in general. Last, but not the least, a heartfelt thanks to all the organizing committee members, the participants of the *Institute*, and all other individuals involved in making the project a success!

Songram Basumatary
Editor
25.11.2020

1

Problematizing the Epistemological and Practical Issues of Ageing Blessing or Curse...!

M. Peter Singh

Conceptions of ageing are relative, relational and complex phenomena that have been left out in theoretical and theological constructions, and no theological discourse sufficiently problematized its nature and issues. Ageing is inevitable but challenging, however there is not enough knowledge about the resources available, and a constructive perspective that promotes the well-being of the elders of our families, society and the Church. Therefore, a systematic diagnosis on how to conceptualize and construct a theory of ageing, how to explore the issues involved in growing older, how to confront their existential realities that treat ageing as an illness, how to understand Heidegger's 'happy elderly paradox'[1] and how to make the most theological and ethical choices for our action and reflection is crucial for a deeper understanding and to make relevant responses to decrease inequalities. More particularly, in a fast-changing society in which the aged beloved ones find it difficult to cope up with the changing existential realities and experience rejection from their own children it is very much relevant as a theological community to reflect upon this concern very seriously.

Contemporary Scenario of Ageing

Ageing is unprecedented in human history due to declining fertility, increasing longevity, and the development of cohorts to the older ages are causing ageing to rise throughout the world. Virtually every country in the world is experiencing growth in the size and proportion of older persons in their population. There were 703 million persons aged 65 years or over in the world in 2019. The number of older persons is projected to double to 1.5 billion in

1 Martin Heidegger, *The Question of Being* (New York: Twayne Publishers 1958).

2050. Globally, the share of the population aged 65 years or over increased from 6 per cent in 1990 to 9 per cent in 2019. That proportion is projected to rise further to 16 per cent by 2050, so that one in six people in the world will be aged 65 years or over.[2] The United Nations classification of ageing into three categories, are as follows (1) Old Age dependency ratio (OADR), (2) The prospective old-age dependency ratio (PODR), and (3) The economic old age dependency ratio (EODR)[3] present the world scenario of ageing. The OADR is one of the most commonly used indicators which shows that since 1990s, the OADR has continuously increased across all regions, although the level and speed of this increase vary. Globally, there were 16 persons aged 65 years or over per 100 persons aged 20-64 years in 2019. In 2050, the global OADR is projected to increase to 28 older persons for every 100 working age persons. Prospective measures that redefine ageing based on remaining life expectancy instead of basing it on the number of years lived, capture increases in life expectancy in a population over time. The PODR is calculated as the number of persons above the age closest to a remaining life expectancy of 15 years relative to the number of persons between age 20 and that age. This pattern can be observed at the global level, where the prospective old-age dependency ratio has slightly declined from 12.9 in 1990 to 11.6 in 2019, but it is projected to increase from 11.6 in 2019 to 17.3 by 2050. Economic measures use labour force participation and examine how economic resources are reallocated across individuals of different ages through the family, the government and the market. The economic old-age dependency ratio is increasing around the world. According to the latest National Transfer Accounts' calculations, population ageing leads to a global increase from 20 effective older consumers (age 65+) per 100 effective workers in 2019 to 33 by 2050.

Epistemological Leap in Ageing

Epistemology of ageing is however more complex. How do we describe what human ageing is? What is ageing and how do we recognize, categorize and define it? How old is old? Ideas and definitions of ageing[4] have changed over time and continue to evolve. Generally ageing is characterized by a progressive

2 See "World Population Ageing 2019," (New York: Department of Economic and Social Affairs, United Nations, 2019), 5.

3 "World Population Ageing 2019," (New York: Department of Economic and Social Affairs, United Nations, 2019), 5.

4 Ageism is not a new concept; the term was first coined by Robert Butler in 1969 to describe discrimination against aged people, patterned on racism and sexism. He defined ageism as a combination of three connected elements: prejudicial attitudes towards older people, discriminatory practices against older people; and institutional practices and policies that perpetuate stereotypes about elderly people. See R. N. Butler, "Age-ism: Another form of bigotry," *The Gerontologist* 9/4 (1969): 243–246.

degeneration of the tissues that has a negative impact on the structure and function of vital organs, loss of physiological integrity, resulting in a progressive decline of homeostasis and reduced capacity to respond to environmental stimuli with age, contributes to an incremental risk of disease and death. In "Performing Age, Performing Gender," Kathleen Woodward suggests that definitions of age can be distinguished by chronology, biology, psychology, culture, and statistics. She defines chronological age as "the number of years a person has lived," differentiating it from biological age or "the state of a person's physical capacities."[5] Kathleen further distinguishes between them by explaining that, people suffering from a severe disease in middle age would be understood to be functionally older than their chronological age.[6] She also defines social age as "the meanings that a society accords to different categories of age, in which ageing women are considered older than men of the same chronological age;"[7] and Cultural age as "the meanings or values that a culture assigns to different people in terms of age."[8] She goes on to say that Psychological age refers to "a person's state of mind in terms of age," suggesting that a person may feel older or younger psychologically than their chronological age.[9] In "The Body, Gender, and Age: Feminist Insights in Social Gerontology," Julia Twigg employs the terms "Third Age" and "Fourth Age." Third Age is taken to approximate the ages of fifty to seventy-five, and Fourth Age the ages seventy-five plus.[10] The modern life stages tie social roles to chronological age and considers old age to begin at sixty-five years with retirement. Helen Small uses philosophical approaches to old age, in her book "The Long Life" and explores the view that to understand old age we have to consider more fundamentally what it means to be a person, to have a life, to lead a 'good' life and to be part of a just society.[11] Erik Erikson by taking the ageing process across gender, race and class says that older adults develop a "comprehensive sense of wisdom" by renewing earlier stages of development and developing mature forms of the psychological achievements that they made throughout the life course. His new model analyzing both positive and negative aspects of ageing reestablishes meaning and purpose for old age.

5 Kathleen Woodward, "Performing Age and Performing Gender," *National Women's Studies Association Journal* 18/1 (2006): 183.

6 Kathleen Woodward, "Performing Age and Performing Gender", 183.

7 Kathleen Woodward, "Performing Age and Performing Gender", 183.

8 Kathleen Woodward, "Performing Age and Performing Gender", 183.

9 Kathleen Woodward, "Performing Age and Performing Gender", 183.

10 Julia Twigg, "The Body, Gender and Age: Feminist Insights in Social Gerontology," *Journal of Aging Studies* 18 (2004): 64.

11 Helen Small, *The Long Life* (Oxford University Press, 2007), 3.

Constructing an Epistemology of Ageing

Constructing knowledge about ageing involves the processes of categorizing, organizing and ranking according to socially and culturally defined imaginaries. It essentially requires an analysis of two main perspectives. First, a chronological measurement of age, which is often based on appearance and activities is the most common way to establish "oldness." This typically takes the form of common-sense criteria for marking out someone as old, as Miller says, "People were classified as elderly based on the appearance of a combination of factors such as grey hair, wrinkled faces and hands, retirement scenarios, ambulatory aids such as canes, walkers and wheelchairs, presence of middle-aged children, and/or presence of grandchildren.[12] Kohli argues that Chronological age is apparently a very good criterion for the rational organization of public services and transfers. It renders the life course – and, the passage of the individual through social systems – orderly and calculable.[13] The fixation on chronological age as a socializing device in a society has established normalizing attributes of behaviour attached to the label of elderliness. This chronologisation paradigm still dominates in our understanding of ageing. The second paradigm of understanding is that ageing is a social and cultural construct. In the recent years academic knowledge makes ageing socially visible as well as relevant and important to the ways in which we perceive the existential social reality. In many contemporary societies, ageing is equated with decline and misery,[14] and old age is seen as a type of trap that spreads around our social and cultural environments.[15] This trap presents old age as a fearsome and frightening disease, and it depicts old people as having no gender, race, religion, class, etc.[16] The development of gerontology – the science of age and ageing – has greatly contributed to such understandings of old age focusing on ageing, a stage that is particularly vulnerable to environmental agents result in age-related changes in functions, the ability to maintain physiologic homeostasis.[17] Therefore, it is not ageing that constitutes the main problem, but the ways that people learnt to categorize, calculate and evaluate them.

---

12 Cited by Richard A. Settersten, Jr. and Karl Ulrich Mayer, "The Measurement of Age, Age Structuring, and the Life Course," *Annual Review of Sociology* 23 (1997): 233-261.

13 Cited by Richard A. Settersten, Jr. and Karl Ulrich Mayer, "The Measurement of Age...."

14 Sara Mosberg Iversen and Monika Wilinska. "Ageing, Old Age and Media: Critical Appraisal of Knowledge Practices in Academic Research," *International Journal of Ageing and Later Life* 14/1 (2020): 126. Available at:. https://ijal.se/issue/view/292.

15 Sara Mosberg Iversen1 & Monika Wilin´ ska, *Ageing, Old Age and Media*, 127.

16 Sara Mosberg Iversen1 & Monika Wilin´ ska, *Ageing, Old Age and Media*, 127.

17 Sara Mosberg Iversen1 & Monika Wilin´ ska, *Ageing, Old Age and Media*, 128.

Problematizing and Paradigmatic Deconstruction of Ageing

Having discussed the global scenario of ageing, now we inevitably proceed to problematizing the concerns of ageing. Problematization is a critical thinking proposed by Michel Foucault that involves asking "how and why certain behaviour or processes become a problem.[18] Alvesson and Sandberg drawing on the work of Michel Foucault, proposes problematization as a paradigmatic deconstruction for identifying and challenging the assumptions embedded in the society[19] and asks what else might be possible. The dominant discourse on ageing is life centered on experiencing a decline in mental functioning, dementia and a loss of mobility. Paradigmatic deconstruction of the shortcomings of the dominant ways of approaching, Walby et al. proposed that an intersectionality encourages a language of inequalities and systems of inequalities.[20] Intersectionality is a paradigm, that explores the interactions of social markers such as psychological, social and political aspects are of equal significance to the meaningful understandings constructed on ageing experience. A growing number of studies explore the interactionality[21] between age, class, gender, race, sexuality, and masculinity. Intersectionality opens a discourse of problematizing.

Individualization of Ageing

The impact of globalization has redefined the social context of ageing, opening up deregulated social order and inequalities. Risks once carried by social institutions have now been displaced onto the shoulders of individuals. Zsuzsa Ferge calls this "individualization of the social."[22] Young refers this as part of a wider shift from an "inclusive to an exclusive society. This erosion of the inclusive world ... involved processes of disaggregation both in the sphere of community (the rise of individualism) and the sphere of work (transformation of ... labor markets). Both processes are the result

---

18 Michel Foucault, "Polemics, Politics and Problematizations," in *The Foucault Reader*, ed. Paul Rabinow (New York: Pantheon Books, 1984), 389.

19 Mats Alvesson and Jorgen Sandberg, "Generating Research Questions Through Problematization," *Academy of Management Review* 36/2 (2011). Available at: https://journals.aom.org/doi/abs/10.5465/amr.2009.0188.

20 S. Walby, J. Armstrong and S. Strid, "Intersectionality: Multiple Inequalities in Social Theory," *Sociology* 46/2 (2012):, 224–240. Available at: https://doi.org/10.1177/0038038511416164.

21 Intersectionality is a theoretical framework for understanding interconnected aspects of people's social and political identities. This theory asserts that people are often disadvantaged by multiple sources of oppression: their race, class, gender identity, sexual orientation, religion, and other identity markers.

22 Zsuzsa Ferge, "The Changed Welfare Paradigm: The Individualization of The Social," (2002). Available at: https://doi.org/10.1111/1467-9515.00035.

of market forces and their transformation by the human actors involved"[23] It is the "human consequences" of globalization in terms of new forms of segregation and exploitation, especially affecting those in deprived and peripheral communities. Dannefer summarizes this process in the following way: "Corporate and state uncertainties are transferred to citizens, protecting large institutions while exposing individuals to a possible catastrophe in the domains of health care and personal finances…."[24] Globalization has led to the rise in income inequality, and weakened the labour organizations that has produced greater cultural and social diversity and inequality to ageing.

Marginalization of Ageing

Marginalization of ageing is an inhuman treatment that the aged individuals experience in their own families and society. The once masters of their own families lose their independence and become dependent for their life, bringing heavy socio-economic pressures on them. Age normality varies among different work organizations. Employees under the age of 40 are considered to be too old by the telemarketing industry, they can also be seen as too young to gain status and prestigious assignments within parts of the academic world. Labour force participation declines as people age. Labour income is an important tertiary or quaternary source that funds about 15 to 25 per cent of consumption of older persons in most countries. In Europe, they are less likely to be in the labour force than populations in other regions, due to its more developed and generous social security systems.[25] In India about one-third of old-age consumption is financed through own work. In countries with low intergenerational transfers, ageing will put substantial pressure on older persons to be self-reliant and will create pressures for families. This makes the ageing process dangerous.

Feminization of Ageing

Experiences of ageing are strongly influenced by gender. Due to differential mortality there are more women than men at older ages, who experience greater strains with fewer resources. This is referred to as the feminization of ageing. Feminist gerontology provides a theoretical framework for understanding social constructions of ageing and gender and holds that men and women experience ageing differently and their experiences of ageing are constructed socially and relationally through interactions and exchanges of power between men and women. This gender paradox shows a lower quality

23 Young Jock, *The Exclusive Society* (London: Sage, 1999), 6.

24 Dannefer Dale, "Bringing Risk Back In: The Regulation of the Self," in *The Evolution of the Aging Self*, edited by K.W. Schaie amd J. Hendricks (New York: Springer; 2000), 270.

25 Cited in *World Population Ageing 2019*, Department of Economic and Social Affairs, 24.

of life for women. Women around the world are paid less than men and therefore more women are in poverty than men. Employment is a typically male dominated sphere and work, particularly housework is done primarily by women, unpaid. Even when women are also engaged in gainful employment, they still have the responsibility for the unpaid housework. This shows that the household work of women has been considered as informal work because it is believed that household work is unproductive.[26] The cheapness of female labour, their submission at work, sexualization of skills and other forms of struggles make women vulnerable and disadvantaged at older ages than men. This is especially problematic for widowed and divorced women, as well as racial and sexual minority women who already receive fewer benefits from the institution of marriage. Additionally, since pensions are relative to income level while working, and there is a gendered pay gap, many women receive lower pensions after retirement than men. The gender paradox is largely explained by gendered patterns of disease, whereby men are more likely to have more life-threatening conditions, such as heart disease and lung cancer, and women are more likely to have less immediately life threatening chronic conditions, such as arthritis and thyroid conditions. Thus, although women live longer, they also spend more time with worse health conditions while having to cope with chronic conditions and experience humiliation and rejection. Gendered ageism[27] points out the discrimination in relation to recruitment, career, and pension, and women are ageing at an earlier chronological age, than men. Clarke and Griffin have shown that women of all ages, more than men, experience ageism based on appearance and sexuality in the labour market.[28] Naomi Wolf explains, patriarchal standards of beauty depend on a woman's ability to project an image of youth rather than maturity.[29] Gendered ageism points to another dimension of physical beauty and looks. Healthism, lookism, and fitnessism, further supported by ideals of consumerism,[30] point

---

26 Ivy Singh, "A Quest for an Ecofeminist Methodological Construction," Paper presented in the Doctoral Methodology Seminar, organised by SATHRI, 2011.

27 Marjut Jyrkinen and Lynda McKle., "Gender, Age and Ageism: Experiences of Women Managers in Finland and Scotland," 2012. Available at: https://doi.org/10.1177/0950017011426313.

28 L. H. Clarke and M. Griffin, "Visible and Invisible Ageing: Beauty Work as a Response to Ageism," *Ageing and Society* 28/05 (2008): 653–674. Available at: https://doi.org/10.1017/S0144686X07007003.

29 Naomi Wolf, *The Beauty Myth: How Images of Beauty are used against Women* (London: Chatto & Windus, 1990), 12.

30 R. Crawford, "Healthism and the Medicalization of Everyday Life," *International Journal of Health Services* 10/3 (1980): 360. Available at: https://doi.org/10.2190/3H2H-3XJN-3KAY-G9NY.

that ageing does not constitute a role, an identity, or an individual attribute, but is rather an expression of the social cultural construct.

Conceptualizing Ageing

Conceptualisation is essential to direct the thinking to specific dimensions. Ageing is a living process that every living being undergoes. Although the process is unavoidable, it is crucial to understand the process. Why do living things age? Aristotle is arguably the first philosopher to show a serious theoretical interest in the natural process of ageing and he detested old age as a natural decline that was both physical and moral.[31] He did not recognize old age as a valuable life stage; rather he made vitriolic remarks concerning the nature of the elderly, saying that the older person is cowardly, distrusting, cheap, and inactive. The aged are loquacious, often subjecting others to protracted speeches and storytelling about their past. They lack passion.[32] For him, old age brings with it not only the physical maladies of decay; it also renders its victim selfish, morally weak, and practically sociopathic. Plato saw old age as a wonderful time of life, and they are in a uniquely fortunate position to achieve the good life, provided they make the best use of the gifts of their time and experience. The Hellenistic thinkers reconsidered the stereotypical woes of old age in the light of Epicureanism which says that the elderly who lived well are fortunate[33] and Stoicism which says that virtue is the only good" for human beings, and that external things—such as health, wealth, and pleasure – are not good or bad in themselves.[34] Plutarch focused on the intellectual capital that an experienced life can offer a community.[35] Cicero says old age is the cessation of life.[36] Seneca, a staunch Stoic thinker considers ageing as a natural part of life so by accepting it, it can change one's perspective from viewing ageing positively based on the tenets of stoicism. The Epicureans maintained that the goal in life is pleasure and that the fear of death and anxiety are a waste of time since there was no threat from the gods and that this life is the only one. Both philosophies sustained the belief that happiness is the goal. Modern biological theories emphasize environmental assaults to living organisms that induce cumulative damage at various levels as the cause of ageing.

---

31 Liat Ayalon and Clemens Tesch-Romer, eds., *Contemporary Perspectives on Ageism* (Switzerland: Springer Open, 2018), 493-516.

32 Cited by Audrey Anton, "Aging in Classical Philosophy" in *Palgrave Handbook of the Philosophy of Ageing*, edited by Geoffrey Scarre (Palgrave Macmillan, 2016), 131.

33 See Daniel Klein, *Travels with Epicurus* (Penguin Books, 2012).

34 See Donald Robertson, *Stoicism and the Art of Happiness* (Great Britain: John Murray, 2008).

35 Cited by Audrey Anton, "Aging in Classical Philosophy," 133.

36 Marcus Tullius Cicero, *On Old Age*, 154. Available at: https://oll.libertyfund.org/pages/cicero-on-old-age.

Goldsmith investigates how organisms have evolved mechanisms that purposely limit their lifespans in order to obtain an evolutionary benefit.[37] Ageing is the result of a sequential switching on and off of certain genes, where biological clocks act through hormones to control the pace of ageing that the immune system is programmed to decline over time, leading to an increased vulnerability to infectious disease and thus ageing and death.

Ageing: A Blessing or Curse?

Now we move on to raise a very fascinating yet a problematic question, for whom is ageing a blessing or curse? Human life is lived through organic bodies which mean that we are essentially interconnected and interdependent with others and the environment. This interconnectedness and interdependence often becomes the source of vulnerable. Martin Heideggar considers Vulnerability as the essential characteristics of human life.[38] Life needs to be preserved on the condition that it remains genuine. We therefore need to take 'the human dignity of life' as a paradigm to address this question of blessing or curse. Life is the greatest blessing of God given to humans. Everyone deserves to live a good life with all basic amenities, respect and dignity. Acceptance or rejection, relationship or manipulation, freedom or control, independence or dependence would result either in a positive or negative impact in the life of the aged people.

Ageing is a blessing. In some Indian societies, caring for the aged ones is a responsibility of both the family and society. Society treats them as the storehouse of knowledge and gatekeepers for the management of life. An African proverb says, "When an old man dies, a library burns to the ground" it points out the significance of ageing. Ageing is a curse too. Aged ones, whether a male or a female, who lived an active social life find a drastic change in the attitude of people towards them when grey hair, wrinkles and marks on their face begins to appear. Some are treated with respect and their advice is highly sought after for their experience, however the majority of them suffer sickness and when they come to the stage of living under the mercy of their children they often experience rejection. Ageing is definitely a bane in India because children begin to see their parents as an economic liability, burden and many are treated poorly by their children, deprived of their basic needs like food, clothing and shelter in their own homes. Their properties are forcefully taken by their children. Caring for the bedridden aged ones is considered an

37 T. C. Goldsmith, Modern Evolutionary Mechanics Theories and Resolving the Programmed/non-programmed Aging Controversy," *Biochemistry* 79/10 (2014): 1049-55.

38 Cited by Patrick L. Bourgeois and Frank Schalow, "The Integrity and Fallenness of Human Existence," *The Southern Journal of Philosophy*, .XXI/1 (1987). Avilable at: https://onlinelibrary.wiley.com/doi/abs/10.1111/j.2041-6962.1987.tb01611.x.

intrusion of independence and personal space and seen as a major drain of their economy. The social prejudices, perceptions, and value judgments refuse to acknowledge the reality of ageing. In this situation, life becomes a burden for them. Old age illness, financial dependency for their medical assistance makes them more vulnerable. The collapse of the nuclear family system, increasing domestic violence and neglect pushed many aged ones to be isolated and many are seen on the streets or end up in old age homes or senior citizen centers. Such homes are considered a blessing for the children, but for the aged ones to live a life in this awful state is either a blessed curse or a cursed blessing.

Theologizing Ageing

The above problematization and conceptualization have vividly identified ageing as cruel or weak and aged people are often ostracized, neglected, and overlooked; and they are seen no longer as bearers of wisdom but as embodiments of shame. In Western thought, old age is an evil, an infirmity and a dreary time of preparation for death. Furthermore, death is often preferred over decrepitude, because death means deliverance.[39] Jan Vijg considers ageing a necessary evil in the logic of life.[40] The question of evil may lead us to a never-ending discussion which focus is not here. There are people who seek to do harm to innocent aged people deriving enjoyment and comfort from the suffering and the situation that are inflicted upon them. This perennial image of evil is perpetuated by individuals who make people to separate "us" from "them." This way of constructing evil is prone to stereotyping and exaggeration and makes us to confront the nature of evil from an objective stance. One way of confronting as Teilhard de Chardin says is Christian charity. He says that Christian charity is not simply a soothing lotion poured over the world's suffering. He viewed it as the most complete and most active agent of hominization. For him charity was the precise means that enables the progressive development of human life to higher and higher levels within the human heart and beyond in charity. Thus, if life is to develop and evolve and mature to a high degree in Christ in this ageing process, then charity to others becomes the essential element.[41] As ageing is not a downward movement, but a continuation of a forward movement, more than charity it is justice concern. Justice is right to live with dignity and free from injustice caused by lack of food, health care and a safe place to live. Taking the preferential option for the

39 Georges Minois, *History of Old Age: From Antiquity to the Renaissance* (Chicago: University of Chicago Press, 1989), 303.

40 Jan Vijg, *Aging Genomes: A Necessary Evil in the Logic of Life*, (E-Book, 2014). Available at: https://onlinelibrary.wiley.com/doi/abs/10.1002/bies.201300127.

41 See Michael McCabe, *Reflections on Aging* (2008). Available at:, http://www.nathaniel.org.nz/bioethics-politics-and-slovenly-language-lessons-from-history/16-bioethical-issues/bioethics-at-the-end-of-life/172-reflections-on-aging.

victims, the aged ones challenge us to take the process that God is enough to be the ground of hope. The cross of Jesus as God's emptying himself, becoming human and, by his own rejection and suffering opened up the "paradigm from below" as a firm hermeneutical ground for all who believe in Christ. The Church must move away from the present authoritarian model of Peter in her ministry and take Mary, the aged mother of Jesus, who was kneeling vulnerable at the foot of the cross, a humble model. Vulnerability is power. Being vulnerable is being open, open for joy and pain. Open to the wounds of life means being open to the bounty and beauty. In this sense kneeling model is not a weak model. Church should become a meeting point of the kenotic ecclesiology and the kneeling ecclesiology, only then she can be an authentic powerful liberative Movement to those who are denied justice.

Conclusion

Life is an affirmation and is intrinsically valuable. By virtue of being alive and being able to recognize the value of life, humanity is responsible for life to live. The existence of life is no longer a given, it can be destroyed too. Destroying others life is destroying ones' own existence. This gives us the imperative to protect life that, we ought because we can. The ontological freedom that we enjoy entails moral responsibility, what we do affects the existence of things that have value. Value can have a claim right on the society. Our existence is based on our collaboration with the aged ones. The "ontological ought" in our relationships is essential. Hans Jonas puts it succinctly; "The perishable qua perishable"[42] can be an object of responsibility. Our responsibility roots in the object, which by virtue of its vulnerability that holds us accountable for our attitudes towards the aged ones. The call and command directly come from the object. We can inhumanly resist this, but we cannot humanly contradict it.

42 Michael Hauskeller, *The Ontological Ethics of Hans Jonas*. Available at: https://www.academia.edu/3406849/The_Ontological_Ethics_of_Hans_Jonas.

2

'Ageing' in Jewish Interpretations

John Samuel

Visualizing the 'aged' in Hebrew Bible

The Rabbinic world often presents a joyful and a healthy picture of the aged people. Let me begin by visualizing one of the Biblical images of the aged people here. Our father Jacob was ninety-seven years old or seventy years old (according to two traditions) when he was engaged in a wrestling match with an angelic being. We also read that the angel was not able to overcome Jacob even after a prolonged fight for several hours (Genesis 32:25). How can this happen, a mysterious person, who must have been robust, was not able to knock down a ninety-seven years old man? Jacob was alone (badad) when he wrestled with this man. The word used for wrestle here is 'avek' which means dust. In the verbal form, it would mean, both of them were rolling in the dust and made themselves dusty. That shows that it was a severe encounter. Some exegetes say that it was not a physical encounter, but a spiritual warfare or a mental struggle with an angelic being. If it was so, it must have been even more severe than a physical encounter.

There is a second reading of the story. The core of the narrative, verses 27-30, stands in stark contrast to the rest of the narrative:

> Then he said, "Let me go, for dawn is breaking." But he answered, "I will not let you go, unless you bless me." Said the other, "What is your name?" He replied, "Jacob." Said he, "Your name shall no longer be Jacob, but Israel, for you have striven with beings divine and human and have prevailed." Jacob asked, "Pray tell me your name." But he said, "You must not ask my name!" And he took leave of him there.

This does not look like a wrestlers' language, who are fighting with each other. This looks like an intimate scene between a man and a woman (or other).

The language seems to be powerfully sexual. One partner wants to end sex as day was breaking forth. They are not able to leave each other. One partner is asking to be blessed for what was rendered. When one partner is able to say the name, the other partner pleads not to ask the name. It is between two who do not know who is 'he' and who is 'she.' This is one of the loftiest place in the beauty of Hebrew literature for sexual love.

Rashi interpreted 'avek' as 'embrace.' A sexual battle where the one strives to overcome the other physically. It is a battle for pleasure, strangely, not on the lawns, but on a dusty ground, where both roll upon the dusty ground! The word 'avek' (wrestle) is used only one other time in the whole of the Hebrew Bible, that is in Song of songs 3:6. "What is this coming up from the desert like columns of smoke, perfumed with myrrh and incense from all the fragrant powders (dust) of the merchant?" Hence, it is more probable that it must have been a romantic event rather than a wrestling event. Either it was a wrestling sport or an intimate sexual encounter, the Biblical image of a ninety-year-old man is not what we imagine. Hence there can be an 'image-correction' of the 'aged' according to the Bible.'

Keeping in the Perspectives

We are all aware of the phenomenon of 'ageism' as it is a very important concern in our times. 'Ageing' includes all kinds of discrimination meted out to people, both open and hidden, to those who are advanced in age. Such harsh attitude may be seen in different levels ranging from subtle to extreme. Activities such as denying employment, not giving adequate health facilities, isolating them in public space etc. are subtle forms of discrimination. In extreme cases, it can even go to the level of physical and mental abuse. Aged people deserve a dignified life. When they do not find love in their life, when we do not treat the aged people with respect, it may cause worries to them and at times, it makes them think that their life is not worth any more.

In our times, human life is often viewed as mechanical and utilitarian in this scientific society. We are living in a consumerist society. Not only are raw materials, even human beings are valuable, only so long as they are economically beneficial. A man or woman is valuable when they earn money. When they are not able earn money due to old age, they are considered as not needed any more. Scientists and Utilitarian philosophers advocate the view that life does not have any value more than utilitarian worth. They believe that it is even unethical to spend our resources for the aged people with dementia, depression and mental disorder. They persuade the society not to extend social welfare and health services to such fragile people as communal waste of resources. In Bio ethics, they recommend that, if it is necessary, it is not wrong even to annihilate the aged people, who are an economic burden to the family and the state. They go to the extent of suggesting euthanasia to them, even when they are unwilling to accept such means of termination. One of the writers of this view even suggested for state sponsored euthanasia at the age of fifty-five. Hence, it is imperative for the religious to see the Biblical views of ageing and old people.

Stages in Human Life

Human life has been divided into different stages from time immemorial. They have been grouped differently from infancy to old age by priests, philosophers, poets, politicians and doctors etc. Bible mentions about the division of human life into three stages in Deuteronomy, "for young man and woman alike, nursing child and old grey head" (Deuteronomy 32:25). We can find a similar division of human life in the book of Psalms, "Young men and women alike, old and children together! (Psalms 148:12-13). Rabbis mention this tripartite division in human life as follows:

> When the man is young, he sings songs
> When grown up he abounds in proverbs
> As old man, he speaks empty words.[1]

Pirkei Avot suggests certain age limits to work, based on Numbers 4:23, "From thirty years old up to fifty years old you shall enrol them, all who qualify to do work in the tent of meeting."[2] When the Israelites were travelling through the wilderness, the Levites had to carry the tent of meeting and it may have been difficult for aged persons. Hence, the people above the age of fifty were found unfit for such tasks. However, after they settled in the promised land, the tabernacle was built as a permanent building and the work of the Levites was only to sing hymns in the temple. Their work did not need a strong body of a young person to carry heavy weights. As long as one was able to sing, he/she continued in the divine service. Hence it arose out of a certain need which belonged to the time of sojourning in the wilderness.

Abraham and Old Age

Traditions say that our father Abraham became the first person to become old. Abraham prayed for old age (ziknah) and received it. Until Abraham became old, old age had never been mentioned in Torah,[3] even among those who lived more than hundred years. None of them were ever mentioned 'old.' For them, it was natural to live a long healthy and active life until death.

Abraham and Isaac faced a problem in their life. They both looked very much alike. When they came to a place together, people did not know who

1 Midrash Rabba to the Song of Solomon I.I.

2 Pirkei Avot 5:25.

3 Bava Metzia 87a.

the father was and who was the son. Abraham thought that the people should know who the father was and then only they can give respect to the father. So, Abraham requested for old age for him. God agreed. God said, by your life, this phenomenon will begin with you!" Hence old age came to stay with human beings forever.

The life of Abraham and Sarah portrays a youthful old age. Abraham departed for Canaan at the age of seventy-five. Even from that point, they travelled, acquired wealth, dug wells, conducted wars and met kings. Abraham became the father of Ishmael when he was eighty-six years old (Genesis 16:16). Isaac was born to him when he was hundred years old (Genesis 21:5). Now Abraham was old, well advanced in years; and the LORD had blessed Abraham in all things.[4] Nahum Sarna describes the expression 'old and contented' as unique in the entire Hebrew Bible and this phrase is found with no other persons except Abraham in the whole Bible.[5] This phrase does not imply his longevity, but also about the quality of his earthly existence.

Elders as a Source of Wisdom

It is generally held in all cultures that those who have lived for a long time gain wisdom and knowledge.[6] Talmud says, "Even if the elders tell you to destroy and the young tell you to build, you should destroy and not build, for the 'destruction' of the older people is 'building' and the 'building' of the young people is really 'destroying.'[7] When Rehoboam refused to listen to the advice of the aged people, he lost the ten tribes (I Kings 12:8) and later this attitude came to be referred as 'Rehoboam syndrome.'[8] Those who take the advice of the elders never stumble.[9] When Moses needed wisdom to lead the people, God said to him. "Go and gather the elders of Israel and say to them" (Exodus 3:16.). Later when Moses said that he cannot lead the people alone, God said to him, "Gather for me seventy elders" (Numbers 11:16). These events show that elderly people are endowed with wisdom.

Older people are a reservoir of knowledge. Talmud mentions, "He that learns from the young (teacher), to what is he like? To the one who eats unripe grapes and drinks his wine from the wine press. And he who learns from the aged (teacher), to what is he like? To the one who eats ripe grapes and drinks

---

4 This appears with reference to Isaac (*Genesis 35:29*), Job (*Job 42:17*), and Jehoiada (*2 Chronicles 24:15*). However, each of these passages has the Hebrew word *yamim* (days) in the text, whereas *Genesis 25:8* does not. Hence it is unique for Abraham.

5 Nahum Sarna, *Understanding Genesis* (New York: Schocken Press, 1970), 155.

6 Malbim commentary on Leviticus 19:32.

7 Megillah 31b.

8 Jean Sheldon, "Rehoboam Syndrome and its Cure," *Spectrum Magazine* (July 3, 2017): 1.

9 Exodus Rabbah 3:6.

old wine."[10] The teachers were all aged in olden times. "Moses was in Egypt for forty years, forty years in Midian and led Israel for forty years. Hillel, the elder came from Bavel at the age of forty, studied under the sages for forty years and served Israel for forty years. Rabbi Yohanan Ben Zakkai engaged in business for forty years, studied under sages for forty years and led Israel for forty years. Rabbi Akiba began to learn Torah at the age of forty and served Israel for forty years."[11] Old age never hindered them from their active engagements.

God bids Moses and Aaron to go to the Pharaoh and negotiate for the freedom of the Israelites. After this conversation between God and brothers, Bible says that "Moses was eighty years old and Aaron was eighty-three, when they went to meet the Pharaoh." Why does the Torah leave the main sequence of the events and go to mention about their ages, which cannot be of much importance in this situation?

Rabbi Abraham ibn Ezra writes that this reference to 'advanced age' is very important to understand a significant truth. He also says that we do not find anywhere else in Bible where the age is mentioned for any prophets apart from Moses and Aaron. Whereas, it is usual that any one will try to hide their old age, here, it is mentioned for Moses and Aaron, as a matter of pride because, Talmud mentions that "at 80 -- the age of strength." What is the strength of an 80 years old? A teenager has a strong physique. The shrewdness of a 40-year old is more apparent and a 60-year old is more knowledgeable. But the strength of 80 is the wisdom and maturity that comes from the experience of life. That is why God sent them when they were eighty and eighty-three years old.

Of course, the sages also recognize that sometimes even the wisest of the elders can make mistakes. Job says, "He will remove reason from the elders" (Job 12:20). It is interpreted that this refers to Isaac, Jacob, Moses and Aaron who all made bad decisions in their old age.[12]

Old Age as Fruitful

The fruitfulness in old age is discussed in many places. It is usually held that the older a person grows, his contributions will gradually become lesser and lesser. However, there are many occurrences in the Rabbinic writings which contradict this belief. Rabbi Honi saw an elderly person planting carob trees which takes seventy years to produce fruit. He asked him if he would still be alive to eat the fruits of the tree. The man replied that just as his forefathers planted trees for him, he is planting trees for future generations.[13] There is

10 Ethics of the Fathers 1:1.

11 Sifre Deuteronomy 357.

12 Genesis Rabbah 99:5.

13 Taanit 23a.

another story in Midrash which mentions that a man who was hundred years old was planting trees.[14] This portrays how old age can be fruitful just like other phases of human life!

One day, the wife of the elderly teacher Rabbi Chisda was applying cosmetics. A disciple asked, 'how can an old woman do this which was permissible only for younger women?' Rabbi replied by saying, "I swear, even your mother, even your grandmother, even if she is on the edge of her grave, is permitted to put make up."[15] The rabbi opposed to any objection of older women liking to appear beautiful. Ecclesiastes mentions, "the end of the matter is better than the beginning" and the meaning is, "old age will even be better than youth" (Ecclesiastes 7:8). Rabbis have actively raised their voices against the discrimination of the aged women. Advancing of age need not necessarily reduce the normal activities of life.

It was believed that each earlier generation was one step closer to the revelation of God at Sinai. Hence, the earlier generations were in a higher spiritual plane compared to the later generations. It gave rise to the proverbial phrase, 'decline of generation' (veridot-ha-dorot'). In another place it is written, "If the earlier generations are like angels, then we are like people. But if the earlier generations are like people, we are like donkeys."[16] "The hearts of earlier generations was like the opening of a large hall and ours are like the eye of the needle.[17] In this connection, it was asked, "Why the earlier generations did have many miracles performed for them whereas we do not have many miracles performed for us."[18] When they were asked to give an illustration for something 'which is upside down', they said, "when the youths will embarrass the face of the elderly and the elderly will have to stand before the young", it is something 'upside' down.[19] The normal thing to do would be when the young stand before the elders.

Not to Ridicule the Aged

There are some events remembered about how the aged people were insulted by the young people and how God was in favour of the elders. Sages say that the older people who have led a 'just life' are more acceptable than the young people. It is mentioned that one day King David asked God, I have heard people say, "when will this old man die so that his son Solomon can come and build the temple.' God replied to David, I would have rather one day of your

14 Tanhuma Kedoshim 8, Leviticus Rabbah 25:5.

15 Moed Katan in Talmud 9b.

16 Sabbath 112b.

17 Eruvin 53 a.

18 Berachot 20a.

19 Sotah 49a.

Torah learning than a thousand sacrifices of Solomon."[20] Midrash Tanhuma mentioned, "Aaron's sons Nadav and Abihu would walk behind Moses and Aaron saying, when will these two old men die so that we take over and rule?" But God allowed Nadav and Abihu to die first allowing Moses and Aaron to lead the Jewish people for a longer time.[21] Thus God denounced the evil mind of the younger people who were against the older people.

Bible recalls that Abraham held a feast in honour of Isaac when he weaned (Gen. 21:8). On that occasion, every one gossiped and said: "This old man and old woman, brought a child from the marketplace and claim that he is their son. They are holding a great feast, to make everyone believe that he is their son. How can a son be born for an old man Abraham and an old woman such as Sarah!" God immediately withered up the breasts of the women who had come for the feast. When their children were crying for milk, Sarah stood and revealed herself, and her two breasts spouted milk. The women of all the nations of the world brought their children to Sarah to nurse that day. All those who convert in the world, and all those who fear God in the world, are from among those who nursed from Sarah.[22] Those who spoke ill of Abraham and Sarah due to their old age were humiliated and apologised to Sarah.

Healthy Old Age

Rabbi Hanina said from his own life with what he was able to do even when he was at the age of eighty. He recalled that "the warm bath and oil with which my parents anointed me in my youth have stood me in good stead in my old age."[23] What did he mean by warm water and oil? Judaism is the warm water and Torah is the oil with which we must anoint our children. If so, even in old age, we will flourish like a cedar. "We will be planted in the court yards of the Lord and will bear fruits even in old age" (Psalms 92:12-13). There is a saying, "Today is the time to do, tomorrow to reap the reward." If God has granted a person even a single day in his/her life means that he/she has not yet concluded his/her mission in his/her life and there is something more to be accomplished in this world. Even in the Messianic age, when things will turn to ideal state, there will still be older people and they will all be in good health. "Old men and old women shall again sit in the streets of Jerusalem, each with staff in hand, because of their great age (Zachariah 8:4).

Bible mentions about the barrenness of the matriarchs and the mothers of great leaders such as Samson. They got a child only in their old age. It is actually

---

20 Makkot 10a.

21 Midrash Tanhuma.

22 BT Bava Mezia 87a.

23 Rabbi Bradley Shavit Artson, "Bearing Fruit Even in Old Age," *Va'eira* (January 27, 1962): 1.

a matter of irony. Either they should bear children when they were young or they should not bear a child at all. However, what happens is the opposite. They bore a child when they were advanced in age. Hence the Rabbis tried to respond to this strange phenomenon in a number of ways. It is mentioned in one place that the matriarchs and patriarchs were initially childless "because the Holy One, blessed be He, longs to hear the prayer of the righteous."[24] Others explained that the matriarchs were barren so that their husbands might derive pleasures from them for a long time. When a woman conceives a child, they lose their beauty. Thus, the whole ninety years, our mother Sarah did not bear a child and she was like a bride in her canopy.[25]

Hannah sang a song when she bore Samuel, where it is said, "While the barren woman bears seven," (1 Samuel 2:5). What is the meaning of this phrase, 'bears seven'? Sages explain this as "On seven occasions has the barren woman borne." Sarah, Rebecca, Leah, Rachel, the wife of Manoah and Hannah are the seven older women mentioned here, but one is lacking. The seventh person is not a woman, but it is the city of Zion, as the prophet of Isaiah said, "Sing, O barren one who did not bear; burst into song and shout, you who have not been in labour! For the children of the desolate woman will be more than the children of her that is married, says the Lord." (Isaiah 54:1). This midrash explains how the mothers were fruitful, bearing children, even in their old age.[26]

Menachem Mendel Schneerson, known to many as the Lubavitcher Rebbe or simply as the Rebbe, was celebrating his seventieth birthday, after a meticulous life, serving for many decades as leader and activist. On that day, he received greetings and letters from his well-wishers from all over the world. While they greatly appreciated his contributions and tireless work, they also suggested, with gratitude and love, that it was time for him to 'slow down' and 'take life easy.' However, while the Rabbi fully understood their love, at the same time, rejected the idea of retirement for him. At that moment, he not only continued his work, but also inspired everyone to establish 'Torah Study centres for the aged.' As a response to his words, his followers established hundreds of such study centres all over the world and they were named as 'Tifrret Zkeinim' (the glory of the aged). Some years later, on his eightieth birthday, he delivered a six-hour address that ended after 3 a.m. and called for the massive expansion of Chabads activities. It is said that after the long meeting, he proceeded to distribute a special edition of Chassidic classic 'The Tanya' personally for 10000 men, women and children which ended at 6 a.m.

---

24 Genesis Rabbah 45:4.

25 Genesis Rabbah 45:4.

26 Cf. Baskin, Judith. "Rabbinic Reflections on the Barren Wife," *Harvard Theological Review* 82 (1989): 1–14.

They say these were only a fraction of his activities at his age of 90. Old age does not quench the flame of human spirit![27]

Merits of the Fathers and Mothers

There is a concept, 'merits of fathers and mothers' (*Zekhutavot*) in Jewish spirituality. Rabbis explain that Esther became queen due to the merits of her great grandmother Sarah. Torah mentions that Sarah lived for hundred and twenty-seven years. The hundred and twenty-seven years of Sarah came back to act a thousand years later, when Ahasuerus, who eventually married Esther and ruled over hundred and twenty-seven countries. They ask a question, "Why did Esther merit to rule over hundred and twenty-seven countries?" Said God: "Let Esther, the descendant of Sarah who lived hundred and twenty-seven years, come and rule over hundred and twenty-seven lands." When Sarah lived, she used every year, every month, every day, every hour, every minute and every second fruitfully. Hence Esther became queen over hundred and seventy countries. When Esther was rewarded to be queen over hundred and twenty-seven nations, she attended to the needs in every nation, every province, every city, every street and every household.[28] Thus the merit of the mother to daughter.

A mysterious tradition has been handed over generation after generation which explains about the merits of the fathers/mothers. One day, God allowed all the future generations to pass before Adam. God accepted his request. When Adam was introduced to David as one of the most important persons in his descendants, Adam wanted to give David sufficient time in his life to be able to fulfil the roles for which he was born. Adam, requested God to give David seventy of the thousand years blessed for him. However, it is breath-taking that the sages have written, where they connected the first human originator with the most important person in the history of Israel. It is also to say that Adam helped for the long life of David which was due to the merits of the fathers/ mothers.

Scripture says that the descendants inherited certain blessings from the merits of their fore fathers Abraham, Isaac and Jacob (Leviticus 26:42). The idea of 'merits of the fathers' lost its importance over the time. However, after Bar Kokhba's revolt (132–135 CE), the 'akedha' became the paradigm of 'merits of the fathers.'[29] They even believed that Isaac was actually offered as sacrifice. Rabbi Judah Alter of Gur taught about the merit of the seventy

27 Menachem Mendel Schneerson, known to many as the Lubavitcher Rebbe or simply as the Rebbe, mentioned in Wikipedia.

28 Esther Rabbah 1:8., Gen. Rabbah 58:3.

29 E. E. Urbach, *The Sages* (Jerusalem, 1975), 15:7, 485.

grandchildren of Jacob as received by the later generations.[30] This concept emerged probably to emphasize the blessings the elders brought into the life of the children.

Old Age is a Continuation of the Young Age

Old age is only a continuation of how a person lived throughout his/her life. Old age is not a new beginning. No one becomes a new being when they attain old age. In many cultures, it is often observed that an old man is seen as a burden in the house whereas the old woman is considered as a treasure in a house.[31] Because an old woman is still able to continue the work she was doing all her life, whereas, the old man is unable to do the house hold work (which he did not do when young) when he becomes old. It is not easy for an old man to shift to the work of a woman when he becomes old. Talmud says that the Pharaoh of Egypt gave the woman's work to men and it was considered as harsh.[32]

The preparations of old age should begin while people are still young. They must begin to invest for old age as early as possible. If a person takes sincere efforts to adjust for the old age at an earlier stage, the transition from young to old will be smooth. In recent years, they have introduced 'time banking' in Swiss banks. Swiss time banking initiatives have experimented with the idea of using 'time banking' as part of a retirement plan. The idea behind these experiments is that those who are young and capable may provide care to seniors. While they do such services, they can bank the time they spend in serving the aged people and then exchange the time they have saved for their care when they become old. This is a remarkable way of preparing for old age.

There is a beautiful Midrash which explains how life continues even after death. Talmud says that R. Bana'ah would mark out tombs for the observance of the ritual purity laws. When he arrived at Abraham's cave, Eliezer was guarding at the entrance. When R. Bana'ah expressed to Eliezer that he must visit the tomb of Abraham and Sarah, Eliezer replied: "He is lying in the embrace of Sarah, and she is looking fondly at his head." When Abraham heard his voice, he told Eliezer: "Let him enter." Everyone is aware that the sexual activity ends in this world. So, R. Bana'ah entered, surveyed the cave, and went out.[33] This midrash describes how Abraham and Sarah's "life" continued in the Cave of Machpelah as the extension of their life in this world. The fact

30 Solomon Schechter, *Some Aspects of Rabbinic Theology* (New York, 1909), 175.

31 Arachin 19a.

32 Sotah 11 b.

33 BT *Bava Batra* 58a.

that Abraham lies in the bosom of Sarah, and not the opposite, reveals their relationship that Abraham subordinates himself to Sarah.

Old Age and Death are Inseparable!

Old age and death are inseparable. As much as long-life matters for a person, it is equally important how he/she departs from this world. Enoch, Abraham, Moses, Elijah, they all attained old age and also had deaths in unique ways. One surpasses the other in the way God had ordained their deaths. David had a practice of sitting and studying Torah on all Sabbath days from morning to night. God had already revealed to David that he must die on a Sabbath day. On the day that he must die, the angel of death arrived and stood before him for a long time, but could not take his life, because he did not cease from learning Torah. Finally, the angel shook a tree in the garden before his house. When David went out to see, as he was climbing the ladder, it broke under him. Thereupon he fell down and became silent [from his studies] and his soul had departed. Because of David's constant preoccupation with the Torah, the angel had to resort to a trick to bring his life to an end.[34]

According to Rashi, Moses wanted to see God's face, but God could not grant him this wish. God knew that Moses will die if he was allowed to see God's face. God was in need of the service of Moses to lead the Israelites to the land of Canaan. Now, the situation has changed. Moses has fulfilled his mission. Moses is not permitted to enter the Land, and the time has come for him to die. It is said, "And Moses the servant of the LORD died there. by the mouth of the LORD" (Deuteronomy 34:5), with the interpretation that God kissed Moses. Finally, when the Lord showed his face to Moses and kissed Moses, Moses died. The Lord buried Moses. No one knows where Moses was buried till this day.[35] David and Moses lived a long life. They attained old age as a blessing. Their long life met with a glorious end.

Conclusion

The Biblical view of ageing is in sharp contrast to the view of the utilitarian philosophers. Biblical view of human life is based on creation theology which says that human beings are created in the image of God. All people have intrinsic worth. It suggests not the physical similarities between God and human, but we are imbibed with the attitudes similar to God. God's attributes are subsumed in the words of John 4:16, "God is love." The highest form of divine love was revealed in the cross and it was the sacrificial love. Even when the aged people become burdensome, Bible says that, "we must bear one another's burdens, and in this way, we will fulfil the law of Christ." (Galatians

34 BT Shabbat 30a.

35 TB Moed Katan 28.

6:2). We must seek to embrace them who are neglected by society, including the aged and should not throw them to garbage or euthanise them. Even when we have not attained the old age, we pray and trust in God's protection in old age in the words of the Psalmist, "So even to old age and grey hairs, O God, do not forsake me, until I proclaim your might to all the generations to come" (Psalm 71:18). God also makes the righteous blossom to the end of their life, "They are planted in the house of the LORD; they flourish in the courts of our God. In old age they still produce fruit; they are always green and full of sap (Psalms 92:13). What a farsighted act that even the pension system was introduced in honour of the aged people from the age of sixty in the early church to set an example for the civil communities. (I Timothy 5:9). We are called to be the light for the world! 'Honour your father and mother' is one of the most revolutionary laws introduced by Moses, which argues that it is an 'act of human rights.'

Even in the parlance of poetry, old age was held as honourable. There is a beautiful verse, "Are you the firstborn of the human race? Were you brought forth before the hills?" (Job 15:7). If that is the case, how can you be proud? The Earth, its mountains, are very old.

Humanity is also very old. The same idea occurs in Psalm 90:2, "Before the mountains were born or you brought forth the whole world." This is a poetic attempt to praise the oldness of nature, humanity and God. The more the older, the more they are to be praised. Those who were made later, those who are younger, must hold the 'ancient' in honour. Old age is precious. "Ageing," is it not a blessing from God!

3

Mapping the Gerontological Imageries in *Qohelet* Juxtaposing the Allegorical and Literal Interpretations of *Qohelet* 12:2-5

Aravind Jeyakumar Moniraj

Introduction

The Hebrew Bible's perspective on the theme "gerontology"[1] or "ageing" is complex in understanding since it "is not always easy to distinguish what is theologically intentional in the Bible and what is sociologically taken for granted."[2] There are plenty of references to older people and their experiences which are mentioned in several passages of the Torah, Prophets and Writings of the Hebrew Bible/Old Testament.[3] The Hebrew Bible underscores that "achieving old age is a divine attribute and the process of ageing can be a distinctive triumph, but at the same time growing older also brings out 'definite testing' along with blessing."[4] In the light of multifaceted ideas of ageing that are presented in the Hebrew Bible, this paper is an attempt to explore the reality of ageing by analysing Ecclesiastes 12:2-5.

---

1 *Gerontology* is the scientific study of old age, the process of ageing and the particular problems of old-age. It concentrates on the social, cultural, psychological, cognitive and biological aspects of ageing. The term *Gerontology* is a combination of two Greek words γέρων, (*geron*) – "old man" and λογία, (*logia*) – "study of," and this term was first coined by Ilya Ilyich Mechnikov in 1903.

2 J. Gordan Harris, *Biblical Perspectives on Aging: God and the Elderly* (New York: Taylor and Francis Inc., 2008), xii.

3 D. Gu. M.E. Dupre, ed., "Biblical Perspectives on Aging" in *Encyclopaedia of Gerontology and Population Aging* (Switzerland: Springer Nature, 2019), 4.

4 James Davies, "A Practical Theology of Aging: Biblical Perspectives for Individuals and the Church," *Christian Education Journal* Series 3, Vol. 5, No. 2 (2008): 274.

Sitz im Leben of Ecclesiastes (Qohelet) with Special Reference to *Qoh.* 12:1-8

The name "Ecclesiastes" is the Greek translation of the Hebrew name *Qohelet*. *Qohelet* is not the proper name of a person but a functional title, and it means probably "the one who speaks to the assembly" (קָהָל – *qahal*).[5] The identification of *Qohelet* with King Solomon in the title of the Book (1:1) is no more than a literary convention, for the Book was composed in the third century BCE.[6] *Qohelet* has a complex character and he has been variously called a pessimist, as epicurean, an early existentialist. But in an actual fact, *Qohelet* is a realist with a basic trust in the reality of God's Providence (Eccl. 3:11, 13-18; 8:17; 11:15). He is a realist who plunged deeply into the mystery and experiences of life and its many vicissitudes.[7]

In the face of Hellenistic (Greek) culture which exalts the power of the human mind and human spirit, *Qohelet* proclaims the utter uselessness of all earthly things: "Meaningless…everything is meaningless" (Eccl. 1:2) – wealth, pleasure, work, success, even the search of wisdom (Eccl. 1:17-18; 2:15).[8] However, he affirms a strong belief in God's Providence, even though no human mind can fathom the depths of God's ways. He rejoices in God's creation (Eccl. 11:7) and affirms the right to enjoy the good things of life when God gives them to us (Eccl. 2:24; 3:13; 11:19). But, we should also be prepared to accept the sorrows of life as they come (Eccl. 7:2-3; 7:14-15), for there is nothing eternal under the sun. He categorically opposes the view that earthly happiness is the goal of life, but he could offer no solution to the problem of divine retribution.[9] One of the masterpieces of *Qohelet* is its grand finale, i.e., the "final poem" which is recorded in *Qoh.* 12:1-8. This section has initiated numerous interpretations due to the richness of mysteries

---

5 Peter Enns, "Book of Ecclesiastes" in *Dictionary of the Old Testament: Wisdom, Poetry and Writings* (Illinois, USA: Intervarsity Press, 2010), 121-122.

6 This was the period when the Ptolemies (Greek Kings) who were ruling Egypt held sway over Palestine, and the influence of Greek language and culture was becoming all pervasive. This influence can be noticed in Ecclesiastes, though the writer/teacher remains Israelite in outlook. Roland E. Murphy and O. Carm, Wisdom Literature: Job, Proverbs, Ruth with Canticles, Ecclesiastes, and Esther *The Forms of Old Testament Literature Vol. XIII* (Grand Rapids, Michigan: William B. Eerdmans Publishing Company, 1981), 127-131.

7 Norbert Lohfink, *Qoheleth – A Continental Commentary* (trans. Sean McEvenue; Minneapolis: Fortress Press, 2003), 9-11.

8 Lohfink, *Qoheleth,* 15-17.

9 Lohfink, *Qoheleth,* 15-17.

or paradoxes it carries and therefore, it has been also considered as "the most controversial portion of the book."[10]

Qohelet 12:1-8: A Controversial Portion with Multiple Interpretations

Qohelet 12:1-8 is arguably "the most controversial portion of the book."[11] There is considerable agreement on the unity of the passage, its purpose and poetic quality,[12] but there is a great disagreement in the interpretations. Many attempts have been made to unify Qoh. 12:1-8 under one analogical scheme: some have advocated that the passage describes physiological changes and others have suggested that it depicts a funeral house and still others have indicated that it pictures a ruined house. MICHAEL V. FOX has explored the interplay of three dimensions of meaning in *Qohelet's* final poem – literal, symbolic and figurative/allegorical,[13] and states that the entire passage describes "the events surrounding a death and funeral" rather than the "process of ageing."[14] The traditional reading from the Jewish sources has recognized *Qoh* 12:1-7 as the "allegory of old age" (physiological) – specific parts of the body are associated with particular details;[15] i.e., "the degeneration of the decaying body."[16] However, the traditional reading has encountered considerable opposition from the contemporary biblical scholarship due to its inconsistent interpretation.[17] JOHN F. A. SAWYER suggests that the poem should be read as "parable of a failure house," which represents the failure of human

---

10 So CHOON-LEONG SEOW, "Qohelet's Eschatological Poem," *JBL* 118 (1999): 209; ROLAND MURPHY, *Ecclesiastes*, WBC 23A (Dallas: Word Books, 1992), 114; MICHAEL V. FOX, *A Time to Tear Down and a Time to Build Up: A Rereading of Ecclesiastes* (Grand Rapids, Michigan/Cambridge, U.K.: William Eerdmans Publishing Company, 1999), 333.

11 CHOON-LEONG SEOW, "Qohelet's Eschatological Poem," *JBL* 118 (1999): 209.

12 DANIEL C. FREDERICKS, "Life's Storms and Structural Unity in Qoheleth 11.1-12.8," *JSOT* 52 (1991): 95-114; CHOON-LEONG SEOW, "Ecclesiastes," *AB* 18C, (New York: Doubleday, 1997), 368-369.

13 For MICHAEL V. FOX, the allegorical interpretation can have validity to certain images expressed in the poem, but the poem as the whole is not an allegory. MICHAEL V. FOX, "Aging and Death in Qohelet 12," *JSOT* 42 (1988): 57. For FOX, sections of the poem should be read at it stands, the surface imagery/literal reading which gives literal meaning of the things, actions and events depicted in the poem. HANS DEBEL, "When it all Falls Apart: A Survey of the Interpretational Maze Concerning the "Final Poem" of the Qohelet (Qoh 12:1-7)," *OTE* 23 /2 (2010): 237; cf. FOX, "Aging and Death," 59-60.

14 FOX, "Aging and Death," 61. This was the literal interpretation proposed by CHARLES TAYLOR and FOX strongly subscribes to this view.; Cf. FOX, *A Time to Tear Down,* 355.

15 ROBERT GORDIS, *Koheleth - The Man and His World: A Study of Ecclesiastes* (New York: Schocken Books, 3 1968), 328; DEBEL, "When it all Falls Apart," 238-243; MURPHY, *Ecclesiastes*, 115.

16 DEBEL, "When it all Falls Apart," 238.

17 DEBEL, "When it all Falls Apart," 238; FOX, *A Time to Tear Down,* 344-347.

efforts.[18] CHARLES TAYLOR argues that the poem is a "dirge describing the state of a household/community on an occasion of death/mourning."[19] CHRISTIAN GINSBURG dismisses the physiological reading and perceives the text as a cohesive description of a "gathering storm" meaning "approaching storm."[20] But DANIEL BUZY is of the opinion that the poem deals with ageing and he prefers to read it from a literal perspective (grammatical-historical) which will genuinely describe what actually aged-people in different sections of society irrespective of their class and status experience while ageing (shaking, stooping, infirmity, blindness and isolation – vv.3-4.[21]

Method: Allegorical or Literal?

"Allegorizing is searching for a hidden or a secret meaning underlying but remote from and unrelated in reality to the more obvious meaning of a text."[22] The literal reading is a sort of code, which needs to be deciphered to determine the more significant and "hidden" or "deeper" meaning. In this approach the literal is superficial; the allegorical is the true deeper meaning. The literal reading doesn't mean the face value reading of the text, but rather it is the grammatical-historical interpretation, where meaning of each word is determined by grammatical and historical considerations that the writer had expressed.[23] When allegorical method is applied to *Qoh.* 12:2-5, it limits the meaning of the passage to just referring to the deterioration of parts of an individual's body only. By doing so this method overlooks the semantic nuances that are applied in the text to explain the sufferings of people from various sections of society due to struggles of ageing. Therefore, the grammatical-historical approach enables the reader to unearth the gerontological issues

---

18 JOHN F. A. SAWYER, "The Ruined House in Ecclesiastes 12: A Reconstruction of the Original Parable," *JBL* 94 (1975): 519-531; HAGIA WITZENRATH, *Süss ist das Licht. Eine literaturwissenschaftliche Untersuchung zu Kohelet 11,7-12,7,* (Münchener Universitätsschriften. Katholisch-theologische Fakultät. Arbeit zu Text und Sprache im Alten Testament, 11; St. Ottilien: EOS Verlag, 1979), 46-50.

19 CHARLES TAYLOR, "The Dirge of Coheleth," *JQR* 4 (1892): 533-549.

20 CHRISTIAN D. GINSBURG, *The Song of Songs and Coheleth, Commonly Called the Book of Ecclesiastes: Translated from the Original Hebrew, with a Commentary, Historical and Critical* (New York: KTAV Publishing House, 1861, repr. 1970), 457-469; FRIEDRICH W. C. UMBREIT, *Koheleths des weissen Königs Seelenkampf* (Gotha-Beckerschen Buchhandlung, 1818).

21 DENIS BUZY, "Le portrait de la vieillesse (Ecclésiaste, xii, 1-7)," RB 41 (1932): 329-340; Maurice Gilbert, "La description de la vieillesse en Qohelet xii 1-7 est-elle allégorique?" in *Congress Volume Vienna 1980* (ed. John A. Emerton; Leiden: Brill, 1981), 96-109; cited in DEBEL, "When it all Falls Apart," 243-243.

22 ROY B. ZUCK, *Basic Bible Interpretation: A Practical Guide to Discovering Biblical Truth* (Colorado Springs, Co: Victor Books, 1991), 29.

23 ZUCK, *Basic Bible Interpretation,* 30.

that are discussed in this passage from the social, cultural, psychological, and biological perspectives, which cover people from all the sections of society. Hence, this research intends to re-visit *Qoh*, 12:2-5 in order to understand the suffering experience of the aged-people who ultimately long with hope for a better life.[24]

Decoding The Allegorical and Literal Meanings of *Qoh.* 12:2-5

An Allegory of Ageing: The Degeneration of the Decrepit Body

The allegorical interpretation of *Qohelet's* final poem, first attested in Targum Onqelos, the Midrash (both *Qohelet Rabbah* and *Leviticus Rabbah* 18) and the Babylonian Talmud (*Shabbat* 151a-153a) is still dominant.[25] It has been understood as a veiled description of the physical and emotional ailments from which the aged suffer; in other words, each object mentioned in the poem is transposed into an organ of the body and its deterioration. Here are some of the decodings that have been proposed in the commentaries, ancient and modern:[26]

> *The sun grows dark:* The light of the face or the forehead dims.
> Or the eyes cannot see the
> sun. or the enjoyment of life fades.
> *The light:* The eyes or nose lose their keenness
> *The moon:* The cheeks or the soul grows dim.

---

24 Gordis, *Koheleth,* 339; Wesley J. Fuerst, *The Book of Ruth, Esther, Ecclesiastes, the Song of Songs, Lamentations: The Five Scrolls* (Cambridge: Cambridge University Press, 1975), 152.

25 Many elements from Targum and Talmud were introduced into Christian exegesis by Jerome and his "historical allegory," he draws from Jewish sources. Matthew Kraus, "Christians, Jews, and Pagans in Dialogue. Jerome on Ecclesiastes 12:1-7," *HUCA* 70-71 (1999-2000): 224-231.

26 Fox, *A Time to Tear Down,* 344-345. George A. Barton, *A Critical and Exegetical Commentary on the Book of Ecclesiastes* (Edinburgh: T&T Clark, 1908), 187-192; Abraham Cohen, *The Five Megilloth: Hebrew Text & English Translation with Introduction and Commentary* (London: Soncino, 8 1968), 299-302; Franz Delitzsch, *Hoheslied und Koheleth* (Leipzig: Dörffling und Franke, 1875), 388-409; Christian D. Ginsburg, *The Song of Songs and Coheleth, Commonly Called the Book of Ecclesiastes: Translated from the Original Hebrew, with a Commentary, Historical and Critical* (New York: KTAV Publishing House, 1861, repr. 1970), 458-467; Robert Gordis, *Koheleth - The Man and His World: A Study of Ecclesiastes* (New York: Schocken Books, 3 1968), 341- 348; Sara Japhet and Robert B. Salters, *The Commentary of R. Samuel Ben Meir Rashbam on Qohelet* (Jerusalem: Magnes; Leiden: Brill, 1985), 206-210; Kraus, "Christian, Jews and Pagans," 224-231; Ludwig Levy, *Das Buch Qoheleth: ein Beitrag zur Geschichte des Sadduzäismus, kritisch untersucht, übersetzt und erklärt* (Leipzig: J. C. Hinrich, 1912), 132-138; Charles Taylor, *The Dirge of Coheleth in Ecclesiastes XII, Discussed and Literally Interpreted* (London - Edinburgh: Williams and Norgate, 1874), 57-63.

The stars: The eyeballs or the cheeks grow dim.
The clouds return after the rain: The eyes darken (grow blurry) after weeping.
The keepers of the house tremble: The knees, or ribs, or legs, or arms, or hands, tremble.
The powerful men writhe: The arms, or loins, (or limbs) or spinal column weaken or bend.
The "grinders" cease: The teeth fall out.
Those (fem) looking through the windows darken: the eyes grow weak or blind.
The doors in the street are closed: The feet or bodily apertures or ears or lips suffer or close.
The anus and bladder suffer retention.
The sound of the mill fades low: The appetite or mouth or digestion or voice diminishes.
He arises to the voice of the bird (usual translation)*:* The old man is easily awakened. Or his voice rises in pitch.
The daughters of song bow low: The voice rasps or loses pitch or becomes weak. Or deafness sets in.
They fear a high thing (or: from on high): Non-allegorical: Old people fear heights.
Frights are along the way: Literal: the aged become timid.
The almond tree blossoms: The hair goes white.
The grasshopper becomes laden (or: becomes a burden): The back of the pelvic cavity becomes sore. Or breathing becomes laboured. Or the joints grow stiff. Of the old man in bent over. Or the ankles swell up. Or the buttocks droop. Or sex becomes onerous. Or the penis fails to become erect. Or a (literal) grasshopper feels heavy to the weakened oldster.
The caperberry is annulled (?): Desire is dulled. Or aphrodisiacs fail.

The Days of the Ending: Mapping the Gerontological Imageries in Qoh. 12:2-5

The above paragraph offered the traditional reading of *Qoh.* 12:2-5 as allegory of old age in which the poem is as a description of the physical degeneration of ageing. But the dominant allegorical interpretation failed to look at the literal reading (grammatical-historical reading) in which the multifaceted human images (i.e. men and women belonging to the different sections of society) reveal the miseries the aged-people face in various forms. Therefore, a careful analysis of *Qoh.* 12:2-5 is inevitable in order to determine its specific point of reference. *Qoh.*12:1-8 is framed by referring God as the "Originator of life." Despite the inequalities of life and the terrors of death, God is ever the Creator of both the living (v.1) and the dead (v. 7). God's sovereignty is thus recognized as a regulating element in all human activities.[27]

The entire passage (*Qoh.*12:1-8) can be divided into three subsections (v. 1; vv. 2-5 and vv. 6-8): Before age (v.1); old age (vv. 2-5); and Death and disintegration (vv. 6-7 or 8). *Qohelet* has employed three times the temporal marker, i.e., עַד אֲשֶׁר לֹא (*'ad 'asher lo'* – before…) in vv. 1b, 2a, 6 in order to maintain the flow of thought and to indicate the temporal-psychological shifts in the passage. These markers interlink the subsections and keep intact the entire passage as one unit. The following study will be concentrating only on vv.2-5. The second thematic marker (עַד אֲשֶׁר לֹא „ רהֶסא`רא` לֹ) introduces a series of metaphors (vv. 2-5) which describe the realities of old age encountered by all.

2a	before the sun grows dark, as well as the light and the moon and the stars,
2b	and the clouds return after the rain;
3a	in the day when the watchers of the house tremble, and the men of strength bend themselves,
3b	and the grinding-maids cease because they are few, and those who look through the windows grow dark,
4a	and the doors in the street are closed, as the sounds of the mills fades,
4b	and one rises at the sound of the bird, and all daughters of song are bowed down
5a	also from up high they fear, and the terror on the road,
5b	and the almond blossoms and the locust drags himself along, and the caper-berry bursts
5c	for man is going to his eternal house, and the mourners go about in the street.

The first part of v. 2a mentions that the light of all sorts become dim, i.e., the sun (שֶׁמֶשׁ – *shemesh*) moon (יָרֵחַ – *yaraah*) light (rAa) – *'or*) and stars (כּוֹכָבִים – *khokavim*). This phenomenon can be understood as "affliction and sadness," the fading capacity of joy. Allegorical reading perceives this as failing of one's eyesight.[28] Light and darkness are standard symbols of well-being and evil.[29] Most simply, this clause is expressing the loss of joy and excitement in

27 Barry C. Davis, "Ecclesiastes 12:1-8 – Death, as Impetus of Life," *Bibliotheca Sacra* 148 (1991): 298-317.

28 Fox, *A Time to Tear Down,* 322.

29 Murphy, *Ecclesiastes*, 118.

life.[30] Secondly, the cloud image (שׁא עָב), "the clouds return after rain" in the Hebrew worldview describes, "a day of misfortune."[31] The unexpected return of the clouds soon after a storm, once more shutting out the light, is a bad sign and brings gloom, both literally and psychologically.[32] Therefore, this imagery is not depicting the gradually failing eyesight, but rather the repetitive gloom into which the elderly may be prone to fall as they encounter setback after setback in the final years of their lives.[33] When an elderly person recovers from one injury or illness he/she is again conquered by another which devastates the individual's hopes and dreams.[34]

Most commentators compare the metaphors mentioned in v. 3 with the deterioration[35] of the human body as it becomes old.[36] The watchers are associated with "the arms," the mighty men "the legs," the grinding one "the teeth" and those at the windows "the eyes."[37] In addition, the writer is not restricting the process of old-age to one gender, but both the genders (male and female) are included in the Hebrew text.[38] "The watchers of the house tremble" refers to the workers or keepers who preserve, protect, and guard the house. The word שֹׁמֵר (*shomer* - keeper) refers not only to the guards but also to all kinds of servants.[39] The reason for trembling might be due to the degeneration of nervous and muscular system of the body or a powerful outside force that

---

30 J. M. Fuller, ed., *Proverbs-Ezekiel*, The Bible Commentary (Grand Rapids: Baker Book House, 1972), 111; Michael A. Eaton, *Ecclesiastes: An Introduction and Commentary* (Downers Grove, IL: InterVarsity Press, 1983), 148; Derek Kidner, *A Time to Mourn, and a Time to Dance* (Downers Grove, IL: InterVarsity Press, 1976), 101; J. Barton Payne, *The Theology of the Old Testament* (Grand Rapids: Zondervan Publishing House, 1971), 186.

31 Davis, "Ecclesiastes," 307. Cf. Franz Delitzsch, *Commentary on the Song of Songs and Ecclesiastes – Biblical Commentary on the Old Testament* (trans. M. C. Easton; Grand Rapids: Zondervan Publishing House, 1988), 405.

32 Davis, "Ecclesiastes," 307.

33 James L. Crenshaw, "The Shadow of Death in Qoheleth," in *Israelite Wisdom* (ed. John G. Gammie et al.; Missoula, MT: Scholars Press, 1978), 185.

34 Eaton, *Ecclesiastes,* 148; Delitzsch, *Commentary on the Song of Songs and Ecclesiastes,* 405; Raymond N. Whybray, *Ecclesiastes*, *The New Century Bible Commentary* (Grand Rapids: Wm. B. Eerdmans Publishing Co., 1989), 164; Crenshaw, "The Shadow of Death," 185.

35 Robert B. Y. Scott, *Proverbs, Ecclesiastes*, AB (Garden City, NY: Doubleday and Co., 1965), 255.

36 Whybray, *Ecclesiastes*, 164; Debel, "When it all Falls Apart," 239.

37 Murphy, *Ecclesiastes*, 118.

38 Crenshaw, "The Shadow of Death," 186.

39 Fox, *A Time to Tear Down,* 323.

threatens the watchers. Thus, the aged become defenceless to the increasing attacks in terms of physical, mental and psychological.[40]

The next metaphor in v. 3a describes that the men of strength bend themselves – וְהִתְעַוְּתוּ אַנְשֵׁי הֶחָיִל (*wehit'awwetu 'anshe hehayil*). There is variety of semantic meaning to the term "powerful (men)" (אַנְשֵׁי הֶחָיִל – *'anshe hehayil*) skill, strength, efficiency, ability, wealth, force, army and virtue.[41] They are men with influence and position (referring to social status) in contrast to the servants or keepers.[42] The word bending (וְהִתְעַוְּתוּ – *wehit'awwetu*) connotes that the strong men are neither naturally bent over nor do they choose to be, but rather forces working contrary to their will impose conditions to which they finally surrender.[43] The following set of metaphors (v. 3b) stands in opposition to the guards and influential men who are mentioned in the previous line in masculine form (v. 3a): "and the grinding-maids cease because they are few, and those who look through the windows grow dark, (conjugated in feminine forms). The allegorical interpretation of "grinding maids" is "teeth" and "the woman looking through the windows" is "eyes."[44] The grinding-maids (הַ טֹּחֲנוֹת וּבָטְלוּ – *uvatlu hattohanot*) is plausibly referring to the female servants (טֹּחֲנוֹת הַ – *hattohanot*) who make flour for the household's bread. This can mean that women are few in number to work and they need more labour force. Moreover, the grinding ones are the unspecified group of people in the house who no longer possess the resources to support them.[45]

The metaphor, וְחָשְׁכוּ הָרֹאוֹת בָּאֲרֻבּוֹת – *wehashku haro'ot ba'arubbot*: "and those who look through the window grow dark is referring to women (the lookers הָרֹאוֹת (*haro'ot*)" explains the condition of the aged-women. According to the AWA custom women were not allowed to associate with men in household matters (e.g. decision making) and so they are scrutinized through the repeated-work of the house.[46] They hardly have freedom and eventually their eyes become dim or grow dark (lack of clarity of vision).[47] Due to this condition they have a difficult time to view through the windows which has become dark to them. In any case, women have been increasingly isolated or cut off from the outside world and denied of the joys and pleasures they once

40 BDB, 226; Debel, "When it all Falls Apart," 243-245.

41 BDB, 61; Fox, *A Time to Tear Down,* 325.

42 Fox, *A Time to Tear Down,* 325; Whybray, *Ecclesiastes,* 164.

43 Davis, "Ecclesiastes," 309.

44 Murphy, *Ecclesiastes*, 118. The teeth stand in isolation and no longer stand in a row and some are decayed in the process of ageing. Davis, "Ecclesiastes," 309.

45 Fox, *A Time to Tear Down,* 324.

46 Gordis, *Koheleth,* 342.

47 Murphy, *Ecclesiastes*, 118. Delitzsch, *Commentary on the Song of Songs and Ecclesiastes,* 405.

knew due to the cultural norms. Hence, it is more pitiable for the aged women who are confined to their homes or dependent upon others.[48]

Qohelet continues to portray this isolation-fear imagery in v. 4. "And the doors in the street are closed, as the sounds of the mills fades." If one approaches the text from an allegorical point of view, appropriate parts of the body can be supplied. The doors can refer to the dual organs – two ears, jaws or possibly lips.[49] Doors appear in dual form (דְלָתַיִם – *delatayim*) referring to double doors which are only found at the entrance of cities, temples and exceptionally grand houses, since most houses apparently had only single doors.[50] The doors are closed, perhaps denotes the inattentiveness or a lack of care by those responsible for opening them, or perhaps through their own inability to be opened any more.[51] It can also literally refer to the weak steps of the elderly, who can no longer walk steadily and are hence impeded from going out on the street.[52] In addition, the doors may shut remains as a picture of a self-enclosed, self-isolated group of people.[53] "And the sound of the mill fades" because few people are working there (cf. v. 3). The noise of the mill can be referred to the voice that weakens the age – "feebleness of the voice."[54] Such a condition would be discouraging to the elderly because what they remember as a cheerful indicator of the exciting activities of business is now more and more being shut out of their lives. They in turn find themselves "increasingly cut off from the hum of daily life."[55]

Many interpreters assume that the rising at the sound of the bird (v. 4b) portrays the insomnia of the elderly, whose sleep is so light that even a bird tweeting can disturb it – which, according to the Targumic and Midrashic tradition, makes them afraid of robbers.[56] Others, translating the verb וְיָקוּם (*weyaqum*) impersonally as "it rises to the sound of a bird," explain this phrase as an allusion to the intense of the old man's voice, which was clear as a bell in the vigour of his life, but has now turned treble and resembles the high-pitched sound of a sparrow.[57] The "daughters of song" (בְּנוֹת הַשִּׁיר – *benot hashshir*)

48 Debel, "When it all Falls Apart," 243-244.

49 Murphy, *Ecclesiastes*, 118; Debel, "When it all Falls Apart," 240.

50 Barton, *A Critical and Exegetical Commentary,* 118; Whybray, *Ecclesiastes,* 165; Fox, *A Time to Tear Down,* 325; Murphy, *Ecclesiastes*, 118.

51 Davis, "Ecclesiastes," 310.

52 Debel, "When it all Falls Apart," 240.

53 Fuller, *Proverbs-Ezekiel*, 111.

54 Debel, "When it all Falls Apart," 240.

55 Davis, "Ecclesiastes," 311.

56 Debel, "When it all Falls Apart," 241.

57 Charles H. H. Wright, *The Book of Koheleth, Commonly Called Ecclesiastes. Considered in Relation to Modern Criticism, and to the Doctrines of Modern Pessimism, with a Critical*

have also been associated with the old man's vocal capacities, particularly with his inability to utter songs and the trembling of his lips. The allegorical reading tends to perceive the daughters of song as the mourning women, the professionals who mourn in the funerals.[58] However, it is also suggested that they refer to the upcoming deafness, making it impossible for the aged to distinguish sounds from songs and to appreciate the joyous songs of their youth.[59]

Qohelet's change of tone in v. 5 in terms of existential Anguish[60] can be noted and fear now runs widespread. The elderly "are afraid of a high place and of terrors on the road" – they develop acrophobia or because they are averse to walking up hills. The word גָּבֹהַּ (*gaboah*) is used here which is an adjective, applied to "tall or lofty" entities and could serve as a noun meaning something tall or height, but not height or high places.[61] The other way of rendering this verse is "also from up high they fear," which can also metaphorically connote the fear of God "up high."[62] However, the adjective גָּבֹהַּ (*gaboah*) is not a recognizable epithet for God. Their weakened sight and constrained breathing prevent them from ascending high places. The slightest hindrance on the road is described as "the terror on the road," because they can no longer trust their weak limbs.[63] A straightforward rendering of these two images expresses the person who is old, feeble, and defenceless, which have great risks and physical dangers.[64]

The remaining three metaphors in *Qoh.* 12:5 are difficult to interpret and three nouns are used here, the almond, locust and the caperberry.[65] The first of these three images "the almond blossoms" is a symbolism referring to the white

---

Grammatical Commentary and a Revised Translation. The Donnellan Lectures for 1800-1 (London: Hooder and Stoughton, 1883), 248; WHYBRAY, *Ecclesiastes*, 165; CRENSHAW, "The Shadow of Death," 187. However, a strangeness results from such an explanation, for if the old man's ears have become so impenetrable that he is unconscious to the sounds around him, he would not be awakened by a bird singing. KIDNER, *A Time to Mourn,* 102.

58 FOX, *A Time to Tear Down,* 326.

59 DEBEL, "When it all Falls Apart," 241; WHYBRAY, *Ecclesiastes*, 164; FULLER, *Proverbs-Ezekiel*, 112; HERBERT C. LEUPOLD, *Exposition of Ecclesiastes* (Grand Rapids: Baker Book House, 1968), 280; WHYBRAY, *Ecclesiastes*, 165.

60 CRENSHAW, "The Shadow of Death," 207.

61 FOX, *A Time to Tear Down,* 327.

62 DEBEL, "When it all Falls Apart," 241.

63 FOX, *A Time to Tear Down,* 327; DEBEL, "When it all Falls Apart," 241.

64 DAVIS, "Ecclesiastes," 312; DELITZSCH, *Commentary on the Song of Songs and Ecclesiastes,* 411-412.

65 The almond, locust, and caperberry have most often been read as deliberately obscured sexual organs. FOX, *A Time to Tear Down,* 327.

hair of an elderly person.[66] The word שָׁקֵד (*shaqed*) is "a symbol of watchfulness with which old age is visited.[67] The second metaphor "and the locusts drags himself alone," is often read in the following ways: the stiffness of the joints; the bent figure of an old person; the enormous; appetite of the locust which, becoming weighted down by its full stomach, moves awkwardly.[68] The third metaphor is caperberries, "the caperberry is ineffective." Caperberries were used in ancient times as a "provocative to appetite." This implies therefore, that in old age, not even an artificial stimulant can move the individual to do what they have done in the past.[69]

The concluding section of v.5 explicitly presents about the fact of death – "for man is going to his eternal house" (כִּי־הֹלֵךְ הָאָדָם אֶל־בֵּית עוֹלָמוֹ – *ki ha'adam 'el-bet 'olamo*). The verb הָלַךְ (*halek* – to go) is used euphemistically in classical Hebrew to express the concept of dying.[70] "To his eternal home" indicates that the end of that "going" is the individual's final resting place.[71] *Qohelet* concludes with the promise of eternal home which is not the unknown grave and darkness but eternity and not vanity – "physical death opens the doorway to a new quality of existence."[72]

Conclusion

Qoh. 12:2-5 imprints "the shifting of abilities and adjusting to loss is inevitable with ag(e)ing."[73] The gerontological images unfolded from the above analyzed passage portray old age as the time of affliction, sadness, the fading capacity of joy and so on. The literal reading of Qoh. 12:2-5 unlike the allegorical interpretation, enabled us to unearth the agony of the elderly people in different social levels who face the difficulties of ageing in their respective social contexts. "The guards/keepers" and "the grinding maids" represent the people who struggle for their livelihood. Due to their natural ageing process and health abnormalities they lose their jobs and struggle for their survival and they have no security of life during their older age. Even the skillful men/strong

66 This view is favoured because the almond blossom, which exhibits a pink colour when it blooms and very soon thereafter becomes white at the tip. Delitzsch, *Commentary on the Song of Songs and Ecclesiastes,* 413; Whybray, *Ecclesiastes*, 166; Gordis, *Koheleth,* 345.

67 Ernest W. Hengstenberg, *A Commentary on Ecclesiastes* (Minneapolis: James and Klock, 1977), 248.

68 Davis, "Ecclesiastes," 313.

69 Fuller, *Proverbs-Ezekiel*, 112; Delitzsch, *Commentary on the Song of Songs and Ecclesiastes,* 416; Whybray, *Ecclesiastes*, 166-167.

70 Nicholas J. Tromp, *Primitive Conceptions of Death and the Netherworld in the Old Testament* (Rome: Pontifical Biblical Institute, 1969), 167.

71 Kraus, "Christian, Jews and Pagans," 230; Debel, "When it all Falls Apart," 243.

72 Davies, "A Practical Theology of Aging," 276.

73 Davies, "A Practical Theology of Aging," 283.

men who bend themselves are forced to do so, which signifies that elderly with more innovative abilities are replaced by young personnel forcefully. The plight of women (whether rich or poor) in the patriarchal society becomes more and more devastating during the later stages of their life. The life of isolation, social, economic and physical dependence and denial of opportunities during the older age are expressed through the metaphor of shutting the doors on the streets which leads to self-isolation. The space and voice of the elderly in the family and society gradually fades and their significance diminishes. They are feeble, defenseless and their life encounters great risks and physical dangers and moreover, they are counted as people with less growth and productivity and above all they are considered as incapable for procreation.

Despite all these discouraging realities, the passage (*Qoh.* 12:2-5) underlines the following foundational aspects of ageing in the light of the gerontological imageries: all human life is precious and sacred (God is the creator); physical life is temporal; the ageing process is natural, inescapable and dynamic; ageing provides opportunity for increased growth toward maturity and wisdom and the journey of the faith life enables the aged-people to face difficulties and death with confidence. Moreover, two aspects can be discovered as a lesson for all: ageing is inevitable, we all will face this stage of life; therefore, it is our sole responsibility to revere the aged and give room for their peaceful living; insights can be drawn from their experiences to enrich our lives and above all, the obstacles that hinder them to gracefully age should be removed in order to enable them to live life with all its fullness.

4

Growing Old in the Ancestral Narratives
A Theological Perspective

Nagaiyasamy N. S. Samuel

Introduction

Study of biological ageing was reflected both in the scientific fields as well as in the religious worlds. In scientific researches, the ageing was studied at a biological level; ageing is associated with the gradual accumulation of a wide variety of molecular and cellular damage.[1] The ageing process encompasses changes at the molecular, cellular, and organismal levels which analysed with various methods.[2] In the religious researches, the biological ageing process was perceived from the religio-socio-scientific, cultural perspectives to see ageing as a blessing and in certain cases as a disadvantage to an individual and the community. There are certain pertinent questions raised when one reads about Ageing in the Hebrew Scripture such as how must the life spans of biblical ancestors be understood in the light of those of their extra-biblical contemporaries which, as recorded in their own writings, are considerably at odds with those of the Bible? Can they be taken literally? Must or can they be manipulated in order to bring coherence to them? Do they have symbolical, mystical, or other coded meanings that permit the texts as written to have meaning other than what appears on the surface of the text? This study would attempt with the literary, historical, hermeneutical and theological tools to study *ageing* in the Hebrew Scripture, particularly from the Ancestral Narratives.

Etymological Study of Ageing

The regular Hebrew expression for age or ageing intends a simple designation of advanced age and/or declining years of life. The most frequent Hebrew

1 World Health Organization, *World Report on Ageing and Health*, 2015, 25.

2 Trygve O. Tollefsbol, ed., *Biological Ageing: Methods and Protocols* (New Jersey: Humana Press, 2007), 1.

term used for ageing is זָקֵן[3] *zaḳen* (*old, and old man*). This term is applied first to Abraham[4] and thereafter to other Biblical worthies, such as Isaac, Jacob, Joshua, Eli, Samuel, and David. In a number of instances, the term is defined by the additional expression *advanced in years*. This term! זָקֵן ((*zaḳen*) is connected with the word זָקָן[5] *zaḳan* (*beard, chin, lower jaw*), the gray beard being the most striking sign of age. It also means one who wears a beard, i.e., a fully accredited adult. Though the term defines any person past puberty, it also designates a clan leader, a local official, and an old person.[6] From *zaḳen* are obtained the derivatives זִקְנָה[7] *ziḳnah* and זְקֻנִים[8] *zeḳunim*, meaning *old age*. We find also the following expressions: שֵׂיבָה[9] *sebah* (*old age*), יָשִׁישׁ[10] *yashish* (*an old man*), שְׂבַע יָמִים[11] *seba' yamim* (*satiated with years*), מְלֵא יָמִים[12] *mel` yamim* (*full of years*), כַּבִּיר יָמִים *kabbir yamim* (rich in years[13]). Of the two terms most commonly used for Old Age, *sebah* designated a greater age than *ziḳnah*.

Issues of Lifespan in the Ancestral Narrative

One of the most obstinate problems in the Hebrew Scriptures among many others has to do with the lifespans of Abraham, Isaac, and Jacob, the three together embracing the period from ca. 2150-1860 BCE, the Early Bronze-Middle Bronze era in terms of archaeological description.[14] The genealogy that is presented in the Hebrew Bible Gen. 5:1-32; and 11:10-32[15] have ample

3 F. Brown, S. R. Driver, C. A. Briggs, *Hebrew English Lexicon* (Oxford: Clarendon Press, 1906), 278.

4 This term also used in the pre-flood narrative and also from Noah to Abraham Narratives also.

5 F. Brown, S. R. Driver, C. A. Briggs, *Hebrew English Lexicon*, 278.

6 David Noel Freedman, *Old Age, Anchor Bible Dictionary*, vol. 5 (New York: Double Day), 6491.

7 F. Brown, S. R. Driver, C. A. Briggs, *Hebrew English Lexicon*, 279.

8 F. Brown, S. R. Driver, C. A. Briggs, *Hebrew English Lexicon*, 279.

9 F. Brown, S. R. Driver, C. A. Briggs, *Hebrew English Lexicon*, 966.

10 F. Brown, S. R. Driver, C. A. Briggs, *Hebrew English Lexicon*, 450.

11 F. Brown, S. R. Driver, C. A. Briggs, *Hebrew English Lexicon*, 960. Gen 15:15; 25:8; Judg. 8:32; 1 Chr. 29:28. A similar image appears in Biblical Aramaic describing the – ancient of days who sits enthroned with hair like lamb's wool.

12 F. Brown, S. R. Driver, C. A. Briggs, *Hebrew English Lexicon*, 571.

13 F. Brown, S. R. Driver, C. A. Briggs, *Hebrew English Lexicon*, 460.

14 These dates derive from the data of the Masoretic Texts, specifically from Genesis 12:4; 16:16; 17:1, 17; 21:5; 23:1; 25:7; 35:28; 47:9, 28; 50:22. For the bases of these dates and biblical chronology in general Eugene H. Merrill, "Chronology," in *Dictionary of the Old Testament: Pentateuch*, edited by T. Desmond Alexander and David W. Baker (Downers Grove: IVP, 2003), 113-22.

15 The genealogy of Gen. 11 states about the Post-Flood Biblical Ancestors life span varies from MT, LXX and Samaritan Pentateuch.

textual variations with regard to the age of the Post-Flood Ancestors. The genealogy of Gen. 5 has the purpose of tracing the history of humanity in general whereas Gen. 11:10-32 focuses on the Noah-Abraham connection. The genealogy in Gen. 11:10-32, one could see the textual variations with regard to the age of the Ancestors. The years of giving birth to the first son varies between MT and LXX about 100 years. Samaritan Pentateuch which profoundly depends on LXX agrees with the lifespan of Post-Flood Ancestors. As per MT the total number of years is 2176 with the average of 272 years; the years for LXX are 2525 with 315 years average and in SP 1506 with average of 188 years. The three great Ancestors lived for 502 years, average of 167 years, with the reduction of average that is found in Gen. 11.[16] Probably, they noticed the actual authenticities of their context and found it difficult to square their life expectancies with the biblical records. Thus, they reduced the figures, at least in some examples, thereby providing some relief to their perplexity.[17]

The principal passages in which the lifespans of Abraham, Isaac, and Jacob are in view are, respectively, Genesis 25:7; 35:28; and 47:28. The great manuscripts and versions agree with MT that Abraham lived to be 175, Isaac 180, and Jacob 147. Obviously, one cannot attribute these numbers to text corruption or idiosyncratic interpolations or the like. They are fixed and grounded as far as text criticism is concerned.[18] The three great Ancestors lived between 2200 and 1800 BCE. It is important that when their age lengths compared to those of the contemporary AWA world, the mystery of the ages of the Ancestors has helped a little and to some extent none by the available Ancient Near Eastern literatures which leads to suggest solutions across the broad spectrum of biblical scholarship.[19]

H. Gunkel views the Old Testament as folklore and/or legend and emancipates the Ancestral period from imaginative characteristics, which leads to the historical validity of the Ancestors.[20] K. A. Kitchen states that historicity of the early texts of the Ancestors were exaggerated of the true

16 Eugene H. Merrill, "The Lifespans of the EB-MB Patriarchs: A Hermeneutical and Historical Conundrum," *Southwestern Journal of Theology*, 57 (Spring 2015): 270.

17 Gordon J. Wenham, "Genesis 1-15," *Word Biblical Commentary*, vol. 1 (Waco: Word, 1987), 250-51.

18 Eugene H. Merrill, "The Lifespans of the EB-MB Patriarchs: A Hermeneutical and Historical Conundrum," 270.

19 Eugene H. Merrill, "The Lifespans of the EB-MB Patriarchs: A Hermeneutical and Historical Conundrum," 271.

20 Hermann Gunkel, *Genesis* (Philadelphia: Fortress Press, 1979), 30. With regard to the genealogy of Cain, Gunkel writes that the legend originally existed as an independent narrative in which a few imaginative figures appear.

figures.[21] Westermann who takes a conservative position applies to the age of a literary or genre solution and proposes that the Ancestral accounts are basically historical, employ literary analysis magnification to demonstrate the greatness of God and God's people.[22] Von Rad presumes that the biblical genealogies were borrowed from secular prototypes of Mesopotamian Kings, Sumerian Kings and Egyptian Kings, deviated from their polytheism in favour of Israel's monotheistic God, Yahweh.[23] The Medieval Judaism that engage in Kabbalism[24] or some other form of numerology to view the number of years of the age in the genealogy which obliged to view the numbers as a coding system that has to be "cracked" in order for the true figures to emerge the age of the Ancestors.[25]

In Genesis, Chapters 5 and 11 we read that the early patriarchs lived deep into old age. Adam lived 930 years, Mathuselah 969 years, Abraham 175, Sarah 127, and Joseph 110 years.[26] Living longer is not a new historical fact. In the Old Testament, the ancient patriarchs died at the age of 900 or even older. Methuselah is one such example. Age was probably measured differently in those days.[27] There are some problems with these Genesis numbers. First, from biological evidence men do not live to be eight or nine hundred years. Second, men do not father children when they are over a century old.[28] Such problems

---

21 K. A. Kitchen, *The Authority of the Old Testament* (Grand Rapids: Eerdmans, 2003), 359: "[The patriarchs'] life spans and birth dates are high; a minimal chronology would allow for possible inflation of these figures in tradition, while keeping the overall profile."

22 Claus Westermann, *Genesis I-II.* Trans. John J. Scullian (Minneapolis: Augsburg: 1984), 354: "The genealogy sets in motion and puts into the length and breadth of human history the power of the blessing which God bestowed on his people."

23 Gerhard von Rad, *Genesis* OTL (1961), 66-71; for a summary of this view and a rebuttal to the ANE - Israel sequence is stated in John H. Walton, *Ancient Israelite Literature in Its Cultural Context* (Grand Rapids: Zondervan, 1989), 127-31.

24 The term refers to a system of mystical hermeneutics in Medieval Judaism that, among other things, assigned numerical values to the Hebrew letters of a word or even series of words. As it can be seen in Frank Talmage, "Apples of Gold: The Inner Meaning of Sacred Texts in Medieval Judaism," in *Jewish Spirituality*, edited by Arthur Green (New York: Crossroad, 1986), 328-29, 337- 40; Daniel C. Matt, "The Mystic and the *Mizwot,"* Green, *Jewish Spirituality,* 372-89.

25 Umberto Cassuto, *Commentary on Genesis I* (Jerusalem: Magnes, 1989), 249-72.

26 Elias L. Taylor, "Senior Years: Old and New Testament," *International Journal of Humanities and Social Science,* 1/18 (Special Issue), 103. Available at: http://www.ijhssnet.com/view.php?u=http://www.ijhssnet.com/journals/Vol_1_No_18_Special_Issue/13.pdf.

27 Ana Amélia Camarano, "Living Longer: Are we getting older or younger for longer?" *Vibrant*, 13/1 (Jan. - Jun. 2016): 155.

28 Adam was 130 years old when his son Seth was born; Seth was 105 when his son Enos was born; Mathuselah was 187 when his son Lamech was born; Shem was 100 when his son Arphaxad was born; Abraham was 100 and Sarah over 80 years old when Isaac was born.

disappear, however, if one assumes the following: (a) the original Genesis numbers were not written in decimal notations. They were instead recorded in an archaic, pre-cuneiform, sign-value, number system, similar to what we know today as Roman numerals; (b) the compilers of the original Hebrew text calculated the years/seasons data using one or more archaic number sign for tens, a different sign for tenths, and a different sign for measuring units of weights.[29] This is called sign-value notation. This original text was edited several times. It was edited again in the 5th and 4th century BC and later translated into Greek done in Alexandria, Egypt about 280 BCE known to us as the Septuagint - the sources and the traditions that contributed for the variations of the age in the biblical text.[30]

It appears that the early scribes had difficulty interpreting correctly the archaic sign-value system, since they did not know in which number system the original texts were written and the context in which they were written. When the scribes translated the numbers, probably erroneously assumed they were written in the Sumerian proto-sexagesimal number system. The Sumerians used one system of numbers designed for counting discrete objects such as animals with different notations and a different number system designed for counting volumes of grain. Confusing one system for another creates errors. Such errors converted tens of years to hundreds, years to tens of years, tenths of years to years, and also inflated the ages at death for people who were mentioned in those records.[31] In Genesis 5 was based on these mistranslated numbers representing the ages of Noah, a Sumerian king of Shuruppak, and his ancestors which were written in clay tablets before the river (Euphrates) flood of 2,900 B.C. The archaic (pre-cuneiform) Sumerian number system was probably created by taxation scribes, so that tax collectors would know who was responsible for paying real-estate taxes. Therefore, when the Old Testament numbers are translated properly, Adam lived to be 81 years old and Mathuselah, the epitome of longevity, lived to be 84.9 years old.[32]

Ancestral Traditions on Ageing

As Jacob approached death, his 147 years were summarized as "the years of his life" (Gen 47:28). A rich, full life is one that satiated in time, as Job was "full of years" (Job 42:17; also Abraham in Gen 25:8).

29 Borland, James, A., "Did People Live to be Hundreds of Years Old before the Flood?" in *The Genesis Debate*, edited by Ronald F. Youngblood (Grand Rapids: Baker Book House, 1990).

30 Elias L. Taylor, "Senior Years: Old and New Testament," 104.

31 Klein, R., "Archaic Chronologies and the Textual History of the Old Testament," *Harvard Theological Review*, 67 (1974): 255-263.

32 Elias L. Taylor, "Senior Years: Old and New Testament," 106.

The Pentateuchal traditions, pre-Deuteronomistic sources, and other ancient Near Eastern literature contributed in knowing the Ancestral traditions.[33] These materials on the basis of different traditions had its amalgamation in the form of compilation, on each occasion; older literary materials have been collected and placed in a redactional setting that determined their arrangement, presentation and interpretation. Three great compilations have come down to us: the Pentateuch, the Deuteronomistic historiography and the Chronicles historiography.[34]

All this tells us very little about the organisations of patriarchal society that the family tie was prevalent to care for the aged. There was, however, awareness within the patriarchal tradition of certain links uniting the ancestors of Israel to other groups of people, but these were always expressed genealogically.[35] Lot for example, was Abraham's nephew. He went with him from Ur to Haran (Gen. 11:31) and from Haran to Canaan (Gen. 12:5). He then separated from him (Gen. 13:5-12) and became the father of the Moabites and the Ammonites (Gen. 19:30-38). Again, Nahor, Abraham's brother, had twelve sons who were the ancestors of the Aramaean tribes (Gen. 22:20-24). As we have already seen, Ishmael, Isaac's brother, was the ancestor of twelve *'ummoth*, the equivalent of tribes (Gen. 25:13-16). Finally, Jacob's brother Esau was the 'father' of the Edomites (Gen. 36:6-9), who were divided into clans of *'alluph* (Gen. 36:15-19, 40-43).[36]

Obviously, the sons of Jacob at this time had their individual families yet they lived under their father's headship and were responsible for their parents' welfare. Such socio-cultural family structure was a strategy which the Israelites used in dealing with the elderly demands. The elders on their part provided advisory services and could direct the children hence being a defence for them. Just before the monarchy, the Naomi-Ruth story in the Book of Ruth exemplifies further how the Israelites took care of their elderly ones. Naomi lived with both her sons and her daughter's in-law before the children died. Ruth provided care for Naomi and was able to sustain her.[37]

---

33 Mignon R. Jacobs and Raymond F. Person Jr. eds., *Israelite Prophecy and the Deuteronomistic History Portrait, Reality, and the Formation of a History* (Atlanta: Society of Biblical Literature, 2013), 4.

34 Albert de Pury, Thomas Römer and Jean-Daniel Macchi, eds., *Israel Constructs its History Deuteronomistic Historiography in Recent Research* (Sheffield Academic Press, 2000), 48.

35 M. D. Johnson: *The Purpose of the Biblical Genealogies* (Cambridge: Cambridge University Press, 1969), 77.

36 Roland de Vaux, *The Early History of Israel: To the Exodus and Covenant of Sinai*, Trans. David Smith (London: Darton, Longman & Todd, 1978), 240.

37 Uzonna F. Echeta and Ebere Ifeyinwa Ezeh, "The Igbo Care for the Elderly in Contemporary Times: An Old Testament Evaluation," *International Journal of Development and Management Review*, 12/1 (2017): 146.

Sarah: The Ancestress

In the Hebrew Bible, Sarah is the only woman whose age, death and burial are mentioned primarily to give high honour to the mother of the Hebrew people. She was a channel of blessing to fulfil the promise of God made with Abraham the Father of a great nation. The legacy of Sarah rooted in her commitment to family through the respect and love for her husband Abraham and inherits spiritual motherhood as well. Sarah was hundred and twenty seven years old when she died. The Jewish writers immediately mention that Isaac was when thirty seven years of age with his mother Sarah. Sarah was the only woman whose age was reckoned in the Hebrew Scripture.

Deuteronomistic Tradition on Ageing

The Deuteronomistic tradition glorifies some of its heroes by describing their longevity. Deuteronomic summary praises the good health of Moses at his death (Dt. 34:7), and Caleb brags on his extra vigour at 85 years of age (Josh 14:10–11). A study of fourteen kings from the dynasty of David presents a clearer picture of the average life span during the royal eras of Israel, 926–597 BCE[38] Omitting Jehoiakim, Jehoiachin, and Zedekiah, the age at death of the remaining kings varies between 66 (Manasseh) and 21 (Ahaziah), the average being 44. Premature and unnatural causes of death such as assassination may account for some of these deaths. Nevertheless, in spite of superior diet and medical care, monarchs in stable Judah during this period did not live 70 or 80 years (contra Ps 90:10). Outside of stories about the patriarchs in Genesis, only Moses (120 years), Joshua (110), Job (140), and the high priest Jehoiada (130, 2 Chr. 24:15) are said to surpass 100. One passage suggests that only in the eschatological kingdom would people regularly attain 100 years (Isa 65:20). Generally, transitions to old age began earlier than age 65.[39]

The Deuteronomists urged people to preserve the law within their heart, so that they could live a long time and that all may go well with them (Proverbs 22:28, Deuteronomy: 25:13-16). The Covenant Code, the Decalogue (Exodus 34), each encompassed a wide range of anticipated punishments in the event of particular infringements of the law and gradually came to characterize an Israelite community of faith. The *Tôrāh* was associated with disclosing the divine will, and it gave shape to the Israelites as the elect people of God. Those who embraced the law and who obeyed God would inherit life eternal. By embracing the *Tôrāh* and the law one embraces God.[40] Once Israel was given the *Tôrāh*

---

38 Hans Walter Wolff, *Anthropology of the Old Testament* (Philadelphia: Fortress Press, 1974), 119–123.

39 David Noel Freedman, *Old Age, Anchor Bible Dictionary*, vol. 1 (New York: Double Day, 1987), 11–17.

40 *African Journal of Hospitality, Tourism and Leisure* 1/3 (2011).

they responded, we will do everything the Lord has said, we will obey (Exodus 24:7). God responded to them, "Everything they said was good. Oh, that their hearts would be inclined to fear me and keep all my commands always so that it might go well with them and their children forever" (Dt. 5:28-29).

In Deuteronomy 27:16 there are curses against those who do not honour or who speak ill of their parents. Yahweh in the Old Testament was described as old and wise. Since God was the "Ancient One," He demanded that His people respect and honour Him; therefore, He expected and required that those who were older be respected and honoured as well.[41] There are even more specific God - given instructions to the Israelite nation regarding the care of the destitute and elderly. Deut. 24:19-22 we read that God commanded them to leave some of the grain, olive and grape harvest for *the alien, the fatherless and the widow.*[42]

Theology for the Ageing

The duty to honour the parents appears on every statue or picture of the Ten Commandments.[43] The communal and extended family structure of the patriarchs enabled them to take good care of their elderly folks. This patriarchal family structure vividly exemplifies and typifies the family structure of the Israelites. For instance, Abraham lived with Lot and his family and both families shared everything together until they grew to uncontrollable size (Gen. 13). Even when they separated, it is the same spirit of communal living that made Abraham to muster three hundred and eighteen men to a rescue attack for Lot against Chedorlaomer and the Kings that allied with him. He defeated them and brought back his relative, Lot (Gen 14:14-17). They shared in their joys and sorrows. Isaac lived with his grown children even after Esau married (Gen 28:9).[44]

Numbers 4:3 and 8:24-26 define the age span during which Levites are to perform their tasks in worship and in transporting the Tabernacle in the Sinai Desert, from age 25 (or 30, the difference is not relevant here) till age fifty. After that, according to verse 8:25-6, they may no longer perform the official functions but they may "assist their brethren," meaning, effectively, they were kept on in a "consultant" capacity. The rabbis were troubled by this. They said the mandatory retirement age for Levites applied only in the desert, where heavy physical labour was involved; in the Temple in Jerusalem, where the Levites' main jobs were to sing in the choir and guard the gates, they could

---

41 Elias L. Taylor, "Senior Years: Old and New Testament," 110.

42 Lev. 19: 9-10, 23:22, etc.

43 Exodus 20:12.

44 Uzonna F. Echeta and Ebere Ifeyinwa Ezeh, "The Igbo Care for the Elderly in Contemporary Times: An Old Testament Evaluation," 146.

continue to serve until they "lost their voices."[45] Maimonides was yet more concerned about forced retirement. He ruled that even after a Levite can no longer sing, he may still guard the Temple gates.[46]

Conclusion

Ageing is an indispensable human condition. Whatever has a beginning has a growth and decadence. Therefore, Human Beings are part of nature as Human Beings. Human beings are a rare mixture of physique and spiritual elements. Physique as far as the Human body is a matter. God made Human out of clay and breathed out to make Beings. Human Beings are unique. The uniqueness of Human Beings has two special characteristics. (i) Human Beings are the choice product of God's creation. There are two creation stories in which Human Beings are made as the crown of creations. (ii) God decides to breathe *God's own Beings* which is necessary in nature into the Human physique which is contingent in nature.

Adam lived for 930 years and it indicates that his Being lives; although the spirit lives but the body became aged. If human is part of nature, human being is also a biological phenomenon which is subject to space and time (Abraham and Lot). Advancement in Ageing is considered to be advancement in wisdom (Moses' appointment of Elders), since wisdom was honoured, the advancement aged also must be honoured.

Human Being ageing is no other option but to be lived. Abraham was lived and buried; one has to live in it. Accepting the fact of ageing is psychological preparation. Although, the physique feels aged, the psyche doesn't let it down. In interpreting the Bible requires to permit the context of the particular passage to drive our conclusions. Older adult spirituality has a unique place in Jewish tradition. Older ears may be distinctly able to hear and follow the commandment to continue going forth. We must be wise enough to reach a good old age by traveling new paths for ourselves and for those who will follow us.

45 Babylonian Talmud Hullin 24b.

46 Maimonides Mishneh Torah Hilkhot Klei Hamikdash 3:8.

5

Re-reading Lukan "Birth Narratives" with the Optics of Ageing

Shanthi Sudha Monica

Introduction

Ageing is a process of becoming older. The concept of ageing is a growing field of study in several academic disciplines and is understood from various perspectives — historical, social, anthropological, psychological, and medical. In the process of ageing, it is the whole person who is ageing. Wholeness requires the interfacing of physical, psychological, social, and spiritual dimensions of human growth and development.[1] Hence, the process of ageing is a reflection of a social construct that involves different phases of life situations and experiences. There are attempts to give a clear definition of old age and even to designate its borders, which are not successful because the ageing process is for all people, and the process differs in each individual. There is no general, identical situation for all people, of the final stage of life.[2] The common denominator is that older people become vulnerable in all aspects, physically, socially, psychologically, mentally.

The Hebrew Scriptures provide various insights about growing old.[3] It presents a positive view of old age, especially in understanding faith about older people. From an ageism perspective, the Bible can be viewed as inclusive. In Judaism and Christianity— a just society comprises of honor and respect for the elderly. However, Professor Sarah M. Moses argues that such

---

1 Melvin A. Kimble, "Pastoral Care of the Elderly," *Journal of Pastoral Care*, 41/3 (September 1, 1987): 11.

2 Marina V. Ermolaeva, "Old Age as a Cultural and Historical Phenomenon and its Transformation in Modern Times," *Contemporary Russian Contributions to Vygotsky's Heritage* (Special Issue), 4/1 (2017): 204.

3 Douglas A. Knight, "Perspectives on Aging and the Elderly in the Hebrew Bible," *Interpretation: A Journal of Bible and Theology*, 68/ 2 (2014): 137.

an understanding cannot be taken as an example regarding how the ancient Israelite society treated the aged, and the moral concerns in the texts should not be considered as a proof.[4] In other words, the moral norms contained in the Hebrew Scriptures do not reflect an idealized period in which the elderly always enjoyed respect and adequate care. There are texts in the Hebrew Scriptures that reveal that there was a period of social instability in ancient Israel where the aged were mistreated.[5] Therefore there are diverse views regarding the treatment of the aged in the ancient Israelite society, which continued even during the first century Judaism.

This essay focuses on re-reading Luke chapters 1 and 2, respectively. It will examine how Luke, as the narrator, characterized the ageing people in the Birth Narratives. Luke's narration of Jesus' birth story includes four people who are in the older age group— Elizabeth, Zachariah, Simeon and Anna. It can be noted that each of them plays a unique part in the overarching story of Jesus' birth. The problem is that, the traditional interpretations of this story seem to undermine their role with their focus on the Messianic significance. Hence, this essay attempts to highlight the unique roles of the elders in the Lukan Birth Narrative. Therefore, this essay attempts to enlighten on how these four older people have been depicted in the narratives. In order to understand these texts, it is worthwhile to consider the social world of the time in ancient Israel, and also the surrounding cultures. Also, of importance is evidence from archeological and anthropological studies that can enrich the story of Jesus' birth. They allow a reader to appreciate new meanings that can be drawn from these stories. Theories of ageing and exegetical approaches, particularly ageing perspectives will be used in this study.

Methodology

Lukan "Birth Narratives" refer to the narratives surrounding the Birth of Jesus, particularly Luke chapters 1 and 2. Luke includes four ageing individuals into his story Elizabeth, Zachariah, Simeon and Anna. The text has potential for reviewing their presence and characterization in the textual space. Of importance is the current context of how we as a Christian community treat our older people—parents, and grandparents. Hence, the optics of ageing are deployed in this study as a contextual lens to understand and derive new relevant meanings from the text. In other words, the select texts will be viewed from ageing perspective as theorized in the disciplines of Sociology and Anthropology.

4 Sarah M. Moses, *Ethics and the Elderly: The Challenge of Long-term Care* (Maryknoll, NY: Orbis Books, 2015), 22.

5 Moses, *Ethics and the Elderly*, 55.

Re-reading Lukan "Birth Narratives" with focus on the Older People: An Exegetical Study

Though the Synoptic Gospels reject a part of the 'Traditions of the elders,' Luke, in his Gospel, values elders. Luke records the 'Birth Narratives' of Jesus, which are centered around a few old people, Elizabeth, Zachariah, (Luke 1:18-25) Simeon and Anna (Luke 2:25-35). The Matthean and the Lukan gospel writers alone record the Birth Narratives of Jesus. An earlier tradition becomes the basis for the two evangelists. The accounts shared a few things in common, yet they varied from each other in their emphasis and also the structural forms. Interestingly Luke begins his Gospel narrative after a brief prologue of two older people, Zachariah and Elizabeth, the parents of John the Baptist (Luke1:57). The record of these two elders in the 'Birth Narratives' in the Lukan Gospel tradition is worth noticing. However, though the elders being the stronghold of the Lukan Birth Narratives, most of the Lukan commentators or interpreters do not focus much on the elders recorded in the first three chapters. Fitzmyer mentions that Luke records the temple piety of some of the people of the period of Israel and the beginning of Christian faith. The elders embody piety that foreshadows in early Jerusalem Christians (Acts 2:46; 3:1; 5:2).[6] This implies the continuation of Israel's faith through the four older people who are represented at the Birth of Jesus in the early first century Judaism.

Introducing Elizabeth and Zachariah

Elizabeth and Zachariah were the first major characters in the Lukan Gospel. Both the elders had a rich Jewish background and heritage. Elizabeth and Zachariah were descendants of Aaron. They were from priestly families and represented the best of the social order. Both were considered righteous before God, living blamelessly according to all the commandments and regulations of the Lord (Luke 2:6). It is said that spirituality has been historically associated with adult ageing as part of wisdom in which a person is encouraged to engage oneself in the latter part of one's life.[7] Elizabeth Mac Kinlay has emphasized on the importance of spirituality both in the everyday experience of a long life, and the significance of deep old age.[8] Therefore, psychologically, religion and spirituality play an essential role in the old age. The elders tend to seek comfort and security in the divine.

---

6 Joseph A. Fitzmyer, *The Gospel According to Luke I-XX, The Anchor Bible* (New York: Doubleday, 1970), 316.

7 E. Mackinlay and C. Trevitt, "Finding Meaning in the Experience of Dementia," in *Biblical Perspectives: God and the Elderly*, edited by J. Gordon Harris (New York: The Haworth Press, 2008), 199.

8 E. Mackinlay and C. Trevitt, "Finding Meaning in the Experience of Dementia," 199.

Luke 1:7 Καὶ Οὐκ ἦν αὐτοῖς τέκνον - *But they had no child*

Elizabeth and Zachariah were described as advanced in age (very old) and therefore were not able to bear children, and Elizabeth was portrayed as barren (Luke 1:7). Barrenness in the Israelite culture was considered as disfavor of God. In the Jewish context being childless was particularly an unacceptable state and a misfortune, it is also considered as a disgrace or a punishment for sin.[9] From the biological point of view to conceive at old age was difficult for the couple become vulnerable. However, childlessness creates a sense of insecurity, lack of support and feeling of loneliness in old age, and sometimes they experience poverty. The issue of 'childlessness in Luke's Gospel has connotations in the Hebrew Scriptures (Gen. 16:1-2; 18:11 Gen 25:21; Gen 30:1 Jud 13:21; Sam 1:2). Some of them, as older couples, share the common problem of childlessness in old age.[10] God's intervention overcomes the barrenness of all these women, and similarly, Elizabeth also conceives.[11] Zachariah, her husband, a priest, served as long as he is able; usually, the Levites were superannuated at the age of sixty.[12] Though he was advanced in age, he was able to serve as a priest in the temple. There are incidents in the Hebrew Scriptures where elders were able to take part in the work and responsibilities (Number 11:16-17).[13] Elizabeth and Zachariah could have prayed for an offspring but would have lost hope because of their age, or maybe they did not aspire nor desire for an offspring at this stage. προβεβηκότες – (Far advanced / well stricken), Fitzmyer identifies that the phrase 'advanced in their days' is frequently used in the LXX (Gen 18:11;24:1; Josh13:1; 23:1,2). Elizabeth's barrenness is mentioned, and this term also reveals that she was also beyond the age of childbearing along with Zachariah. Their situation reveals the miraculous aspects of the birth to come.[14] The social construct of

9 Gen 16:4,11; 29:32;30:1; Lev 20:20-21;1 Sam 1:5-6;2 Sam 6:23.

10 Jacob M. Caldwell & Diana Caldwell, "Reading Luke for Community Formation Against Ageism," *Journal of Religion, Spirituality & Aging* 22 (2010): 211–219.

11 Joseph A. Fitzmyer, *The Gospel According to Luke I-XX,* 323.The significance of women's barrenness is linked with the plan and the purposes of God, who withholds fertility from these importance women in the history of Israel for a period of time. However, in the course of time God gives them the capacity to bear children. *Expository Dictionary of Bible Words: Word Studies for Key English Bible,* edited by Stephen D. Renn (Massachusetts: Hendrickson Publishers, 2005), 91.

12 Alfred Plummer, "The Gospel According to Luke," *The International Critical Commentary* (Edinburgh: T&T Clark). Available at: https://archive.org/details/criticalexegetic28plumuoft/page/10/mode/2up Accessed on 23rd April 2019.

13 Klaas Spronky, "Aged Jacob: Jacob's Final Years as The Biblical Ideal of Old Age," *Communio Viatorum* 58/3 (2016): 287.

14 Joseph A. Fitzmyer, "The Gospel According to Luke I-XX," *The Anchor Bible* (New York: Doubleday, 1970), 323.

the elders is said to be based on ageist notions of elders as frail, dependent and feeble. This construction assumes that the age of sixty-five marks inevitable bodily and mental decline and a consequent need for health and medical care.[15] Nevertheless, both Zachariah and Elizabeth seemed to have regained their strength in their old age, as portrayed in the phrase that 'Elizabeth is pregnant.'

Vs.18. Zachariah Said to the Angel: "*How will I know that this is so? For I am an old man, and my wife is getting on in years.*"

'How will I know this': This would be the natural response of any old person who is advanced in age when he/she is said to bring up an offspring. The same question is asked by Abraham (Gen 15:8) because physical changes take place in the process of ageing. The response, '*For I am an old man…*', reflects the psychological mindset of the aged who accept their incapability, since they become physically weak as they grow old. However, on the contrary, both regained their strength to conceive through divine intervention. Stephen Sapp argues concerning Elizabeth and Zachariah that the choice of characters reveals something about God's way of working: "God can use any vehicle to accomplish his purposes, even one that seems to be past its usefulness. The story also contains an implicit warning to the elderly not to let their age become an excuse for doubting God's concern for them."[16] However, Zachariah was not able to speak because he doubted. The loss of speech amounted to a loss of power in the ancient world. Though Zachariah is identified as a praiseworthy male with essential public responsibilities, he was not able to talk (Luke 1:22).[17] Yet, even at an old age, Zachariah fulfilled his responsibility in the temple, being able to perform his duties until his service ended (Luke 1:23).

Therefore, being advanced in age does not necessarily mean a person is not capable of doing anything physically. Stoneking notes that "anyone who lived a life of hard work, faith, and self-discipline could preserve health and independence into a ripe old age, which would be followed by a quick, painless, natural death."[18] The emphasis here is that such positive and active living could help in successful ageing. As Joel Green notes, both sets of questions are raised concerning God's covenantal promise. From the Lukan perspective, it is neither accidental nor unusual that God would use older adults, even to

15 Laura Talarsky, "Defining Aging and The Aged: Cultural and Social Constructions of Elders," in U. S. Arizona Anthropologist Association of Student Anthropologists, Department of Anthropology, University of Arizona, Tucson, 13, 1998, 101-107.

16 Stephen Sapp, *Full of Years: Aging and the Elderly in the Bible and Today* (Nashville: Abingdon, 1987), 126.

17 Brittany E. Wilson, *Unmanly Men: Refigurations of Masculinity in Luke-Acts* (Oxford, UK: Oxford University Press, 2015), 79.

18 C. B. Stoneking, "Modernity: The Social Construction of Aging," in *Growing Old in Christ,* edited by S. Hauerwas, et.al. (Grand Rapids, MI: Eerdmans, 2003), (63–89), 71.

accomplish tasks for which youth would seem to be a prerequisite. Rather, Luke would want his recipients to believe that older adults are especially suited to participate in the work of God.[19]

Vs. 24. συνέλαβεν – *became pregnant*

Luke alone who uses this term for conceiving offspring, and he uses this only in the first two chapters (1:31, 36; 2:21).[20] To conceive in old age is not common, therefore the context in which Elizabeth was in, and the possibility was an incomprehensible issue. Therefore, for this reason, Luke could have mentioned that Elizabeth περιέκρυβεν ἑαυτὴν - *hid herself* -for five months on becoming pregnant. The reflexive pronoun ἑαυτὴν brings out more forcibly that the act was entirely her own, and the compound verb περιέκρυβεν implies *all-around complete* concealment. The five months are the first five months, and during the coming months, it will be visible, and she would be seized to be called barren. During these five months, she wished not to hear the reproach that she was barren, since she is conceived. Therefore, she withdrew herself until all must know that the reproach has been removed.[21] There are varied views and interpretations regarding her hiding as it seems a strange action for many reasons because a woman presumably would go into seclusion for the last five months of her pregnancy rather than the first few months.

There are assumptions by a few ancient commentators as to why Elizabeth acts in this way. Origen understood that, "she was embarrassed because she was an old and feeble woman and had gone back to what young people do."[22] Rick Strelan draws on Church Father Leontius's view that Elizabeth hid herself either out of embarrassment among her relatives that she, an older woman, has a child, or possibly because she did not think the child would be born.[23] However, the pregnancy of Elizabeth is the creative work of God, which removed her reproach within the society and also within herself, which could have affected her psychologically. In the recent New Testament scholarship, it is intended that it was a literary device used by Luke. Maybe Luke wanted only Mary to first know about Elizabeth's pregnancy. It can also be used as a sign for Mary (Luke 1:36). Raymond Brown also suggests that he

19 J. B. Green, "The Problem of a Beginning: Israel's Scriptures in Luke 1-2," *Bulletin for Biblical Research*, 1994, 61–85.

20 Alfred Plummer, "The Gospel According to Luke," *The International Critical Commentary* (Edinburgh: T&T Clark), 19. Available at: https://archive.org/details/criticalexegetic28plumuoft/page/10/mode/2up (23rd April 2019).

21 Alfred Plummer, *The Gospel According to Luke*, 19.

22 Origen, "Homilies on Luke; Fragments on Luke," in *The Fathers of the Church: A New Translation* (Washington, DC: Catholic University of America Press, 1996). Cited in Rick Strelan, "Elizabeth, Are You Hiding? Luke 1: 24," *Neotestamentica* 37/1 (2003): 87.

23 Strelan, "Elizabeth, Are You Hiding? Luke 1: 24," *Neotestamentica* 37/1 (2003): 87.

sees no need to posit any mystique or obscure purpose in the Lucan mention of the five months of seclusion: it is a literary device to prepare for the sign to be revealed to Mary in 1:36.[24] Robert Tannehill views that Elizabeth remains in seclusion so that "her pregnancy does not become public knowledge."[25] Since the First Century Jewish society in which she lived could ridicule her for she being old and pregnant. Therefore, the characterization of Elizabeth as old and pregnant could be a sight to be wondered at, in the early first century Jewish context—a society which considered Elizabeth as a 'barren woman.' Elizabeth acknowledges her situation and says in **Vs. 25.** *This is what the Lord has done for me when he looked favorably on me and took away the disgrace I have endured among my people.* She expresses her joy over the divine removal of her embarrassment. He saw fit: the Greek word ἐπεῖδεν means "fixed his gaze on," "looked at" "He looked with favour," the term expresses God's concern for human beings. ἀφελεῖν ὄνειδός μου - *to take away my reproach* - the reproach was childlessness. [26] Elizabeth though described as advanced in age, is seen as the bearer of new life, which is a sign of hope.

The angel says **Vs. 36.** "*And behold, Elisabeth your relative has also* ***conceived a son in her old age*** *and this is the sixth month for her the one being called barren.*

καλουμένῃ - *being called* barren. Elizabeth is viewed as the one who is still barren. Though she was six months pregnant, people would not have known and believe that she is conceived.[27] She was known as such, maybe to distinguish her from another Elizabeth who is with children. This could be the reproach that Elizabeth speaks of in Vs. 25 her common name among the people who knew her, being 'Elisabeth the barren.'[28] **Vs. 37**. οὐκ ἀδυνατήσει – *will not be impossible* - This word is used as a thing too hard for human beings but not too hard for God (cf. Job 42:2; Zac 8:6; Jer. 32:17).[29] Elizabeth regained her strength in her old age to conceive and bear a son, John. Zachariah, in his old age, was able to have a son. Both acknowledged their weakness and at the same time experienced their strength to conceive. Old age should not always be understood in negative connotations like weak, unprofitable, vulnerable, and incapable but rather view them positively.

---

24 Brown, Raymond E., *The Birth of the Messiah: A Commentary on the Infancy Narratives in the Gospels of Matthew and Luke*, updated edition (New York: Doubleday, 1999), 282.

25 Robert Tannehill, *Luke* (Nashville: Abingdon, 1996), 47.

26 Rebecca's words were also similar "*God has taken away my reproach*" (Gen 30:23).

27 Nicol, W. Robertson, "Commentary on Luke 1:36," *The Expositor's Greek Testament,* 1897-1910. Available at: https://www.studylight.org/commentaries/egt/luke-1.html.

28 Clarke, Adam. "Commentary on Luke 1:36," *The Adam Clarke Commentary,* 1832. Available at: https://www.studylight.org/commentaries/acc/luke-1.html.

29 Alfred Plummer, *The Gospel According to Luke*, 26.

Another aspect in the Lukan "Birth Narrative" is the song or the prophecy of Zachariah, which is worth noticing where he begins to speak (Luke 1:67-79). Luke wants his readers to see Zechariah's canticle as a hymn directed to God (εὐλογῶν τόν θεόν-*praising God* 1:64). It is uttered in response to the intervention of the Holy Spirit (1:67), which was foretold in the vision of the angel in the temple (1:20).[30] **Vv. 76-77** these two verses are closely related to the question posed by neighbors and relatives (v. 66b).[31] These words of Zachariah reveal the prophetic role of his son, John who is born. Zachariah, though old, portrayed his wisdom in all aspects and also is noted for his active participation in the temple. Many writers regarding ageing highlight the participation of the potential of older people in society, especially in the social and intellectual activity. However, this is possible only if a person realizes the need for continuous creation of themselves and their living conditions.[32] This understanding is true in the life of both Zachariah and Elizabeth; they were conscious of the society around them, and they both in their own framework portrayed their active roles in their old age.

Introducing Simeon and Anna

Simeon and Anna are the other prominent figures in the Lukan Birth Narratives, both in the process of ageing. Simeon is described as one among the representatives of the faithful Jews of Palestine, who is an example to a proper response to God's messianic activity.[33] (Luke 2:26). It can be assumed that Simeon was an older adult. Another possibility is that Simeon (Luke 2:25-35) is paralleled with Anna, who is described as "of great age" (Luke 2:36-38).[34] Anna is also portrayed as a woman, active at the temple.[35]

---

30 Krzysztof Mielcarek, "Prayers of Old People: Zechariah, Simeon and Anna," *Verbum Vitae* 22 (2012): 79.

31 Krzysztof Mielcarek, "Prayers of Old People, Zechariah, Simeon and Anna," *Verbum Vitae* 22 (2012): 79.

32 Marina V. Ermolaeva, "Old Age as a Cultural and Historical Phenomenon and its Transformation in Modern Times," *Revue internationale du CRIRES: Innover dans la tradition de Vygotsky,* 4/1 (2017): 1.

33 Krzysztof Mielcarek, "Prayers of Old People, Zechariah, Simeon and Anna," *Verbum Vitae* 22 (2012): 87.

34 Jacob M Caldwell& Diana Caldwell, "Reading Luke for Community Formation Against Ageism," *Journal of Religion, Spirituality & Aging*, 22 (2010): 211–219.

35 Simeon and Anna are looking for God to intervene by sending the promised Messiah, since Israel was under oppression by the Romans. Israel was looking for God to intervene in this circumstance (Isa 7:14; 9:1-7; 11:1-19:40:1-11; 66:13).

Simeon the Elder (Luke 2:25-35)

Simeon, would not see death until he sees the Messiah-Luke 2:25-35. Simeon is depicted as a righteous and devout person in Jerusalem, who was associated with the Temple (Luke 2:25, 27). This description is expressive of reverence in the presence of God,[36] who was waiting for or 'looking forward to the consolation of Israel' (2:25). There was a belief that before the Messiah comes, there would be a time of great troubles, and therefore the Messiah was referred to as "the Consoler"[37] or "the consolation."[38] Simeon is portrayed as a God-fearing person waiting for his death. Simeon recognizes Jesus as the promised Messiah, the one who would bring salvation to the people of Israel. Such a characterization of the elders is already familiar to the reader of Luke's Gospel; Simeon is closely paralleled to Zechariah, who is known to be an older adult. However, Luke does not explicitly mention that Simeon was advanced in age, but in the course of his actions, it does imply that he was old. He should have been an old man since he is described as a person who by the revelation of the Holy Spirit '*would not see death before he has seen the Lord's Messiah.... now you are dismissing your servant in peace.*' (Luke 2:26,29). These words imply that Simeon could have been an old man. He was not waiting passively, but rather he was eager and active in waiting patiently for the Messiah despite his old age without losing hope. The activity that followed, '*Guided by the Spirit, Simeon came into the temple and when the parents brought in the child Jesus, Simeon took the child in his arms'* (Luke 2:27, 28). Luke depicts Simeon as an example of active devoutness, a model of spiritual and intellectual awareness; he is also portrayed as an authoritative, and as a discerning interpreter of Israel's scriptures. Another noteworthy aspect of his attitude toward his death.[39] Simeon who has been waiting for the consolation of Israel realized this by Jesus' presence. When Simeon sees baby Jesus, Luke records the words of Simeon, where he is prepared to "*depart in peace*"—a euphemism for death. It can be assumed that Simeon does not have the desire to die a premature death.

Luke records Simeon's statement, "And he received him (baby Jesus) in his arms, and blessed God and said "Master, *now you are dismissing your servant in peace, according to your word.*" (Luke 2:29) indicates that he joyfully recognizes that his purpose is realized and he can depart in peace. Simeon, in his old age, does not look forward to his death but rather was continuously

36 Joseph A. Fitzmyer, *"The Gospel According to Luke I-XX,, " The Anchor Bible* (New York: Doubleday, 1970), 426.

37 In the later *rabbinic* tradition, the 'Messiah' was sometimes given the title of "Consoler." Joseph A. Fitzmyer, *The Gospel According to Luke I-XX,* 427.

38 Alfred Plummer, "The Gospel According to Luke," 66.

39 Jacob M, Caldwell and Diana Caldwell, "Reading Luke for Community Formation Against Ageism," *Journal of Religion, Spirituality & Aging*, 22 (2010): 215-216.

waiting for the opportunity for constant involvement in the ongoing activity of salvation history.[40] He was able to see with his eyes the salvation[41] though old (Luke 2:30). Francois Bovon, the Swiss exegete, stresses the role of the verb in the present tense form ἀπολυεις - *you dismiss*, which may emphasize the imminent character of Simeon's death and his readiness for it. He sees the song of Simeon *as* "a conversation with God at the moment of death."[42]

In the process of ageing, older people get more into the spiritual realm and experience a close relationship with the divine in this activity; they accept their ageing as a reality and live to face it boldly. Stephen Sapp says that, "the first requirement for dealing successfully with growing older is to acknowledge that it is inevitable and is, in fact taking place every moment one is alive. And there is only one outcome of ageing. Thus, truly accepting one's ageing, and the ageing of others is of necessity to acknowledge one's mortality, which in a fundamental sense is also the cause of ageing."[43] This opinion is seen in the life of Simeon, where he accepts and acknowledges the ageing process in his words "*Master, now you are dismissing your servant in peace*" (Luke 2:29).

Anna the Elder (Luke 2:36-38)

Anna is described as a prophetess,[44] daughter of Phanuel, of the tribe of Asher and was of great age. She lived with her husband seven years from her virginity, and herself a widow for eighty-four years (Luke 2:37). As a widow, she would have felt lonely. Persons of all ages experience the pain of loneliness; they also experience the pleasures of solitude. Beginning in infancy, human beings know both the terror of feeling abandoned and lonely and also the joy of contentedly being alone.[45] She is portrayed as residing in the temple, and she never leaving it but worshipping there with fasting and praying night and day (Luke 2:37). When the moment came for her to see the child, she began to praise God. In other words, she kept acknowledging the Messiah of God and praising God

40 Jacob M. Caldwell and Diana Caldwell, *Reading Luke for Community Formation Against Ageism*, 215-216.

41 Since Simeon utters his prayer, holding Jesus in his arms it is clear that the term "salvation" is another metonymy and implies Jesus himself. Krzysztof Mielcarek, "Prayers of Old People," in Foot note, 85.

42 Francois Bovon and Christine M. Thomas, *Luke 1: A Commentary on the Gospel of Luke 1:1-9:50*, ed. Helmut Koester (Minneapolis, Minn.: Fortress Press, 2002), 103. Cited in Krzysztof Mielcarek, "Prayers of Old People: Zechariah, Simeon and Anna," *Verbum Vitea,* 22 (2012): 86.

43 Stephen Sapp, "Mortality and Respect: Aging in the Abrahamic Traditions, Generations," *The American Society on Aging,* XXXII (2008): 20.

44 Though she is described as a prophetess she does not utter any prophesy.

45 Barbara Pittard Payne and Susan H. McFadden, "From Loneliness to Solitude: Religious and Spiritual Journeys in Late Life," in *Aging and the Religious Dimension*, edited by L. Eugene Thomas and Susan A. Eisenhandler (Westport, Conn.: Auburn House, 1994), 13.

(ἀνθωμολογεῖτο). She was constantly (or repeatedly) speaking (ἐλάλει) about him to all those 'who were looking for the redemption of Jerusalem' (cf. Luke 2:36-38). The emphasis here is that her age was not a hindrance for her to be one of the early witnesses to the Messiah. Anna sets an example that even in advanced age, she was actively waiting for the Messiah, therefore rightly being described as a prophetess. Interestingly the manifestation of Jesus is made not only known to the aged Simeon (man) but also to aged Anna (woman).[46]

She is also described as being a widow for a long time. In most of the societies and cultures, the widows usually are looked down upon. Moreover, being old and being a widow from an early stage of marriage, she would have faced much discrimination and also would have faced stigmatization. They could also face financial, social and sexual abuse and therefore they are vulnerable people. Widowhood is considered the most vulnerable state in the Israelite society; it is a harsher reality when one is a widow and has no children.[47] Anna, as an old widow, would have also suffered social barrenness, which describes the situation of women who biologically may be able to conceive and give birth, but due to social factors such as widowhood, she is unable to have children outside of this context.[48]

R. E. Brown suggests that the description of Christian widows in 1 Tim 5:3-16 has some striking similarities to the portrayal of Anna. It suggests either some influence of the Jewish idea of widowhood and presenting it in a Christian way or the picture of Anna as portrayed by Luke, which was affected by the later developed Christian model.[49] However, Anna being Jewish is viewed as a source of identity and continuity for Jewish women as they age.[50] Anna sets a model for younger Jewish women and also a model for both young and old widows in India, where they face social discrimination. Mohini Giri laments that "widowhood is considered as social death."[51]

Vs. 37 ἕως – *until* - This term describes the great length of her widowhood. Despite her early widowhood, she did not marry again, which keeps her very

46 Joseph A. Fitzmyer, *The Gospel According to Luke: I – IX,* 430.

47 Janice P. De-Whyte, *Wom(b)an: A Cultural-narrative Reading of the Hebrew Bible Barrenness Narratives* (Leiden: Brill, 2018), 254.

48 De-Whyte, *Wom(b)an: A Cultural-narrative*, 255.

49 Raymond E. Brown, *The Birth of the Messiah*, *The Anchor Bible* (New York: Doubleday, 1970), 467-468.

50 Dena Shenk, "Honor Thy Mother: Aging Women in the Jewish Tradition," in *Aging and The Religious Dimension*, edited by Eugene Thomas & Susan A. Eisenhandler (USA: Greenwood Publishing Group, 1994), 115.

51 Sara Barrera, "The Ongoing Tragedy of India's Widows," *Women's Media Center,* (Accessed on 25th June 2020).

honorable within society.[52] Anna's widowhood did not deter her from moving forward, mostly when all sense of mutuality in the relationship was lost.

Simeon and Anna were old and they were in the later stage of their life where they were able to perform great tasks. However, many proponents of gerontology associate old age with the withdrawal of the elderly from active life and deepening into their inner world.[53] Contrary to this statement, it becomes evident that both Anna and Simeon maximized their role in public life.

Our Grandfathers and Grandmothers

Grandparents who live in Indian homes are treated with respect, and sometimes, also with disdain. The common assumption that they are unproductive and have nothing to contribute to the family or society is a flawed one. Older parents have become a burden to the family comprising of other members apart from their children. Taking care involves many aspects: concern, love, affection, oneness, respect towards the elders within the family, which has been ignored in most of the families both in the urban and rural societies, among the educated and the uneducated, among the poor and the rich. It is because of such unsympathetic attitude, most families all over the world are seen enrolling their elderly parents in old age homes and nursing homes. In such a situation, the older people feel a sense of rejection and loneliness. Sometimes the old parents are happier to live in such homes with people of their age, instead of suffering ill-treatment within the families.

Hummel Cornelia termed such a phase of the aged as an "unpleasant old age," a perspective in which older adults are seen as isolated, suffering diminishing autonomy, dependent, indeed, in a state of physical or mental impairment or degeneration.[54] On the other hand, Sonia Douek affirms that as people become old, they tend to connect themselves with their community. How people express their faith or spirituality may not manifest itself in practice but be more about inclusion and connectedness. Life circumstances in which they live will determine people's faith, identity and approach to spirituality.[55] Even today, most of the older people of all faiths are inclined more to the religious and spiritual dimension of their selves. Apart from the faith aspect, most of the present grandmothers and grandfathers are active,

52 Alfred Plummer, *The Gospel According to Luke*, 72.

53 Marina V. Ermolaeva, "Old Age as a Cultural and Historical Phenomenon and its Transformation in Modern Times," *Revue internationale du CRIRES: Innover dans la tradition de Vygotsky* 4/1 (2017): 204.

54 Hummel, Cornelia, "Social Representations of Ageing," *Ageing and Society* 32/06 (August 2012): 986.

55 Sonia Douek, "Faith and Spirituality in Older People - A Jewish Perspective," *Working with Older People*, 19/3 (2015): 114-122.

and it is evident that they are not just consumers of resources but also as those who make a valuable contribution to the societies in which they live. It can be considered as productive ageing. Proponents of this approach are aware of the need to be cautioned regarding the limits to such productive ageing where the older people were not obliged or exploited in undertaking activities.[56]

Conclusion

The focus on the issue of ageing demands importance, alongside other practical theological concerns. The Gospel traditions do not focus much on the elderly but instead derive certain conclusions based on the teachings of Jesus. It can be noted that Jesus, on the cross demonstrates a positive attitude towards the elders (parents) and care for widows. A customary practice which is also in line with the Jewish traditions that insist on honoring the elderly. It is worth noting that the Lukan gospel tradition has highlighted the roles of the elders in the 'Birth Narratives.' Luke's inclusion of the four older people into his birth narrative transcends both traditional and contemporary labeling of the ageing population as inadequate, unproductive and a burden to the society. It also is a telling example of the narrator's emancipatory philosophy that each human being is important irrespective of age. Luke also characterizes them as having special roles as potential mothers, priests, prophetesses, and devoted to a life of prayer. Old age does not curtail their potentialities. It is the systemic ageism which discriminates them and focusses on their limitations, as if there are not people in the younger generation who are rendered unproductive by the same system.

Thus, the re-reading Luke's Birth Narratives with the optics of ageing challenges our limited pseudo perceptions about the so-called limitations of the ageing older population, when as a matter of fact, we all are ageing together towards old age, and eventually death- the cessation of life. Reading with the optics of ageing also teaches us that we have to be cognizant of the life itself as a gift of God and we learn to live it harmoniously. In our contemporary stories we need each other, and we all collaborate with each other in fulfilling our own purposes in our age and in our generation. Therefore, viewing them from the sociological and anthropological perspectives has put them into a wider spectrum. Such interpretations transcend what ageing is all about and also goes beyond the contemporary understanding of ageing. The medical paradigm teaches that death is the cessation of growth. Therefore, every individual can offer something unique through his/her life at all stages. The Church has the responsibility of teaching adherents to be sensitive to the needs

56 Paul Higgs and Ian Rees Jones, *Medical Sociology and Old Age: Towards a Sociology of Health in Later Life* (London, UK: Routledge, 2009), 24.

of elders in the family and community, and encourage them to continue their valuable contribution so the Church and Society. Such a harmonious condition of human co-existence is made possible only by a conscious, responsible effort by all members of the society towards the older people.

6

Graceful Ageing and Intergenerational Conflict in the New Testament Towards Aged-Friendly Communities

Edwin Jebaraj

Introduction

Ageing is a beautiful gift from God. It is a normal and continuous process of change in the body as it is designed in that way. With age comes wisdom and understanding (Job 12:12). Older people are a blessing to the society as they pass on their knowledge and experience to the younger generations. According to Albert Jewell, old people should be respected for their special 'charisms' such as disinterestedness, memory, experience/wisdom, interdependence, and a more complete vision of life that emphasises "being over having."[1] Erdman Palmore lists out fourteen advantages of older persons to the society which include their lower criminal activity, greater political participation, increasing voluntary organization participation, and work abilities, to mention a few.[2] However, the negative stereotypes of ageing, including in the media, which presents the aged as unreliable, selfish, seriously ill, dependent on others and a burden to the society has shattered the traditional approach towards the aged. The higher participation of women in the labour force, the increasing mobility of workers and divorces has created fresh challenges in the area of elderly care.

This essay is an overview of graceful ageing in the New Testament using intergenerational solidarity approach. For the sake of clarity it is divided into six sections: the first section explores the different sociological perspectives which are employed for the study of ageing and finds the intergenerational

1 Albert Jewell, "The Churches and Older People: Gift or Burden?" in *God, Me and Being Very Old: Stories and Spirituality in Later Life*, edited by Keith Albans and Malcolm Johnson (London: SCM Press, 2013), 41.

2 See Erdman Palmore, "Advantages of Aging," *The Gerontologist*, 19/2 (April 1979): 220–224.

solidarity approach as ideal for the study of graceful ageing in the New Testament; the second section analyses various terms used in the New Testament for ageing; the third and the fourth sections explore the meaning of intergenerational solidarity for graceful ageing in the Gospels and Acts; the fifth section discusses the theme of power of the old and solidarity between the young and the old in the Epistles with particular focus on Pauline letters, and in the sixth section the friendliness of Jesus towards the aged in the book of Revelation is discussed.

Sociological Perspectives on Ageing

Theories in sociology provide us with different perspectives with which one can view ageing in the New Testament. These theories explicate how social, religious, economic, and political forces shape the Ageing experience. One theory, proposed by social scientists Elaine Cumming and William Earle Henry, gives a functionalist explanation of the Ageing process, and this is called *disengagement theory*.[3] The theory states that older people are no longer capable of performing their previous roles quite well. Therefore, they must disengage from their earlier roles and select roles that are more suitable for their present condition. This theory no longer finds acceptance among researchers today.

The second theory gives an interactionist explanation of the Ageing process. Called as *engagement model* or *activity theory* it assumes that older people will benefit both themselves and their society if they remain active and try to continue to perform the roles they had before they aged.[4] One problem with this theory is that it fails to take into account the ability level of all the aged to perform as before.

The third sociological perspective for the study of ageing is called *conflict model* which emphasizes competition between generations.[5] It analyses the impact of negative views about old age and prejudice and discrimination against the elderly. Within the conflict perspective three classic theories of Ageing are proposed. They are: *modernization theory* (which focuses on conflict as a result of industrialization and modernization), *age stratification theory* (which analyses conflict that arises due to stratification on the basis

---

3 E. Cumming and W. E. Henry, *Growing Old: The Process of Disengagement* (New York, NY: Basic Books, 1961), 14. A critical problem with this theory is its assumption that older people are no longer capable of adequately performing their previous roles.

4 H.-M. Joung and N. J. Miller, "Examining the Effects of Fashion Activities on Life Satisfaction of Older Females: Activity Theory Revisited," *Family and Consumer Sciences Research Journal, 35*/4 (2007): 338–356.

5 Intergenerational conflict is understood as the difference, gap, distance or conflict of values between the adult and the adolescent generation. K. D. Gangrade, "Inter-Generational Conflict: A Sociological Study of Indian Youth," *Asian Survey*, 10/10 (1970): 925.

of age for social control) and *exchange theory* (which examines conflict that arises due to the demand that the aged submit to the will of the young in exchange of care and support).[6]

Even though each theory has its own merits they are flawed because they fail to address the concerns of both the aged and the young. When it comes to the analysis of the theme of graceful ageing in the New Testament, these theories are found to be wanting. Therefore, in this essay I propose *intergenerational solidarity approach* as the interpretative tool for the study of texts to better understand the theme of graceful ageing in the New Testament.

Intergenerational solidarity is more than reciprocity;[7] it is an intentional bonding between persons of different age groups.[8] Intergenerational solidarity involves the idea of shared responsibility and is influenced by a sense of moral duty and social ethics. In a sense, intergenerational solidarity can be seen as a social equaliser, in which each party exchange with the other to obtain what they lack.[9] Thus intergenerational solidarity, as a hermeneutical tool, will unearth the deeper meaning of the New Testament's teaching on graceful ageing.

Terminology for Ageing in New Testament

In the New Testament several Greek terms are used to refer to ageing or to persons advanced in age.

***Geron*:** The noun *geron* which means "*old man*", appears only once in Nichodemus' question to Jesus (Jn. 3:4).[10] However, two related terms are found in the New Testament: the noun *geras* ("old age") found only in Lk. 1:36 and the verb *gerasko* ("grow old") in Jn. 21:18 and Heb. 8:13.

Presbytēs: As in the Old Testament, the New Testament term *presbytēs* ("elder") can denote simply a person of advanced age. Both Zechariah (Lk. 1:18) and Paul (Phlm. 9) use this term to refer to themselves as "old men." Further, Paul uses the term *presbytas* (plural of *presbytēs*) for "old men" (Tit. 2:2) and the feminine plural *presbytidas* for "old women" (Tit. 2:3).

6 See N. R. Hooyman and H. A. Kiyak, *Social Gerontology. A Multidisciplinary Perspective,* 9th ed. (Upper Saddle River, NJ: Pearson, 2011), 73-74; also see, "Theoretical Perspectives on Ageing," available at: https://courses.lumenlearning.com/sociology/chapter/theoretical-perspectives-on-aging/ (accessed, 20/11/2020).

7 "Reciprocity" works on the principle of giving back to society or looking after one's parents in the same way that they looked after them.

8 María Amparo Cruz-Saco "Intergenerational Solidarity," in *Intergenerational Solidarity: Strengthening Economic and Social Ties*, edited by María Amparo Cruz-Saco and Sergei Zelenev (New York: Palgrave Macmillan, 2010), 9.

9 Jana Kitlinska, "Students of Social Pedagogy and Intergenerational Solidarity," *Procedia – Social and Behavioural Sciences* 174 (2015): 1444.

10 The word gerontology (the study of aging) comes from the Greek noun *geron.*

Presbyteros: The adjective *presbyteros* is the most commonly used term in the New Testament for 'elder.' This term is used in the sense of a mature man who has experience. In several places it is used for leaders who presided over the churches,[11] and in Mat. 21:23 it refers to leaders in the Synagogue. However, in 1 Tim. 5:1-2 the terms *presbyteros* and *presbytera,* the masculine and feminine respectively, refer to the aged who have no official responsibility in the church. Further, in Heb. 11:2 the plural of the term is rendered as "forefathers." It can reasonably be argued that the terms *presbyteros* ("elder"), *poimen* ("pastor") and *episkopos* ("bishop") are simply different names for the same office in the early life of the church, and that it is not limited to the aged alone, but is also held by young leaders like Timothy and Titus who were thought of matured (1 Tim. 5:19–22; 2 Tim. 4:5; Titus 1:5).

Intergenerational Solidarity and Graceful Ageing in the Gospels

The aged persons play an important role in the opening chapters of Luke's Gospel. In the infancy narrative Luke informs that the priest Zachariah and his wife Elizabeth were both getting on in years (Lk. 1:7). Moreover, in Luke's story they are the first two figures filled with the Holy Spirit (Lk. 1:41, 67).[12] Despite being childless, God miraculously blessed them with a child who would later play the role of Elijah in calling Israel to repentance (Lk. 1:13-17). Richard and Judith point out that this motif of surpassing fruitfulness in old age parallels the story of Abram-Sarah and highlights God's power in the life of the aged: "For nothing will be impossible with God." (Lk. 1:37; cf. Gen. 18:14).[13] Luke further points out that young Mary, who is also pregnant, goes to Elizabeth's house and greets her. Elizabeth calls Mary "blessed among women" (Lk. 1:42) and uttered prophetically "the mother of my Lord" (Lk. 1:43), the first to ascribe the title *kyrios* to Jesus.[14] The Lukan infancy narrative clearly shows that intergenerational solidarity can play a key role in the life of the aged, causing ageing a graceful experience.

As the infancy narrative in Luke progresses two more aged characters, Simeon and Anna (an eighty four year old prophetess) serve as prophetic voices (Lk. 2:22-28). They recognised the infant Jesus on the occasion of his purification in the temple, rejoiced over seeing him and proclaimed about

11 Acts 11:30; 14:23; 15:2,4,6,22; 20:17; 16:4; 21:18; 1 Tim. 5:17,19; Tit.1:5; Jas 5:14; 1 Pet. 5:1, 5; 2 Jn. 1:1; 3 Jn. 1:1.

12 Judith C. Hays, Richard B. Hays, Christopher B. Hays, "Ageism in the Bible," *Encyclopedia of Ageism*, edited by Erdman B. Palmore, Diana K. Harris, Laurence G. Branch (Binghamton, NY: Haworth Press, 2005), 24.

13 Richard B. Hays and Judith C. Hays, "The Christian Practice of Growing Old: The Witness of Scripture," in *Growing Old in Christ*, edited by Stanley Hauerwas, et.al. (Grand Rapids, Michigan: Wm. B. Eerdmans, 2003), 3-18, on 6.

14 Richard B. Hays and Judith C. Hays, "The Christian Practice of Growing Old...," 6.

Jesus' mission (Lk. 2:21-38). The advanced age of Simeon and Anna signifies their time-tested wisdom[15] which helped them to relate to the infant Jesus and testify about him. It also points to the religious practice which occupies a key place in their life, and it is an important element for graceful ageing. With his presence Jesus causes their hearts to rejoice as their hopes are now being fulfilled in him.

In Matthew's gospel, the birth of Jesus triggered intergenerational conflict as King Herod ordered the slaughter of all infants below two years of age to ensure the death of infant Jesus (Mat. 2:16-18). In contrast, Luke carefully structures the narrative to announce the arrival of a new era in which the young and the old will accept one another and care for each other. It sees the aged not as a problem but as delightful, not as a burden but as a blessing. Thus, the infancy narrative in Luke serves as a model for intergenerational solidarity and graceful ageing.

In Mark 7:9-13 Jesus is confronting the Pharisees who had concocted a scheme to avoid parental responsibility. The Law of Moses required that the Israelites honour their parents (Ex. 20:12; Deut. 5:16; cf. Mat. 15:4; 19:19; Mk. 10:19; Lk. 18:20; Eph. 6:2). The term "honour" suggests more than mere "lip service"; it is 'caring for the aged parents in their needs.'[16] Those Jews who wanted to avoid parental responsibility would designate certain of their financial resources as "corban." The word "corban" is derived from the Hebrew *hikrib* ('bring near') and denotes an offering made to God.[17] That means, anything offered to God as a corban becomes holy and cannot be made available for ordinary use,[18] including for the care of the parents. Cranfield puts it succinctly: "It did not always mean that the thing concerned had actually to be offered; rather, that it was withdrawn from its originally intended use and was no longer available for a particular person or persons.[19] Jesus condemns this act of going against the fifth commandment to "honour one's father and mother" as it would hinder their graceful ageing. Here, Jesus affirms the right of the aged parents, as enshrined in the Torah, for care and support by their children.

Jesus' movement was inclusive in nature in which everyone regardless of differences in age is promised equal status. It countered the commonly held notions that undermined the rights and the dignity of the aged. Jesus' healing of

15 Richard B. Hays and Judith C. Hays, "The Christian Practice of Growing Old...," 7.

16 Wayne Jackson, What Is the Meaning of "Corban"? available at: https://www.christiancourier.com/articles/1086-what-is-the-meaning-of-corban (accessed, 26/11/2020).

17 C. E. B. Cranfield, *The Gospel According to St Mark: An Introduction and Commentary*, Cambridge Greek Testament Commentaries (Cambridge: Cambridge University Press, 1959), 237.

18 C. E. B. Cranfield, *The Gospel According to St Mark,* 237.

19 C. E. B. Cranfield, *The Gospel According to St Mark*, 237.

Peter's mother-in-law (Lk. 4:38-39) and his raising from the dead of a widow's son (Lk. 7:11-17) demonstrate his concern for the aged. Jesus' mention of God's provision to the widow of Zarephath through Prophet Elijah (Lk. 4:26) and the parable of persistent prayer by a widow before a corrupt judge for justice (Luke 18:1-5) can be seen as a rebuke to a system that neglected one of its prime duties of caring for the aged and thus deny graceful ageing to the old.

The prayer of Jesus that his followers might be one (Jn. 17:20) is a clear hint that Jesus' ministry was aimed at intergenerational solidarity. Jesus' act of committing his mother Mary to John's care even while he was dying on the cross express his commitment for intergenerational solidarity and for the aged to have graceful Ageing (Jn. 19:25-27). Moreover, in the last chapter of John's gospel, the risen Jesus prophesies Peter's eventual death as an old man, and implies that both he and John (the beloved disciple) despite their different manners of death will continue into their old age as key leaders of the early Christian movement,[20] another perfect example of graceful ageing in the New Testament.[21]

Intergenerational Solidarity and Graceful Ageing in the Book of Acts

The book of Acts describes events that unfolded in the church, the larger family of God that offered an alternative vision for unity and solidarity among people belonging to different age groups. Joel's prophecy of everyone speaking in tongues which finds its fulfilment in the outpouring of the Spirit at Pentecost (Acts 2:1-11) suggests that in the newly constituted family of God conflict and tensions between the old and the young will give way to intergenerational solidarity. Further, the early Christians' act of selling everything that belonged to them and bringing the money to the apostles to take care of the needy (Acts 4:32-37), the majority of whom are from the group of the aged, particularly the widows (cf. Acts 6:1) is clear indication that the early church, like Jesus, promoted intergenerational solidarity among the believers.

The role of the younger missionaries in easing the burden of Paul in his mission is remarkable. The book of Acts informs about the assistance rendered

---

20 Judith C. Hays, Richard B. Hays, Christopher B. Hays, "Ageism in the Bible," 24.

21 It should be stressed here that Jesus' teaching on hating one's parents and snapping family ties (Lk. 14:26) needs to be understood against Mat. 10:37 where hatred means "hatred by comparison." However, E. L. Taylor sees it as "a break" from the old attitudes and values of an established system. See Elias L. Taylor, "Senior Years: Old and New Testament," *International Journal of Humanities and Social Science*, 1/18 (2011): 108.

by Timothy[22] and Apollos[23] (Acts 16:1-5; 18:24-28), though there are others whom Paul mentioned in his letters. In one of his letters Paul comments on Timothy's solidarity as, "I have no one like him" (Phil. 2:19–23). Another young person who assisted Paul in his mission was Titus.[24] In his second letter to the Corinthians Paul calls Titus as "my brother" (2 Cor. 2:13), "my partner and co-worker for you" (2 Cor. 8:23). The assistance rendered by the young missionary companions must have brought comfort, encouragement and strength to Paul even when he was facing hardships due to ill health and opposition.

Intergenerational Solidarity and Graceful Ageing in the Epistles

Is Paul a Victim of Ageism?

Ageism is prejudice toward and discrimination against the older persons by the other age groups. It produces a mindset that despises old age. According to gerontologist Robert N. Butler, the discrimination against old people is similar to actions and attitudes present in racism and sexism.[25] The letters of Paul appear to present a grim picture of ageism in Pauline churches. 1 Corinthians gives hints about a tension that existed among the Corinthian Christians over intergenerational differences. Apollos was a young missionary who came to Corinth after Paul founded a church there. He was an eloquent speaker. In few months time after his arrival to the church at Corinth a group predominantly of the young chose Apollos as their leader. The Corinthian Christians particularly those who sided with the young Apollos refused to consider Paul as their leader despite the fact that the church was founded by him. It appears that the young were not happy with the moral and ethical rules Paul was trying to impose on them (1Cor. 5).

Moreover, verses like 1 Cor. 1:12; 3:3 indicate a tension Paul had with the followers of the young and the eloquent preacher Apollos. Many complained of Paul's unattractive, weak and unimpressive appearance and his simple preaching style (1 Cor. 4:9-13; 2 Cor. 10:10) arguing that Paul was not a genuine apostle. The conflict of Paul with the young finds its expression in one of the second century writings of the New Testament Apocrypha, the *Acts*

22 Timothy is believed to have been the son of a Gentile father and Jewish mother, Eunice (Acts 16:1; 2 Tim 1:5) In 2 Timothy 1:5, his mother and grandmother are noted as eminent for their piety and faith. They are examples of intergenerational solidarity and graceful ageing.

23 Acts 18:24 where it says, Apollos, a native of Alexandria, came to Ephesus. He was a powerful preacher, and competent in the Scriptures."

24 The name 'Titus' though mentioned 13 times in the Pauline and Deutero-Pauline letters Acts does not mention it and the reason is not clear.

25 Robert N. Butler, "Age-Ism: Another Form of Bigotry," *The Gerontologist,* 9/4 (1969): 243-246.

of Paul and Thecla. Here Paul receives a full physical description that may reflect oral tradition. In the Syriac text it reads:

> "He was a man of middling size, and his hair was scanty, and his legs were a little crooked, and his knees were projecting, and he had large eyes." His eyebrows met, "his nose was somewhat long, and he was full of grace and mercy. At one time he seemed like a man, and at another time he seemed like an angel.[26]

Though it is difficult to say with certainty if the description of Paul by *The Acts of Paul and Thecla* is correct, it appears to agree to some extent the description given in 1 Cor. 4:9-13.

L. Welborn in his book *The Young Against the Old: Generational Conflict in First Clement*[27] argues that First Clement[28] was written to crush the revolt of the young against their elders. In other words, the letter responds to a crisis in the Corinthian church by enjoining an ethic of subordination especially to the *presbyteroi* and *episkopoi*. Welborn convincingly demonstrates that the late first-century church in Corinth suffered intergenerational strife-discord.

Despite the conflict Paul was striving for intergenerational solidarity in the Corinthian church and the affectionate letter which he wrote to the church (2 Corinthians) is a testimony to this factor. In the end Paul succeeded in his attempt and the church members rectified their errors and restored solidarity among the intergenerational believers (2 Cor. 3:1-3; 5:18-19).

Paul the Aged

Paul is understood in different ways such as the persecutor, the missionary, the apostle, the pastor, the letter writer, the sufferer for Christ etc. However, in Phlm. 9, Paul describes himself as *Paulos presbytēs* ("Paul an old man"). Paul was probably between 50 and 60 years of age when he penned a personal letter to *Philemon*, a wealthy Christian from Colossae.[29]

Ronald F. Hock draws attention to Paul referring himself as old man in his letter to Philemon (v. 9).[30] He argues that in Phlm 9, the word *presbytēs*,

26 Edgar Johnson Goodspeed, *The Book of Thekla* (Chicago: The University of Chicago Press, 1901), 186.

27 L. Larry Welborn, *The' Young Against the Old: Generational Conflict in First Clement* (Philadelphia: Fortress Academic, 2018).

28 First Clement *is one of the oldest Christian documents outside the New Testament canon. It is assumed that the letter was addressed to the Corinthian Christians around 70* C.E.

29 J. A. Fitzmyer, "The Letter to Philemon," *in The New Jerome Biblical Commentary*, edited by Raymond E. Brown, Joseph A. Fitzmyer, Roland E. Murphy (Bangalore: Theological Publications in India, 1991), 870.

30 Ronald F. Hock, "A Support for His Old Age: Paul's Plea on Behalf of Onesimus," in *The Social World of the First Christians: Essays in Honor of Wayne A. Meeks*, edited by L.

translated as old man, is a better rhetorical and social choice. He reviews Roman literature, especially romantic comedy, to find analogies for social cues and norms related to old age, and finds that older people are typically portrayed as miserable and in need of support, especially the support of children. Hock argues that Paul portrays himself an aged parent who needs his (adopted) child Onesimus (Philemon‘s slave) to care for him. Paul uses this relationship as leverage with Philemon to strengthen his plea for Onesimus' release.[31] Murphy-O‘Connor agrees with this picture of Paul as an old man at the end of his life, stating Paul presents himself as a pathetic figure.[32] Perhaps in Phlm. 9 Paul meant to utilize the power of older age to influence a younger person due to his precedence.

Often the expression *presbytes* is seen as expression of Paul's feeble condition, but J.D.G. Dunn sees it differently:

> Since the term does not of itself imply someone near the end of his life or with failing, we should not see the appeal here as one for compassion - for the younger man (Philemon) to act out of pity for someone once so active and now so weak. Rather, since age usually brought with it the wisdom of experience, the appeal is for the respect that a younger member of the same family or circle should pay to the elder (cf. Lev. 19:32: Sir. 8:6).[33]

It is difficult to deny Paul's ill health as he himself mentioned it in few occasions (1 Cor. 2:3-5; 2 Cor. 12:7; Gal. 4:13). However, in Phlm. 9, Paul, as an old man, is using his age to make a plea of love to Philemon to accept Onesimus back into his house. Paul's age must have brought increased respect for what Paul has to say. This is in line with the view in antiquity that wisdom and authority go with age. Thus it can be stated that intergenerational solidarity is an essential factor for graceful ageing.

"Body" as a Metaphor for Intergenerational Solidarity

The body metaphor which Paul uses in Rom. 12:1-8 and 1 Cor. 12:1-31 offers a viable model for intergenerational solidarity. Through this metaphor Paul encourages the church, which is divided by reason of gifts, talents, abilities, knowledge and status, to be united. The members of the human body are united to the extent that when one member suffers, the whole body is affected.

Michael White and O. Larry Yarbrough (Minneapolis: Augsburg Fortress, 1995), 67-81.

31 Ronald F. Hock, "A Support for His Old Age," 68.

32 Jerome Murphy-O‘Connor, *Paul: A Critical Life* (Oxford: Clarendon Press, 1996), 4.

33 James D. G. Dunn, *The Epistles to the Colossians and to Philemon: A Commentary on the Greek Text*, The New International Greek Testament Commentary (Grand Rapids, Michigan William B. Eerdmans, 1996), 327.

In the same way, every member of the body shares the joy together as all are interlinked and interdependent (1 Cor. 12:5). Though each member has unique gifts and functions, they all function in unity. Moreover, in the body the members who seem to be weak are given more importance, the weakest is given an honourable position and the unattractive are clothed with more care. Just as the human body's disparate organs and tissues are joined by "ligaments" into one organism, so too are the members of the church joined together by "the bond of love."[34] Thus, love becomes the driving force for every member to work for the common good. The body metaphor challenges intergenerational conflict which is prevailing in the society and calls for intergenerational solidarity as it affirms the uniqueness and worth of each person for a healthy society.

Treating the Aged with Dignity and Love in the Church

In his letter to the young pastor Timothy, Paul gives important instructions concerning the way the aged should be treated in the church (1 Tim. 5:1–2). Paul directs Timothy that older men are not to be spoken harshly but to be exhorted as a father (5:1). The Greek verb for speaking harshly is *epiplēssō*, and this is the only place in the New Testament this word is used. It literally means "to strike at." Paul's instruction is not that Timothy must never rebuke older men, but that he is not to attack older men with overly harsh words.[35] Paul also encourages Timothy to treat older women like mothers, with the respect and honour due their age. Similarly, in 1 Tim. 5:8 Paul is illustrating how important it is for adult children to take care of their family members as the failure to do so brings shame upon the family members.

In Gal. 6:2 Paul encourages the members of the Galatian church to bear each other's burdens. The word "burden" here means all kinds of weakness (cf. Rom. 15:1), suffering, and pain; in short, any and every load that is hard to bear.[36] Paul has a radical understanding of the responsibility believers have for one another. According to him, sharing each other's burdens, particularly that of the aged, is another way of fulfilling the "law of Christ," that is, the command to love neighbour as self (Gal. 5:14).

The epistle of James, which is an intensely practical book, sees intergenerational solidarity as a form of pure religion. In the opening chapter,

---

34 Walker Mimms, "A Model of Christian Charity Symbols: The Human Body," available at: https://www.litcharts.com/lit/a-model-of-christian-charity/symbols/the-human-body (accessed, 27/11/2020).

35 Drawing upon Cicero, Augustine argues that there are three basic styles of oratory – the subdued, the temperate, and the majestic. Augustine thinks "Paul is advocating the use of the temperate style." Quoted by Jay Twomey, *The Pastoral Epistles Through the Centuries, Blackwell Bible Commentaries* (West Sussex: Wiley-Blackwell, 2009), 75.

36 Ronald Y. K. Fung, *The Epistle to the Galatians*, The New International Commentary on the New Testament (Grand Rapids, Michigan: Wm. B. Eerdmans, 1988), 287.

James affirms that pure and undefiled religion is not outward illustrations and ceremonial observations but it is taking care of the less fortunate and striving for personal purity (1:27). During the time of the writing of James, widows and orphans represented the most marginalized and vulnerable groups of people. In such a context James points out, "true Christianity is composed of a simple and sincere devotion to God expressed through compassionate relationship with one's neighbours in general and the aged in particular."[37] These instructions are meant to maintain intergenerational solidarity which would ensure graceful ageing.

Jesus, the Elder-Friendly in the Book of Revelation

An in-depth reading of the book of Revelation will help us to understand the book's portrayal of inter-generational conflict. In the opening chapter, the book reveals a conflict between John the apostle, the author who was in his nineties and Domitian, the Roman Emperor who was in his forties.[38] The young ruler Domitian banished the aged John to Patmos due to his commitment for an egalitarian society where the young and the aged will live together in peace and harmony as the phrases in Rev. 1:9 suggest: "kingdom, the word of God and the testimony of Jesus." John's banishment is intended to exclude him from the community and it is similar to the aged being driven out of his/her home in the present context.

John personifies the Empire of Rome as a beautiful young and elite woman who has the power to seduce and commit adultery with the kings of the earth and sexually attract the inhabitants of the earth. John calls her as "the mother of the prostitutes and of the abomination of the earth (Rev. 17:1-5).[39] The Empire inflicted a great harm to the aged John and his people by disallowing them from involving in normal economic activities. They were being coerced to bow to the dictates of the Empire (Rev. 13:16-17).

Revelation presents Jesus as the firstborn of the dead, and the ruler of kings on earth (Rev. 1:4). It is very interesting to note that John presents

---

37 Daniel Dei, "A Discussion of James 1:27 and its Impact on Efforts in Evangelization and Discipleship in the Ghanaian Christian Context," *Ilorin Journal of Religious Studies*, 5/2 (2015): 52.

38 Domitian was born on 24 October 51 C.E. He was Roman emperor from 81 to 96 C.E. According to R. H. Mounce the book of Revelation was written around 95 CE when Domitian was the Roman Emperor. Robert H. Mounce, *The Book of Revelation*, The New International Commentary on the New Testament (Grand Rapids, Michigan: Wm. B. Eerdmans, 1977), 34-35.

39 Feminist scholars often question Revelation's use of female imageries in the criticism of the Roman Empire. Surekha Nelavala in her study of Rev. 17:5 by using Postcolonial Feminist approach argues that Revelation is written in the context of Roman imperialism with a patriarchal mindset. See Surekha Nelavala, "Babylon the Great Mother of Whores' (Rev 17:5): A Postcolonial Feminist Perspective," *The Expository Times*, 121/2 (2009): 60.

Jesus as an ideal young man who comes to the aged John who was forced out of his own place for a remote island where he was lonely and abandoned. An important aspect of John's presentation of Jesus is seen in his use of two contrasting images: the Lamb and the Lion. The Lamb image brings to mind Jesus' sacrificial mission for the helpless victims of oppression (here in the book of Revelation the aged), the image of Lion points to a powerful young man who can challenge the abandonment and victimisation of the aged by the young. Thus John presents Jesus as a counter to the Emperor who has no regard for the aged. Jesus is also presented as one who honours and helps the aged John and all the victims of Empires' anti-human policies.

The last two chapters in the book of Revelation are portrayed in terms of a beautiful home with a lovely garden where the young and the old live together and enjoy a healthy life. In The phrase "Now the dwelling of God is with men (and women) and he will live with them (Rev. 21:3) points to an ideal home which has God's presence in Spirit. Moreover, the phrase "there was no longer any sea" (Rev. 21:1) implies a happy home. This is because in Revelation Sea is a symbol of oppression, economic exploitation, conflict and disorder.[40] The absence of sea ensures the presence of peace and harmony among the intergenerational members of the household.

The phrase in "Rev. 21:4, "there will be no more death or mourning or crying or pain" must have brought much relief to the aged of John's time as now death is challenged with the promise of a long life. The household experiencing health and harmony is further described in Rev. 22:1-5, in that, the healing of all pain and suffering is the concrete consequence of an intergenerational community living in harmony with its creator and with the Lamb as its shepherd. The New Heaven and New Earth metaphor in Rev. 21-22 points to an age-friendly physical environment which if realised can promote healthy interaction and caring among the members of different ages in a household.

Conclusion

Ageism is of increasing concern due to the growing older population worldwide and youth-centered focus of many societies. Nevertheless, ageing is not only honourable but also a right of every human being. Ageing populations are "our only growing natural resource." In the thought of Paul ageing is becoming younger: "Though our outer nature (body) is wasting away, our inner nature is being renewed day by day" (2 Cor. 4:16). This means that ageing is to be celebrated; it is not to be endured but to be enjoyed. Nevertheless, statements that denigrate older people's functioning, thinking

40 Donald W. Richardson, *The Revelation of Jesus Christ: An Interpretation* (Virginia: John Knox Press, 1939), 183.

and appearance can lead to old people being stigmatized, isolated, ignored, politically disadvantaged and treated as "others." The New Testament vividly portrays the constant struggle the young and the aged faced in their day to day life at home, church and in the society. In this age of conflict between the young and the old, the New Testament offers an alternative model of Intergenerational solidarity, which is 'love oriented action", for graceful ageing.' The New Testament presents Jesus as the model for the care of the aged: the Lamb model that goes out of the way to care for the aged and the Lion model that resists the negative forces that deny a graceful ageing. It calls the church to emulate the model shown by Jesus in her ministry of elderly care. To sum up, love is the binding principle which the New Testament emphasises for intergenerational friendly communities.

7

Issue of Ageing in the Early Writings of History of Christianity A Response

Babu. C.

Introduction

Church's teaching on old age has always addressed and affirmed the importance of recognizing and nurturing intrinsic values in people of all ages. The Greco-Roman and Jewish society viewed old people differently as ancient society divided people based on capability and productiveness of adult males. While the Greeks and initially the Romans had positive attitude towards older people emphasized on wisdom and capabilities, the Jewish teachings focused on moral-ethical and spiritual advantages attached with old age. The early Christians drew much of their teachings on old age and ageing people from these three diverse societies. The Christian social action fostered a new vigor of human and spiritual values in despised old people of all genders. However, in the early Christian writings, old age was interpreted more in the light of life, death and judgment that followed old age and paid little attention to ageing related problems stemmed from social, economic, religious, cultural and political aspects. The early Christian historical writings and of the early church leaders focused more on theological and organizational growth and expansion of Christianity. Nevertheless, in the writings of the early church leaders one still finds references old age associated with spirituality and otherworldly transition, somehow spiritualized old age. Old age was greatly upheld among Christians as final stage of life to enter the eternal life. Therefore, and attempt is made in this essay to unravel the understanding of old age in the early Christian writings and make a response to the social engagement of the early church towards the aged people.

Ageing in the Ancient Greco-Roman World

To understand the early Christian perception of old age, one has to understand the *sitz-im-leben* of the Greco-Roman worldview of old age in its socio-cultural and political context. The recently discovered Sappho fragment (P Köln 21351 and 21376) reflects on old age and its sad physical effects.[1] Among Greek philosophers, old age was interpreted both positively and negatively as it had goodness and sadness. George Minois in his book, *History of Old Age: From Antiquity to the Renaissance,* brings out the inferred status of the old, even in the best of times for old their position was ambiguous and contradictory.[2] The Roman vocabularies *puer, puella, iuvenis, adulescens, virgo, senex, anus* were used to refer to males and females without any specific age attached to them.[3] Both Greeks and Romans had no definite number that defined the beginning of old age, but the age was rounded-off to the nearest five. Tim G. Parkin, in his book *Old Age in the Roman World: A cultural and Social History,* attempts to clarify "aged" or "old" from cultural and social history perspective.[4]

In the ancient Greek and Roman society, a minimum age to qualify for old age a person should be sixty years and above.[5] Twenty years was considered as young age that was given responsibilities in administration and participation in war. Plato and Cicero offered a philosophical and somewhat idealized view of old age, fifty years considered being old. Aristotle says that as long as an individual is capable of participating in war and political life of the state, considered young, but once retreats from it and become self-sufficient, considered old.[6] Physical changes in a person's body ability marked the ageing process that also brought changes in their involvement various responsibilities.

The Greek world always looked at old age with respect filled with wisdom and spirituality. While Aristotle looked at old age "characterized people as overly pessimistic, distrustful, malicious, suspicious and living to nothing more than staying alive,"[7] Plato in his *Utopia* states that though old

---

1 Angelo Di Berardino, ed., *Encyclopedia of Ancient Christianity: Produced by the Institutum Patristicum Augustinianum* (Ilinois: IVP Academic, 2014), 957.

2 For more details, see George Minois, *History of Old Age: From Antiquity to the Renaissance,* Translated by Sarah Hanbury Tenlson (Chicago: The University of Chicago Press, 1989).

3 Tim G. Parkin, *Old Age in the Roman World: A Cultural and Social History* (Baltimore: The John Hopkins University press, 2003), reviewed by T. McClain, 13 July 2020. https://bmcr.brynmawr.edu/2003/2003.09.49/.

4 For more details see Tim G. Parkin, *Old Age in the Roman World: A Cultural and Social History* (Baltimore: The John Hopkins University Press, 2003).

5 Parkin, *Old Age in the Roman World: A Cultural and Social History,* 105.

6 Richard Macklon, *The Basic Works of Aristotle* (New York: The Modern Library, 2001), 1130.

7 "Confronting aging, a world in transition, Before 1500," 22 July, 2020: https://www.confrontingaging.com/before-1500.html.

age had an important role to play, yet it was a curse, vanishing of pleasures and ill treatment at the end, but it has positive aspects too.[8] Though physically one may be weak but wisdom can still be used in public life as Plato in his *Republic* presented much positive aspects of old age who are free from passions. Before Plato there was an overtly negative tendency of old age as seen in Socrates' preference to die than to bear the disabilities of the old age.[9] Parkins argued that Seneca the Younger and Pliny the Elder better expressed the realities of old age issues. Parkins quotes Seneca saying that old age "…is the final stage of life the dregs, or is it the clearest and purest part of all, provided only that the mind is unimpaired, and the senses, still sound, give their support to the spirit, and the body is not worn out and dead before its time? For it makes a great deal of difference whether a man is drawing out his life or his death."[10] Despite the respectful place for the aged in the Greek society, Seneca the Younger (Epistle 108:28) terms old age to an incurable disease and dying better than living with impaired faculties.[11] Juvenal lists negative depictions of old age issues related with grief, weakness, dementia and ugliness.[12] However, philosophers such as Plato, Cicero, Seneca and Plutarch refuted the overtly negative old age and highlighted the advantages and noblest aspects of old age. Positively looking at the old age, Galen argued that old age was not a disease but a natural process just as to die of old age is natural.[13]

However, there are different understanding of old age among Greeks and the Romans. While the Greeks had placed the old people at a respected place for wisdom and guidance, the Roman society though initially favored, in the gradual shift from Republic to Empire deprived the aged of their political, administrative and familial control. Hugh Last observes that "to the Roman manliness was its connotation… manliness was most prized in the form of courage on the field of battle, so that the chief association of virtues was always with physical bravery."[14] The end of the Roman period marked fatal for the aged as they almost lost their respectful place in society and were left on the streets without care and support.

---

8 Angelo Di Berardino, ed., *Encyclopedia of Ancient Christianity* (Illinois: InterVarsity Press, 2014), 957.

9 Angelo Di Berardino, ed., *Encyclopedia of Ancient Christianity,* 957.

10 Parkin, *Old Age in the Roman World: A Cultural and Social History,* 70-71.

11 Parkin, *Old Age in the Roman World: A Cultural and Social History,* 71.

12 Angelo Di Berardino, ed., *Encyclopedia of Ancient Christianity,* 958.

13 Tim G. Parkin, "Status of Older People; the Ancient and Biblical World," 22 July 2020, https://www.encyclopedia.com/education/encyclopedias-almanacs-transcripts-and-maps/status-older-people-ancient-and-biblical-worlds.

14 Hugh Last, "Family and social life," in *The Legacy of Rome,* edited by Cyril Bailey (Oxford: The Clarendon Press, 1923), 211.

Unlike the Romans, the Greeks had strong laws that made children to take care of their aged parents. Plato in his *Republic* writes that those who neglect their parents will be guilty, and teaches to care for their old parents.[15] In spite of such laws the aged people continue to face the old age issues as Cicero argued that "old age will only be respected if it fights for itself, maintains its rights, avoids dependence on anyone, and asserts control over its own to the last breath."[16] In the Roman Empire, the elderly gradually lost their guiding and advisory roles and lost confidence in their potentialities and capabilities as they felt marginalized, sidelined, or pushed to solitary life.[17] Thus, one finds clearly the changed status of people, especially the aged in the socio-political and family life during the Greco-Roman world that had bearings on women.

Challenges of Ageing among Women

One cannot deny that despite being the patriarchal society, the Greco-Roman world placed women with respect and dignity in the family, social and religious life until they lost their procreation ability. Initially, women enjoyed freedom at home and in public but gradually there was a shift that confined women to home and child bearing. The Greek virtuous woman lived in seclusion and was not permitted to leave her home, however, there are references to women leaving their homes for business and to socialize.[18] Women exercised freedom and at the same time restrictions. But, Hugh Last argues that it is difficult to understand the status of women since theory and practice did not agree.[19] The gradual shift from Republic to Empire marked loss of freedom for women and at best tolerated miserable experience at the worst. Women gained their limited freedom in their post-menopausal state when they no longer produced children. Parkins observed that when the aged women became no longer useful in the family and social life, she was left on the street.[20] In a highly patriarchal social and political context, women experienced a low standard of life as old people of poor and marginalized combined with men and women

15 "Republic" translated by F. M. Comford, in *Greek Philosophy: Thales to Aristotle, Readings in the History of Philosophy,* edited by Reginald E. Allen (New York: The Free Press, 1966), 180, 217.

16 Cicero, 22 July 2020: https://www.confrontingaging.com/before-1500.html.

17 See "Growing Old in Ancient Greece and Rome: How History helps us see ourselves as we age," 22 July 2020, https://www.psychologytoday.com/us/blog/the-art-and-science-aging-well/201704/growing-old-in-ancient-greece-and-rome.

18 Julian Andrew Barr, *Tertullian's Attitude towards the Human Foetus and Embryo,* Doctor of Philosophy thesis submitted to the University of Queensland, Australia, 2014, 193.

19 Hugh Last, "Family and social life," 221.

20 See Tim G. Parkin, *Old Age in the Roman World: A Cultural and Social History* (Baltimore: The John Hopkins University Press, 2003), Review by T. McClain, BMCR 9/49 (2003), 22 July 2020, https://bmcr.brynmawr.edu/2003/2003.09.49/.

faced ageing challenges. The neglect of the aged and unproductive people can be best seen in the Romans slogan "Throw the sexagenarians off the bridge,"[21] that clearly showed the horrible place. The Hellenistic Greek view of women was that she should be silent servant of husband/men, while the Romans placed women at margins. While the legal codes of Greek/Hellenistic world obligated the children to look after their elderly members and see their aged parents' welfare, Rome had no legislative enforcement for familial support of the aged parents.[22] The most affected of such law were the women as they always forced to depend on men for support.

Rooted in such a diverse context of the Greco-Roman world, Christianity emerged as a new force that cared for the uncared. In the NT, references are found caring of the widows and women. Deriving its social responsibility rooted in the teachings of Jesus Christ's love your neighbor marked a paradigm shift among early Christian towards the elderly, poor, widows and the abandoned.[23] The Jewish ethical teachings, the Hebrew Bible, and the teachings of Jesus helped the early Christians to develop a holistic approach to old age and address its challenges.

Judeo-Christian Understanding of Ageing/Old Age

The Judeo-Christian community, which shares socio-cultural and spiritual context of the Greco-Roman world and Jewish heritage, developed the attitude of respect and honor as common obligation and rule towards the aged. Except in few places (Ecc. 11:10; Ps: 90:10), Bible portrays old age positively and exhorts reverence to old people. The sufferings associated with old age were seen as a divine purpose, but the long life was God's benevolence (Ps 71:17-18). OT emphasizes proper responsibilities of the children to honor parents and the elderly as presented in the Decalogue, the fourth and the fifth Commandment (Ex. 20:1-17). Torah and the entire OT clearly mark the consequences of neglecting aged parents and mocking the elderly. Israelites have imbibed a careful and positive attitude towards and place for the elderly in all its aspects of life.

Judaism follows the life stage and the intersection of ageing that begins with birth, growth and development of a human being. In the process of human development, according to Rachel Dulin, "The ancient Israelite writers viewed ageing as the last part of an ongoing developmental process. Each face of life

21 "The Art of Aging in Christian Life," 17 July 2020: https://www.eurozine.com/the-art-of-aging-in-christian-life./.

22 Tim G. Parkin, *Old Age in the Roman World: A Cultural and Social History* (Baltimore: John Hopkins University Press, 2003), Reviewed by David G. Troyansky, *The Gerontologist* 44/2 (2004): 282.

23 Margaret M. Mitchell and Frances M. Young, eds, *The Cambridge History of Christianity: Origins to Constantine,* vol. I (Cambridge: Cambridge University Press, 2006), 156-159.

was marked by physical and psychological changes as maturity set-in and old age approached.... Ageing is inseparable part of human experience."[24] In the OT, Old age was associated with having wisdom, reservoir of knowledge, and fruitful experience. The book of Wisdom of Solomon clearly says that "An honorable old age comes not with the passing of time, nor can it be measured in terms of years; rather, understanding is the hoary crown for men, and an unsullied life, the attainment of old age" (4:8-9). The word 'old' or 'old man' (sic) is not attributed by the virtue of old age but to honor a mature judgment and life full of gravity, and full days of expression. Long life and years was seen as reward for righteous living as the Apocryphal wisdom of Ben Sira 25:4-6 says that "How beautiful is the wisdom of old people and thoughtful advice of individuals who are honored. Much experience is the crown of old people. Their enchantment is reverence for Adonai." In other words, in the OT and Apocryphal literature considered old age, a blessing associated with life and death as joy and a curse as maladies would prevent them from activities. However, the Jewish notion of reverence reinforced the laws of respecting the aged. This attitude became a social system in Judaism, caring for the elderly.[25] What was significant here was that Jesus without despising the elderly taught his disciples to follow the OT and Jewish ethical teachings towards the aged. This we can see throughout the ministry of Jesus and the early Christians.

Ageing in the New Testament and Early Christian Teachings

Unlike the OT, which consists of more stories of old age people, the New Testament though consists of references to old people there is an entirely contrasting picture of the aged. Except few people like Zacharias and Elizabeth, Joachim and Anne, parents of Virgin Mary, Simeon, Anna, Paul and, Timothy, there is certain youthfulness as Jesus taught and spoke, and died of young age, and his disciples were young followers. In the NT, one does not speak anything beyond the age of Jesus that limits our understanding of old age in the NT writings and the early church. There is a different understanding of old age in the NT that connects with eternal life. Hence, there are more references to death and eternal life than speaking of old age issues, a concept different from the idea of the blessings of earthly longevity. Christ's teaching about old age and elderly men and women is simple and clear as he spoke of material aid for the widows, help for elderly parents and regard for parents.[26] The *Korban*

24 Rachel Z. Dulin, "The Elderly in Biblical Society," *Journal of Ageing and Judaism* 1/1 (1986): 50-51.

25 Kerry M. Olitzky and Eugene B. Borowitz, "A Jewish Perspective," in Ageing, *Spirituality, and Religion: A Handbook,* edited by Melvin A. Kimble, et. al (Minneapolis: Fortress Press, 1995), 392.

26 Anna Sanecak, "Christianity Facing the Ageing of Global Population," *Journal of Education Culture and Society* 2 (2015): 243.

mentioned by Jesus to a young man shows that Jesus grew-up in Judaism and trained in Torah upheld its teachings to care for the parents and the elderly as seen in his new command to "love your neighbor." Though the teachings of Jesus do not offer much directly on the aged, yet his attitude to marginalized sections shows his emphasis to care for the aged. Jesus attitude towards old people and his own response in defending the elderly paved the way for his followers and the early Christian community to care for the aged people.

In the early writings of the NT, Paul exhorts to Titus to be sensible of old people and give due honor to old people (2:2-3). To Timothy he says that "Do not rebuke an older man harshly but exhort him as if he were your father... older women as mothers.... Give proper recognition to those widows who are really in need.... (1Timothy 5:1-5). Here, one finds a positive attitude of the early Christians to the aged and a combination of OT teachings of honoring the elderly and the aged, the Greek emphasis on wisdom of the aged and Jesus' teaching on love. Deriving from Jewish and Jesus ethical teachings, the early Christian NT writings placed the aged people with honor and wisdom who would give guidance to the community. Therefore, during the persecution when many people were left without help, when the Romans did not take care of the old people as it did not have any binding law on children to care for their parents, the NT showed a new life and love that became the backbone of the early church towards the aged people.

Ageing in the Writings of Early Christianity

What really does early Christianity speak of the old age? NT and the early historical writings delve more on the physical and spiritual angle of old age associated with death and life than with the issues of old age. Placing the elderly at a high place, the early church outlined two important roles for them: a *guide* and *intermediary* advisers, kind teachers and experienced intermediaries between the contingent world and thereafter, between certainty and mystery, between life and death, between death and resurrection, the role of aged was determined.[27] Elders were leading the church with wisdom and spiritual knowledge.

From the second century onwards, there was a strong eschatological approach to old age. The early church leaders such as Clement, Origen, Eusebius, Gregory of Nyssa, St. Ambrose, John Chrysostom, Jerome and others viewed old age in the eschatological context and thought of a world free of weakness, disease, and death and full of peace and eternal life. Tertullian, the early Church father, speaks of life, death and judgment that follows a person

27 Andrei Plesu, "The art of aging in Christian life," 13 July 2020, https://www.eurozine.com/the-art-of-aging-in-christian-life/.

but does not speak of old age.[28] He says that "the bodily weakness inherent in our human nature which we feel and suffer are not a punishment but a warfare. Fortitude is strengthened by infirmities and misfortune is frequently a training school for virtue, finally, both mental and physical powers become torpid without laborious exercise."[29] Gregory of Nyssa in the context of persecution where Christians face imminent death writes about the troubles and maintaining the resurrected body.[30] Further, he expresses perplexities on what kind of body resurrects on the day, and if the same body that lived at the death, it will be more horrible than to live. In response to Gregory, Macrina writes that in resurrection our nature will be restored in its original condition and not the state of our body at the time of death, not as babies or old, but perfect body as willed by God.[31] This new body will be free of physical misery but of divine image detached from all aspects of corruptions and decay. There will be altogether a new body absence of old age and death. Accordingly, Gregory of Nazianzus writes that there is no old age in the other world, and one does not grow or body will not become immature or old, but all perfect in their spiritual age.[32] He followed Gregory of Nyssa's conception of the absence of old age in the other world and death as liberation from enslavement of corruption.

St. Ambrose, writing a commentary on St. Luke, talks about old age as venerable and not because of duration or number of years, but for their wisdom.[33] In a letter to his brother Anysius, Ambrose writes that "old is blessed, for old age is truly venerable when it grows hoary not with grey hairs but with good deeds."[34] Wisdom attributed to growing age that comes with experience and learning, St. Jerome too praises old age connected with wisdom, a sense developed in the early Christianity. John Chrysostom and St. Augustine both speak of old age not perfect in it but only if equated with wisdom that does not necessarily depend on age.[35] It was generally an attributed notion that old age plays along experience and wisdom. Old was glorified and celebrated than mourning over it. For, old was overcoming the physical behavior with highest spirituality. Jerome in his work, like Origen and Gregory of Nyssa who placed

---

28 Rudolf, Daly and Quain, trans., *Tertullian Apologetical Works and Minucius Felix Octavius* (New York: Fathers of the Church, Inc., 1950), 396.

29 Rudolf Arbesmann, Emily Joseph Daly and Edwin A Quain, trans., *Tertullian Apologetical Works and Minucius Felix Octavius,* 396.

30 Angelo Di Berardino, ed., *Encyclopedia of Ancient Christianity,* 959.

31 Angelo Di Berardino, ed., *Encyclopedia of Ancient Christianity,* 960.

32 Angelo Di Berardino, ed., *Encyclopedia of Ancient Christianity,* 960.

33 Andrei Plesu, "The art of aging in Christian life."

34 Mary Melchoir Beyenka, Trans, *Saint Ambrose Letters* (New York: Fathers of the Church, Inc. 1954), 69.

35 Andrei Plesu, "The art of aging in Christian life."

ascetic life as incarnate ideal, presents death as overcoming physical age and gender.[36]

Old age is not to be seen as something easy to pass without any issues. St. Augustine with regard to death connected with the age writes that "if a man begins to die, to be, that is "in death" from the moment that his death gets under way, that is, when the cessation of life begins..., the conclusion is that he is in death, from the moment of birth. For what else is taking place throughout each moment, hour, day of man's life until, the dying over... after death begins, replacing the time in death which lasted while life was ebbing away."[37] John Chrysostom investigating the relationship between the death or thantology and self-fashioning, viewed multi-directional flow of death in the old age that lies between theology, ethics and physiology. He writes that the ageing of the body was considered a cooling and drying process in which the body becomes monastic and virginal.[38] Cooling and drying dietary regimen was seen as a regiment of ageing and mortification. Here, ageing associated with death was seen beyond earthly realms into eternal life.

In the construction of Christian history and faith, old age was associated with death and life in an eschatological concept. There was a highest reverence given to the old age as this was the final stage to transmit into eternal life. The early writers gave importance to the fact that ageing was not the end but continued life after the death. Therefore, the church's ministry to the aged became significant in developing a futuristic notion of old age.

A Response from Christian Social Responsibility Perspective

What then we have to say about ageing and the aged people in the writings of early history of Christianity? Most writings in Christianity focused on the elderly and the aged deriving from Greco-Roman and Jewish social context. The issue of ageing was some-how submerged under the eschatological understanding of old age connected with life, death and judgment. Unlike the OT, which taught old age associated with long life and wisdom, in the NT, old age continued even after death. Old age has been considered as a process of human life that continues even after death. Therefore, the early writers did not exclusively focus on old age but rather they gave theological and eschatological interpretations. Fred van Tatenhove observes that though there is no separate theology of ageing, this does not mean that the Christian

36 Angelo Di Berardino, ed., *Encyclopedia of Ancient Christianity,* 961.

37 Gerald G. Walsh and Grace Manhan, trans. *Saint Augustine: The City of God,* books VII-XVI (New York: Fathers of the Church, Inc., 1952), 311.

38 Chris L. de Wet, "The practice of everyday death: Thanatology and self-fashioning in John Chrysostom's thirteenth homily on Romans," 23 September 2020, http://www.scielo.org.za/pdf/hts/v71n1/75.pdf, 5.

community intentionally excluded the human experience of the ageing from its writings.[39] The early Christian historical writers viewed human condition worthy of special attention than the importance of ageing. Nevertheless, according to Maldonado the intent is "not to separate ageing from the broader ongoing theological task" … but "to recognize ageing… in such a way that a concern with ageing will become an intentional component of the broader theological inquiry."[40] With many aged people lived/living to the fullest for the growth of Christianity and building on theological foundation of the future church, therefore, ageing needs attention in historical writings of Christianity.

The early Christian approach to old age was developed in a peculiar context of persecution and social and economic exploitation of Roman imperialism, and a section of the society continued to experience alienation and neglect. The early Christians who themselves faced such alienation and negligence by the government and their fellow people, developed a holistic approach towards poor and the needy, the old and the widow. When the Roman Empire threw the old and the weak, women and unproductive people from economic and political life, the early church came forward to help. In the NT writings and in the early church fathers, we see the social responsibility towards the aged integrated with Christian witness and love. When many became homeless and helpless, the Christian charity and ministry to the aged attracted many to Christian faith. From the day of Pentecost, work of the church towards poor, needy and the elderly shows its social and humanitarian ministry.

Church continued the early Christians work of caring for the aged and the elderly. Metropolitan Anthony speaking on "the Spirituality of Old Age" underlined both "the situation of taking care of old people by their families and friends and the difficulties of receiving the care by the elderly people themselves."[41] He further said that the biblical teaching on aged was not to turn to people of older generation for guidance but turn to them for wisdom and humility. In a Letter to Elderly, Pope John Paul II explained what it means to honor your parents. He said that "Honouring older people involves a threefold duty: welcoming them, helping them and making good use of their qualities."[42] He further said that as the number of elderly population increases it is more important to promote a wide spread attitude of effective social assistance for the elderly. Caring for the elderly and addressing the issues of ageing is

39 Fred van Tatenhove, "Evangelical Perspective," in *Aging, Spirituality, and Religion: A Handbook,* edited by Melvin A. Kimble, et. al (Minneapolis: Fortress Press, 1995), 417.

40 Maldonado, cited in Fred van Tatenhove, "Evangelical Perspective," 417.

41 Christianity Facing the Ageing of Global Population, 13 July 2020, https://www.researchgate.net/publication/307789565_Christianity_Facing_the_Ageing_of_Global_Population, 247.

42 Christianity Facing the Ageing of Global Population, 246.

important in Christian ministry. The Protestantism derives much its theological teachings of social concern from the early Christianity and the Reformers of the 16th century. Luther had direct bearings on ageing as he supported the idea of charity and obligations of honouring elderly, loving other people and supporting the people in need.

In the context of growing old age communities in the churches and in the society, Christianity, like any other studies in the secular world, is interested in the study of old age and ageing. Though the early Christian historical writings shed light on the old age as preparing for the death and judgment, there is a need of change in approach towards the issue of ageing. Ageing is a process and comes across many experiences and challenges. Christianity has addressed the issues related to old age, elderly or the aged, ageing which is a process of life, between birth and death, has received less attention. Often the old age, ageing, aged and ageism synonymously is understood and pronounced. Church should understand ageing properly and address them from a holistic point of view firmly based on the ethical teachings of the Bible.

Since this essay is a response to the issue of ageing from social responsibility perspective effort has been made to dig out to unravel the teachings and approaches to ageing in the biblical and writings of early history of Christianity. Though a number of materials are available in the forms of books and essays on ageing in the secular domain, in the early Christian writings we find references to old age in general terms. Christian writers though referred to old age, they were only limited and there was no exclusive studies or writings that focused on old age and its challenges. Such writings focused on family, individuals, communities and societies, growth of organizational Christianity and its theology. Since one cannot deny ageing and issues associated with it, a fresh look at church's ministry the aged in the early Christianity can help in understanding diverse factors linked with old age. Therefore, the issue of ageing in the early Christianity becomes important to understand church's theological, sociological, humanitarian and ministerial approach to old. Life and death spoken very often among Christians cannot deny the realities of old age. Therefore, a fresh look at Ageing can help further enhance the ministry of the church to the old age people in our present context where Aged people continued to face multiple challenges.

Conclusion

As seen in this essay, the Christian teaching and theoretical approach to the issue of ageing presented in early Christianity shed new light in understanding of old age and issues and challenges associated with it. The teachings of the Bible and Jesus Christ, Christians/churches demand honouring, caring and helping the old people. Charity, caring and honouring is an accompaniment to the elderly people. The early Christian writings mainly focus on organizational and theological growth and the issue of ageing shrinks in the larger narrations. A new historiographical documentation of early Christianity can focus on the challenges of old age in the early times and how it shaped church's ministry to the elderly. History of Christianity is not just record of events and actions of people, but it should also focus on how ageing continues with events and actions in shaping Christian social responsibility in the present ecclesial and social context.

8

Ageing in World History An Overview of Programmes and Policies

S. David Joseph Raj

Introduction

Ageing is a natural process, which occurs in each individual's life. The whole world see grey hairs, wrinkled skin, loose tooth, walking with stick and bended-back are seen as sign of ageing. According to Aparna Sarkar, "Ageing is not merely getting old, wrinkles, tumbling feet, diseases but it's an achievement of a lifetime innocence, exuberance, reverence and perseverance."[1] In many society, ageing is considered as honourable because aged person's knowledge, experience and capability to take right decisions and advice. It would not be wrong to say that experience brings maturity in an individual's life. In early times aged people were considered a treasure of the family and they were given respect and honour not only in the family, but in the entire community. But with the advancement of society, the status of elderly is steadily degrading. Today, they are considered as undue burden for the family members. In many cases, even children are not ready to take care of them. The world trends show that the lonely and dreadful old age is what awaits each and every living beings. Sooner or later we all have to live through this dreaded stage in our lives. In Weeraperuna's words: "those who live long enough will someday have to face the unpleasant fact that they are no longer youthful. Unless a person passes away early in life, he or she is fated to experience the problems that arise from having an ageing body and mind."[2] Considering these facts, this essay tries to present a broad overview of ageing, its geographic and temporal spread over different regions of the world and over different countries of Asia. The essay

1 Aparna Sarkar, "Molecular and Cellular Parameters of Ageing: An Overview," *Al Ameen J Med Sci* 9/1 (2016): 4.

2 Susunaga Weeraperuma, *Being Blissful As the Years Pass By Reflections on Ageing* (Delhi: ISPCK, 2012), ix.

also highlights the "World Assembly on Ageing" Programmes and Policies and Policies, Programmes on the ageing in India with special focus on rights of elderly in India.

Ageing

The World Health Organization defined Ageing as having were two different aspects namely biological level and life transitions level. At the biological level, ageing results from the impact of the accumulation of a wide variety of molecular and cellular damage over time. This leads to a gradual decrease in physical and mental capacity, a growing risk of disease, and ultimately, death. But these changes are neither linear nor consistent, and they are only loosely associated with a person's age in years. While some 70-year-olds enjoy extremely good health and functioning, other 70-year-olds are frail and require significant help from others.[3] Beyond biological changes, ageing is also associated with other life transitions such as retirement, relocation to more appropriate housing, and the death of friends and partners. In developing a public-health response to ageing, it is important not just to consider approaches that enhance the losses associated with older age, but also those that may reinforce recovery, adaptation and psychosocial growth.[4]

Common Health Conditions Associated with Ageing

Common health conditions in older age include hearing loss, cataracts and refractive errors, back and neck pain and osteoarthritis, chronic obstructive pulmonary disease, diabetes, depression, and dementia. Furthermore, as people age, they are more likely to experience several conditions at the same time. Older age is also characterized by the emergence of several complex health states that tend to occur only later in life and that do not fall into isolated disease categories. These are commonly called geriatric syndromes. They are often the consequence of multiple underlying factors and include frailty, urinary incontinence, falls, delirium and pressure ulcers. Geriatric syndromes appear to be better predictors of death than the presence or a number of specific diseases. Yet outside of countries that have developed geriatric medicine as a specialty, they are often overlooked in traditionally structured health services and in epidemiological research.[5]

---

3 World Health Organization, "Ageing and Health." Available at: https://www.who.int/news-room/fact-sheets/detail/ageing-and-health (accessed, August 2020).

4 World Health Organization, "Ageing and Health." Available at: https://www.who.int/news-room/fact-sheets/detail/ageing-and-health (accessed, August 2020).

5 World Health Organization, "Ageing and Health." Available at: https://www.who.int/news-room/fact-sheets/detail/ageing-and-health (accessed, August 2020).

Spread of Ageing: Over Time and Regions

In the whole world 'ageing' is spreading rapidly with time and over regions. Some of the major characteristics that mark the global spread of ageing are as follows;

> The number of the elderly has tripled over the last fifty years and this number is expected to further triple in the next fifty years
> The growth rate of the elderly is much faster than the growth rate of the total population almost all over the world
> The proportion of the elderly in total populations will double within the next fifty years
> Though currently the more developed regions of the world have relatively high proportions of the elderly, the older population is concentrated in the less developed regions and is growing at a faster rate.[6]

Since 1950, the number of persons aged 60 years or older was 205 million. Their numbers surged to 606 million in 2000. By 2050, these numbers are projected to rise to two billion. Before 1950 and after 1950, the whole world only three countries had more than one million aged people; namely China, India and the United States of America. In the year 2000, Japan and the Russian federation joined the list. By 2050, there are 33 countries expected to be on the list. The United Nations, 'World Population Ageing' data clearly portrayed in terms of percentage, the aged constituted 8.2 percent of the total population since 1950; this percentage rose to 10 percent of the world's population in 2000. It is projected to rise to 21.1 percent in 2050, by which time the world population of the aged will be larger than the population of children between the ages 0-14 years. The current growth of the older population, which is 1.9 percent, is significantly higher than that of the total population, estimated to be at 1.2 percent. As the baby boom generation enters into old age, the difference between the two can be expected to increase in the near future. The projections indicate that by 2025-2030, the aged population will grow by 2.8 percent compared to 0.8 percent for the total population. There will, however, be a fall in the growth rate of the elderly in 2045-2050.[7]

Causes of Ageing

Frank W. Notestein the demographer stated that the causes of ageing 'viewed as a whole the problem of ageing is no problem at all. It is only the pessimistic

6 Rajagopal Dhar Chakraborti, *The Greying of India* (New Delhi: Sage Publications, 2004), 34-35.

7 Rajagopal Dhar Chakraborti, *The Greying of India*, 34-35.

way of looking at a great triumph of civilization.'[8] There are two important ageing causes described by Andrei Cursaru the first cause is 'Increase in life Expectancy' and second cause is 'Declining Fertility Rates.'

Increase in Life Expectancy

Life expectancy during the 19th century was much lower when compared today. By 1870 the highest life expectancy in the world was in Europe with 36 years and the lowest in Asian and Africa at 26 years. Globally the life expectancy by the end of the 19th century was at 29 years. As of the middle of the 20th century, the life expectancy has risen significantly in the developed world. By 1950 the world life expectancy was at 48 years and it would rise up to 71.4 by 2015. Europe still remains the region with the highest life expectancy as by 2014 this was at 80.67 years. The most impressive increase has been in Africa, which has only seen an increase until 1920, where its population is expected to live until the age of 60. With such increases in life expectancy worldwide it has been predicted that by year 2050 individuals aged 60 and older will be the most common age group. The dramatic shift in the age demographics is most noticeable in a population pyramid that shows the change in modal age groups. In 2100 it is predicted that 22.3 percent of the world population will be aged 65 and over which is a significant increase from the 7.6 percent in 2010. This increase in life expectancy is mostly attributed to medicine and major developments in medical technology.[9]

Declining Fertility Rates

The life expectancy has substantially increased in developed countries, but the total fertility has fallen below the stable rate level. In order for a population to remain stable across every generation, women need to give birth to around 2.1 children during her life 'to replace both her and the father in the population.' This fertility rate is called the 'replacement fertility rate.' In the 19th century there were high birth rate provided each generation with a robust population, today birth rates have fallen drastically. From 1960 until 2015 the fertility rate of most countries has decreased. For example, in 1960 census report Mexico had the highest total fertility rate of 6.8. The present census reports the highest

8 Rajagopal Dhar Chakraborti, *The Greying of India*, 81.

9 Worldwide around 180 out of 1,000 children (18 percent) died under the age of 5 in 1960. However, the infant mortality rate has declined significantly as by 2005 we reached a historically low level where only around 75 out of 1,000 children (7.5 percent) died under the age of five. The reasons as vaccine and awareness have significantly lowered the mortality rate of children by effectively eliminating common problems such as smallpox, scarlet fever, malaria and cholera. Andrei Cursaru, "What are the main causes of ageing and its consequences on the provision of health care?" Available at: https://www.researchgate.net/publication/332303878_What_are_the_main_causes_of_population_aging_and_its_consequences_on_the_provision_of_healthcare.

fertility rate is in India with 2.4. The largest decreases have been in China from 5.7 to 1.6 and Canada from 3.8 to 1.6. A theory, although disputed by some, why there were more births during the lifetime of a woman was that children were 'an effective form of savings by parents.' The children were seen in the past as an investment as they could take care of their parents when they grow older. Fertility has declined because industrialization and globalization made it possible for children to be self-sustainable and social insurance programmes have provided income security when their parents got older.[10]

Ageing Awareness

The primary task of ageing intervention is to recognize the importance of aged persons in human life and to understand the ageing process. Throughout the world history the aged people's life time experiences and their values recognition of the authority, wisdom, dignity and self-control are neglected in some societies. They are unreasonably accused of being a drain on the economy, with their increasing demands for health and support services. Although, healthy ageing is becoming an increasingly important issue for older persons, the public focus on maintaining the aged has sometimes fostered a negative image of ageing. The older women were being shown as weak and dependent, are particularly affected.[11] But, the fact remains that, the human race is characterized by a long childhood and by a long old age. Throughout history this has enabled older people to educate the younger and pass on values to them. The presence of the older people in our home, the neighborhoods and in all forms of social life still teaches an irreplaceable lesson of humanity. Not only by their life, but indeed by their death, older persons teach us all a lesson. Through grief the survivors come to understand that the dead do continue to participate in the human community, by the results of their labour, the works and institutions they leave behind them, and the memory of their word and deeds. This may encourage us to regard our own death with greater peacefulness and to grow more fully aware of the responsibilities towards future generations.[12]

Promoting Graceful Ageing

Denis Goulet suggested that there were three core principles to promote graceful ageing, such as life sustenance, self-esteem and freedom. Life sustenance means the provision of basic needs during the time of old age. Self-esteem demands respect for the elderly from all institutions of civil society.

---

10 Andrei Cursaru, "What are the main causes of ageing and its consequences on the provision of health care?"

11 Rajagopal Dhar Chakraborti, *The Greying of India*, 304-305.

12 Ibid. 305.

Freedom is the ability to choose and be free from bondages of dependence and ill health. Once the people in a country are able to secure these core values in their old age, they can be said to be 'ageing gracefully.' Graceful ageing is a process of optimizing opportunities for physical, social and mental well-being throughout life, in order to ensure a healthy, independent, quality life in older age.[13] Since the late 1990s onwards the World Health Organization has termed this process known as 'active ageing.' Likewise, other international organizations, academic circles and governmental groups (including the G8 countries), the Organization for Economic Co-operation and Development, the International Labour Organizations and the Commission of the European Communities are also using the term 'active ageing.' The 'active ageing' primarily is to express the idea of continuing involvement in socially productive activities and meaningful work. Though the word 'active' implies continuing involvement in all facets of life and not just the ability to be physically active, it may send wrong signals both to the aged and others.[14]

Global Ageing Demography

The twenty-first century, population ageing is poised to emerge as a preeminent worldwide phenomenon. This phenomenon is complex, and has various social, political, and economic dimensions. The world's population aged sixty-five and over has been estimated to be 420 million in mid-2000 and was growing at the rate of over 7,95,000 people per month. Lowered fertility, improved health, and increasing longevity have resulted in an expansion in the elderly population throughout most of the world in terms of both absolute number and proportion. This trend is evident not only in the developed countries of Europe and North America, where there are high absolute numbers of elderly people. But also, in developing countries, which are repeating the trend of the developed world with rates of natural population growth falling sharply. The number of elderly residents is growing in virtually all countries. Developed and developing nations differ in that the former have relatively high shares of people sixty-five and over, whereas the latter are experiencing the fastest growth in elderly populations. Over three-quarters of the global increase in the elderly population since 1999 took place in the developing world.[15]

World Assembly on Ageing Policies and Programmes

The demographic, social, and economic dimensions of the ageing world have placed the issues discussed thus far on the world political stage. In the early

13 Rajagopal Dhar Chakraborti, *The Greying of India*, 306.

14 Ibid. 307.

15 Israel Doron "From national to International Elder Law," 48-49. Available at: https://papers.ssrn.com/sol3/Delivery.cfm/SSRN_ID2286579_code330270.pdf (accessed, August 20,2020).

1980s the United Nations (UN) launched a combined effort to deal with issues concerning the expanding elderly population. The first International Plan of Action on Ageing, which was adopted by the World Assembly on Ageing in Vienna, Austria, in 1982. In this assembly there were 125 nations delegates that attended and discussed the various concerns on ageing to protect the rights of older persons all over the world. It provided specific recommendations for action in seven areas of concern to "ageing individuals", in other words – in areas requiring policy action that is ageing specific. Those seven areas included health and nutrition; protection of elderly consumers; housing and environment; family; social welfare; income security and employment; and education. Following the Vienna International Plan of Action on Ageing, the UN Principles for Older Persons emphasized the need for policies and programmes to ensure independence, participation, care, self-fulfilment and dignity of older people.[16] In 1991, the General Assembly issued the United Nations Principles for Older Persons, which were grouped into five categories namely independence, participation, care, self-fulfilment, and dignity. It corresponds to the rights listed in the International convention on Economic, Social and Cultural Rights (ICESCR). The Assembly in 1991 adopted global targets on ageing for 2001. They issued a Proclamation on Ageing, which promoted national initiatives on ageing and designated 1999 as the International Year of Older Persons.[17]

The Second World Assembly on Ageing (WAA) was held in Madrid, Spain, from 8 to 12 April 2002. There were 150 states represented at the Assembly along with a number of United Nations bodies.[18] The participating countries adopted two key documents: A Political Declaration and the Madrid International Plan of Action on Ageing, 2002. Both documents included commitments from Governments to devise and implement measures to address the challenges posed by ageing. The documents also put forward over 100 recommendations for action based on three priority themes: older persons and development; advancing health and well-being into old age; and ensuring enabling and supportive environments. The Assembly gave the United Nations regional commissions responsibility for translating the International Plan of Action on Ageing into regional action plans reflecting, inter alia, the demographic, economic and cultural specificities of each region and serving

16 Vienna Report, Available at: https://www.un.org/esa/socdev/ageing/documents/Resources/VIPEE-English.pdf (accessed, August 2020).

17 Israel Doron "From national to International Elder Law," 52-53.

18 united-nations-second-world-assembly-on-aging. Available at: https://www.msd.govt.nz/about-msd-and-our-work/publications-resources/journals-and-magazines/social-policy-journal/spj18/ (accessed, August 2020).

as a basis for implementing the recommendations.[19] Diego Rodriguez-Pinzon and Claudia Martin summarize the Madrid Plan as follows:

> The Madrid Plan includes recommendations aimed at implementations and follow up. At the national level, the plan places the primary responsibility with national governments. At the international level, the United Nations Department of Economic and Social Affairs is responsible for facilitating and promoting the plan, the regional commissions are responsible for translating the plan into regional action plans, and responsibility for follow-up and review rests on the Commission for Social Development. However, the Madrid Plan failed to call for the development of a specific instrument that would afford protection to elderly…[20]

Policies and Programmes on the Ageing in India

The Central and State Government of India's policies and programmes towards the betterment of old age people is based on the socio-economic, cultural, religious and health policies. This will create age friendly environments and provide long term cares.

Constitutional Provisions

The Indian Constitution Article 41 deals with the state's role in providing social security to the aged. This article provides that, "The State shall, within the limits of its economic capacity and development, make effective provision for securing the right to work, to education and to public assistance in cases of unemployment, old age, sickness and disablement, and in other cases of undeserved want."[21] In the Constitution of India, Entry 24 in List III Schedule VII deals with the "Welfare of labour, including conditions of work, provident funds, liability for workmen's compensation, invalidity and old age pension and maternity benefits."[22] Item No. 9 of the State List and Item Nos. 20, 23 and 24 of the Concurrent List relate to old age pension, social security and social insurance, and economic and social planting. The right of parents without any means to be supported by their children having sufficient

19 https://www.un.org/en/development/devagenda/ageing.shtml (accessed, August 2020).

20 Diego Rodriguez-Pinzon & Claudia Martin, "The International Human Rights Status of Elderly Persons," *American University International Law Review* 18/4 (2003): 950. Available at: https://digitalcommons.wcl.american.edu/cgi/viewcontent.cgi?article=1199&context=auilr (accessed, August 2020).

21 https://www.mhrd.gov.in/directive_principles_of_state_policy_article-41 (accessed, August 2020).

22 http://interstatecouncil.nic.in/wp-content/uploads/2015/06/CHAPTERII.pdf (accessed, August 2020).

means has been recognized by the Section 125 (I) (d) of the Code of Criminal Procedure 1973 (details of the provision are given here), and Section 20 (3) of the Hindu Adoption Maintenance Act, 1956.[23] Under the Muslim personal law, both son and daughter are bound to maintain their parents who are poor if they have means to do so. Since the concept of adoption does not exist in the Muslim community, the personal law is silent on the right to maintenance of adoptive parents.[24] The Christians and Parsi have no personal laws providing for maintenance for the parents. The Christian and Parsi parents who wish to seek maintenance from their children need to claim it under Code of Criminal Procedure.[25]

Older Persons (Maintenance, Care and Protection) Bill, 2005

The Central Government introduced a bill in Parliament for better care of rapidly growing elderly population in India. The bill titled "Older Persons (Maintenance, Care and Protection) Bill 2005" is intended to overcome the lacunae existing in the current legislation on maintenance and to make relief simpler, speedier and less expensive. It also aims to cover new areas of care and protection that have not so far been covered by any existing legislation. The bill has taken into account three thrust areas for legislation, viz., Maintenance, Care and Protection. Maintenance includes a) financial b) housing requirement c) protection of life and property d) recreational and spiritual needs e) grievance. Maintenance from the family will hitherto be a matter of right for the older persons. Care embraces a) financial b) housing requirement c) clothing requirement d) health requirement e) companionship requirement, from families and/or the state government in the case of persons without family support or living below the poverty line. Protection covers protection of life and property of the old against exploitation including physical and mental abuse.[26]

---

23 The Code of Criminal Procedure, 1973 section 125 (1) (2) makes it incumbent for a person having sufficient means to maintain his/her father or mother who, is unable to maintain himself or herself and on getting proof of neglect or refusal, may be ordered by a first-class magistrate to make a monthly allowance not exceeding Rs. 500/-. It is applicable to all, irrespective of their religious faith and religious persuasions, and includes adoptive parents. This section has been interpreted by the Supreme Court in its ruling so as to make daughters and sons, married or unmarried, equally responsible to maintain their parents. The Hindu adoption and Maintenance Act, 1956 gives a statutory recognition to the well-established normal obligation of a Hindu Child (male/female) to maintain his/her aged or infirm parents, as long as they are not able to maintain themselves. Available at: https://nhrc.nic.in/sites/default/files/ResearchStudyReport_Sense_Security_HumanRightsOlderPersons_Agewell%20Foundation.pdf (accessed, August 2020).

24 https://blog.ipleaders.in/rights-senior-citizens/ (accessed, August 2020).

25 https://blog.ipleaders.in/rights-senior-citizens/ (accessed, August 2020).

26 http://ncwapps.nic.in/PDFFiles/olderpersonMaintenancebill.pdf (accessed, August 2020).

Maintenance and Welfare of Parents and Senior Citizens Act, 2007

The Maintenance and Welfare of Parents and Senior Citizens Act, 2007 a legislation initiated by the Ministry of Social Justice and Empowerment, Government of India passed in the Parliament of India, and it received President's assent on December 29, 2007. The Act states that, a Senior citizen is any citizen of India of 60 years and above whether living in India or not. Parent is the father or mother even if not of 60 years yet. Children are adult son, daughter, grandson and grand-daughter. Relatives are those who are either in possession of the property of the senior citizen or would inherit it. The parents and grandparents who are unable to maintain themselves from their own income can demand maintenance from their children as defined above. The Childless Senior Citizens who are unable to maintain themselves from their own income can demand maintenance from their relatives as defined above. The Maintenance includes provision for food, clothing, residence, medical attendance and treatment. Maximum amount which may be ordered for maintenance of a senior citizen by the Tribunal shall be such as prescribed by the State Government which shall not exceed Rs. 10,000/- per month.[27]

National Policy on Older Persons

The National Policy on Older Persons (NPOP) was announced in January 1999 to reaffirm the commitment to ensure the well-being of the older persons. The Policy envisages State support to ensure financial and food security, health care, shelter and other needs of older persons, equitable share in development, protection against abuse and exploitation, and availability of services to improve the quality of their lives. The primary objectives are:

- To encourage individuals to make provision for their own as well as their spouse's old age;
- To encourage families to take care of their older family members;
- To enable and support voluntary and non-governmental organizations to supplement the care provided by the family;
- To provide care and protection to the vulnerable elderly people; to provide adequate healthcare facility to the elderly;
- To promote research and training facilities to train geriatric care givers and organizers of services for the elderly; and
- To create awareness regarding elderly persons to help them lead productive and independent live.[28]

---

27 http://socialjustice.nic.in/writereaddata/UploadFile/Annexure-X635996104030434742.pdf; http://legislative.gov.in/actsofparliamentfromtheyear/maintenance-and-welfare-parents-and-senior-citizens-act-2007 (accessed, August 2020).

28 https://www.helpageindia.org/wp-content/uploads/2017/06/senior-citizens-guide-2016.pdf 8-9. (accessed, August 2020).

The National Policy on Older Persons seeks to assure older persons that their concerns are national concerns and they will not live unprotected, ignored and marginalized. It aims to strengthen their legitimate place in society and help older people to live the last phase of their life with purpose, dignity and peace. It provides a broad framework for inter sector collaboration and cooperation both within the government as well as between government and non-governmental agencies. The Policy also recognizes the role of the NGO sector in providing user friendly affordable services to complement the endeavours of the State in this direction. While recognizing the need for promoting productive ageing, the policy also emphasizes the importance of family in providing vital non formal social security for older persons.[29] In the year 2010, the Ministry constituted a review Committee under the Chairpersonship of Mrs. V. Mohini Giri to assess the present status of various issues concerning senior citizens and to draft a new National Policy on Older Persons; in view the changing demographic pattern, socio-economic needs of the senior citizens, social value system and advancement in the field of science and technology over the last decade. The Committee, after holding several consultation/regional/subcommittee meetings with the stakeholders, submitted the draft National Policy on Senior Citizens, 2011 on 30.03.2011. A New National Policy for Senior Citizens is under consideration.[30]

National Old Age Pension (NOAP) Scheme

Under the National Old Age Pension Scheme, in 1994 Central Assistance is available. The amount of old age pension varies in the different States as per their share to this scheme. It is implemented in the State and Union Territories through Panchayats and Municipalities. The assistance was available on fulfillment of the following criteria: a. 65 years or more should be the age of the applicant (male or female) b. The applicant must be a destitute in the sense that he/she has no regular means of subsistence from his/her own source of income or through financial support from family members or other sources. The amount of old age pension is Rs. 75 per month. The Ministry is now implementing the Indira Gandhi National Old Age Pension Scheme (IGNOAPS). Under this scheme Central assistance in form of Pension is given to persons, above 65 years Rs. 200/- per month, belonging to a below poverty line family. This pension amount is meant to be supplemented by at least same

29 https://www.helpageindia.org/wp-content/uploads/2017/06/senior-citizens-guide-2016.pdf 8-9. (accessed, August 2020).

30 Annual Report of the Ministry of Social Justice & Empowerment. Available at: http://socialjustice.nic.in/pdf/dnpsc.pdf http://socialjustice.nic.in (accessed, August 2020).

contribution by the States so that each applicant gets at least Rs. 400/- per month as pension.[31]

Conclusion

A brief survey made on the ageing in the world history and the programmes and policies shows that ageing has been a prolonged problems in every society. The crime against elderly people around the world is increasing and various laws on elderly seem to be ineffective to combat the problem. The special legislation – "The Maintenance and Welfare of Parents and Senior Citizens Act 2007' in certain extent appears to be successful in curbing the menace of elders' abuse. However, due to physical and psychological weakness elderly have to depend on their children. Dependence of elderly on others can be the root cause of elder abuse. The care of older persons particularly those in the age groups 50-60, 60-70, 70-80 years and above and those with disability or severe disability pose serious questions for the informal caregivers. Hence, the best, affordable and friendly environment of care for old people is 'Home-based Care.' This care is needed in this hour. It is in fact prevalent in most of the developing countries and is also now steadily growing in the developed countries. In India, due to inadequacy of medical facilities, most ailments are treated in the home itself. Home based health care is defined by the National Clinical Homecare Association (2011) as 'the provision of medical treatments, medical supplies and clinical services directly to patients in the community.'[32] Home-based care includes medical, psychological/social assessment, wound care, medication education, pain management, disease education, physical therapy, speech therapy, pastoral care and prevention. Home based health care is usually less expensive, more convenient than and as effective as care received in a health care facility. To act as care, compassion, console and comfort providers for the home care services by the community and family members is leading to a society which is sensitive and caring for its elderly. This will lead to the creation of 'Elderly Friendly Communities' to the vision of building a better future for our beloved elderly people.

31 Rajagopal Dhar Chakraborti, *The Greying of India*, 373.

32 "WHO Report: the growing need for home health care for the elderly people." Available at: https://applications.emro.who.int/dsaf/EMROPUB_2015_EN_1901.pdf?ua=1 (August 2020).

9

Ageing
Awakening the Mission Mandate of the Church

Rebecca Azariah

Introduction

We all go through the process of Ageing. In this process, an important thing to remember is that only our physical appearance go changes, not our spirit. James A. Garfield beautifully put it in these words: "If wrinkles must be written upon our brows, let them not be written upon the heart. The spirit should not grow old."[1] Roger L. Gould in his book *Transformations Growth and Change in Adult Life* explains: "Ageing is a process in which one finds oneself worthless and periods of passivity, rage, depression and despair are experienced in its highest forms. Most of us oscillate in small swings between the denial and the acceptance of our vulnerability."[2] Here a question arises as to whether the Church is providing help to the growing population of older adults to finish the race well. Regrettably many older adults do not receive spiritual nourishment, care and encouragement. People are living longer, but older adults especially aged women often feel useless in the fast changing world that seems to have left them behind. Therefore, an attempt is made in this essay to focus on mainly, the plight of aged women and bring challenge to the mission of the Church to counter the emerging culture against older adults with a message of God's comforting presence and purpose in their lives. Since, ageing brings challenges as well as opportunity for deep spiritual growth, it is important that an in-depth missiological discourse on ageing is done in order to awaken the mission mandate of the Church as David Bosch appropriately

1 "Ageing." Available at: http//www.un.org/issues-depth (accessed, 20 March 2020).

2 Roger L. Gould, *Transformations: Growth and Change in Adult Life* (New York, Simon and Schuster, 1978), 217.

expresses: "The church is not made up of spiritual giants; only [the] broken men and women can lead others to the cross."[3]

Meaning of the Mission

The word mission comes from the Latin word *mittere*, which means "to send." It is the equivalent of the Greek word *apostello*, which also means "to send." Mission means sending of people to carry the Good News and to attain the purpose of kingdom of God. The original understanding of mission was perceived to be the restoration of Gospel into the life of the people at all levels. With the passage of time, a new theological understanding of mission emerged *Missio Dei*, the mission of God (*Missio Dei*) has no limits or barriers; it has been addressed to and has been at work within the entire human race and the whole of creation throughout history. Mission belongs to God and the followers of Jesus are mere participants in the process of witnessing, proclamation, worship, inculturation and contextualization God's mission in the world. The church, empowered by the Holy Spirit, is sent out to the world to announce the Gospel of Jesus Christ in word and deed, witnessing to the Kingdom of God.[4] Thus the church is a healing and caring community for all humanity in the world, standing in solidarity with the oppressed, downtrodden, marginalized participating in the process of liberation from the various bondages and bringing in transformation in people's life. Therefore, mission is God's gift and a compelling responsibility from God.

K. Rajaratnam envisioned that the Mission in the present-day context, more specifically in India, should be based on the realization that Jesus and His message of the Cross must be proclaimed through engagement in the lives of the people. Engagement in the life of the people is the key phrase here. Only we involve ourselves closely in the lives of the people only then we will be able to relate to varied aspects of their individuality. Mission expresses faith in Jesus Christ, facilitates the transformation of human relationships and signifies hope for the poor and oppressed.[5] David Bosch in his excellent book "Transforming Mission" speaks of mission as transforming people. According him mission is integral to evangelism and the nature of evangelism is mediating good news which transfofms life. The Gospel that is the good news is always

3 David Bosch, J., *A Spirituality of the Road* (New York: Wipf and Stock Publishers, 2001), 77.

4 The purpose of Mission is the Kingdom of God. The church is a means to achieve it through its witness. (Dr. K. C. Abraham says Witness is the expression of God's love for humanity for which Christians are to be the effective tools. It involves the right relationship with God, the humanity and the world are large. It involves loving one's neighbour as oneself and engaging in such activities in the society for the glory of God).

5 Victor Premasagar, *New Horizons in Christian Mission A Theological Exploration* (Chennai: Gurukul Lutheran Theological College & Research Institute, 2000), 265.

contextual and does bring peace and joy being in the lordship of Christ in all realms of life. The gospel is said to be contextual when it holds theory, praxis and *poiesis*, the *poiesis* Stackhouse says need evocative images which involves beauty, love, piety, worship awe and mystery. Thus, in this meaning of mission that is handed over from generation after generation, we are only co-workers and participants.[6] Mission is God's mission, universal and never changing. Therefore mission is for all, it becomes our responsibility to reach the people be it child, woman, man, poor, rich, affluent, oppressed, neglected, tribal and the ageing.

Issues Facing Ageing Women

Ageing the period of the lifespan between younger and older adulthood, has been described as a period of transition in women's lives. This essay is focused on women from 45 years of age, who typically experience multiple social, psychological and biological challenges, among them the menopausal transition. Women during this process face a diverse array of stressful events, for example, health concerns, family problems, work-related issues, deaths, frustrated goal attainment, and financial worries. Family challenges included challenges with adolescent children, domestic violence, divorce or separation from a spouse, and the ending of relationships. Work problems includes difficulty finding work, workplace conflicts, and downsizing of workplaces. women in the process of ageing also face challenges due to racism such as derogatory remarks, and discriminatory actions such as sexual harassment.

It is estimated that women constitute 55% of all ageing population and a majority of them live in developing countries. Most of the women outlive their spouses, which affects women's living arrangements as well as economic and emotional wellbeing, especially when they carry higher burdens of ill health and disability. The level of vulnerability among the aged women often increases when younger women decide to migrate for employment. In this transition between modernity and tradition the perceived values of the aged women get diminished. Women in the process of ageing experience a longer period of ill health, poverty, financial insecurity, high levels of dependency and gender based discriminatory practices. Moreover, if a woman has unfortunately lost her husband there are many of the harmful traditional and cultural practices associated with her. Bakkaiammal, my grandmother who lived to the age of 96, left us a magnificent testimony. She confided to a friend: "I am old but I am strong. Physically I have disabilities, weaknesses, and sickness, but spiritually there is nothing I am not able to do. I don't suffer old age. The only way to live well as we enter the process of ageing is to live it with God." The essay

6 David Bosch, *Transforming Missions: Paradigm Shifts in Theology of Mission* (New York: Orbis Books, 1992), 107-120.

affirms that life is a gift of God and the presence of the aged people and the people approaching ageing in the society needs to be recognized as a gift, a new human and spiritual potential for enrichment.

In the mission and ministry of the Church women still face varied challenges. Most of the time it is in the process of ageing that women face these challenges in the ministry. Men continue to have exclusive claim to perform God's ministry debarring women even in the present context. The patriarchal tradition continues to uphold male superiority and female inferiority, and also subordination of women to men. The natural biological functions of women such as menstruation and child bearing is generally seen by men as problems and hindrances for which women are not accepted to full and equal participation in the ministry of the church. The unreasonable excuse given by men are women cannot conduct holy communion, give baptism and travel from one place to another. They are denied leadership roles and decision making roles particularly in the ministry of the church.

Mission and Ageing women in the Bible

In the Bible we read that ageing is a gift from God, the aged people are in the precise plan of God. In the Hebrew society the aged people were held in honor and respect (Lev. 19:32). As aged people reach old age which was greatly desired and its attainment was regarded as a divine blessing (Gen 15:15; Ex. 20:12). This blessing accompanied the divine assurance which is read in Isaiah 46:4, "Even to your old age I am he, even when you turn grey, I will carry you. I have made, and I will bear; I will carry and will save." Aged people are also believed to be superior in wisdom (Job 12:20; 15:10; 32:7, 9), which gives them positions of guidance and authority.

Aged women were treated with respect and honor. One of the most respected and honoured aged women we see in the Bible is Sarah, who is the only woman whose age, death and burial are mentioned (Gen. 23:1[7]). This might be to honour her as the venerable mother of the Hebrew people. Sarah was childless until she was 90 years old. God promised Abraham that she would be "a mother of nations" (Gen. 17:16) She is also mentioned in the faith Hall of fame (Heb. 11:1[8]). Her greatest legacy is rooted in her commitment to family: her love and respect for Abraham. As wife to Abraham she inherits his spiritual offspring and becomes the mother of a nation.[9] Sarah is a source of inspiration to the aged women and stands as a witness to the generations that

7 'Sarah lived one hundred twenty-seven years; this was the length of Sarah's life.'

8 'By faith he received power of procreation, even though he was too old-and Sarah herself was barren – because he considered him faithful who had promised.'

9 Dora Weithers, "Four Aged Bible Women and their Spiritual Legacies." Available at: https://owlcation.com/humanities/Four-Old-Bible-Women-Worthy-of-Imitation (accessed, 18 April 2020).

God is a promise keeping God. Also, Sarah bears witness to the promise read in Isaiah 43… "Even in your old age I will carry you."

The Book of Ruth tells how Naomi the old woman influenced the life young Ruth. Even in her homeland she mentored Ruth in the Hebrew lifestyle. She spoke about the almighty God, Jehovah, God's wonderful works, and the loving, merciful way God dealt with God's people. Ruth's words are remarkable and perfectly reveal a precious quality, loyal love. The love that Ruth felt was so strong and so loyal that she would stick with Naomi wherever she went. Only death could separate them. Naomi's people would become her own people, for Ruth was ready to leave behind everything she knew in Moab. She was a positive mentor to Ruth and to her son.[10] A model of encouragement where Naomi shows to the ageing women that they can have positive influence on the lives of other people. The Widow of Zarephath in I Kings 17:8-24, who had lost her husband is a striking example of how ageing women are faithful in their journey of life. She had hopes, dreams, experienced joy and despair, suffered real pain. In this passage we read that she had the last handful of flour and a small quantity of oil enough for the day's bread. Even that she offered to Elijah which shows her sacrifice and her willingness to give to Elijah. The woman's sacrifice stands as a model for women in every generation to be sacrificial and have given generously for the Lord's work. Anna in the Gospel of Luke 1:1-2:40 is one of the Bible's honorable woman. She is introduced in the Birth narrative. She is called a prophetess (Luke 2:29-32, 34-36), Anna is the New Testament's only named female prophetess. she recognizes who this child is and tells of his significance to selected people in Jerusalem. Her actions affirm Amos 3:7: "Surely the Sovereign Lord does nothing without revealing his plans to his servants the prophets." She is advanced in age. Luke says she was married for seven years, then widowed. Anna. W. Clarkson remarks, "Woman as well as man to utter reverent joy on this supreme occasion…. For in the Kingdom of Christ there is neither male nor female, all distinction of sex is unknown." Anna was the first female who gave the testimony of Jesus, the Christ, she demonstrated that sincere devotion brings joy and fulfilment.[11] That's what the Psalmist says In you, Yahweh, I take refuge, I shall never be put to shame (Ps. 71:1) This psalm, striking for its beauty, is only one of the many prayers of older people that we find in the Bible and that testify to the religious feelings felt by the soul in the presence of the Lord.

All the Biblical narratives on aged women gives us a sense and value of old age; the rich spiritual, moral and theological resource for social transformation. The Scriptures teach that older women play vital roles. In Titus 2:3-4, Paul encourages older women to "teach what is good . . . and so

10 Weithers, "Four Aged Bible Women and their Spiritual Legacies…."

11 Weithers, "Four Aged Bible Women and their Spiritual Legacies…."

train the young women." The biblical narratives on aged women not only can inspire aged women to face the challenges in the process of ageing, but also tremendously influence among the next generation of women.

Mission by the Aged

Ageing is a time of possibility, opportunity and influence. A process where the aged are seen with respect and value for all their contributions in society. The ageing people have great diversity and are always committed to communicate and work collaboratively ethically, openly, honestly and with accountability in all their endeavors. Though women life experiences may seem to be adverse, there are evidences that the ageing process is positive for women. There are studies says Susan Holen Hoeksema that women as they age feel a greater sense of fulfilment and self-actualization than during their younger years.

Evangeline Cory Booth daughter of General William and Catherine Booth a committed woman remained a single woman, held the position of National Commander in Salvation Army, USA for 30 years and became the Army's first woman general. She through her nature of compassion, thoughtfulness, kindness, dedication and a clever administrator stands as a remarkable influence for women even in the present who are a part of the Salvation Army.[12] Gladys Aylward, was an effective missionary to the Chinese people. Without prejudice, armed with her skill as a story teller and motivated by her determination to live her Christian beliefs, Gladys succeeded. Amy Carmichael stands as an inspiration for women of all ages for selfless discipleship and bold faith. Through her action of grace, compassion and motherly love she founded the fellowship at Dohnavur. This is a home for the girls and boys without protection and were sold to temple prostitution. The home is still active even in the present with entirely Indian leadership. As Amy aged, she was involved in the process of writing books, songs, poems and thousands of personal letters. Some of the few aged people grow sweeter with age, they teach the younger generation to follow God, work hard and respect one another. Through mentoring others and harvesting one's life,[13] a spiritual elder has the capacity to offer wisdom, awareness and harmony by living out those values and sharing them with others.[14] Despite the obstacles, spiritual growth is both possible and desirable for the continued well-being of elderly people. Rabbi Zalma Schacter Shalomi in his book,[15] speaks to the

12 Helen Kooiman Hosier, *100 Christian Women Who Changed the Twentieth Century* (Grand Rapids: Baker Book House Company, 2000), 206.

13 Schacter-Shalomi Zalman, *From Ageing to Sage-ing: A Revolutionary Approach to Growing Older* (New York: Time Warner Books,1997), 85.

14 Zalman, *From Ageing to Sage-ing…*, 6.

15 Zalman, *From Ageing to Sage-ing…*, 5.

value of purpose in the ageing process, especially around the idea of being a sage, something he calls "Spiritual Eldering"[16]

Ageing is a time to grow spiritually with Christ. James Houston and Michael Parker explain the experience of ageing adults in how they relate to God. The ageing population they say provides character, hope and wisdom, crucial to the expressions of the church.[17] "The life of older people helps to cast light on the scale of human values; to reveal the continuity of the generations and wonderfully to demonstrate the interdependence of the People of God."[18] It is notable in the Church that this interdependence is expressed: it is there that the various generations are called to share in the plan of God's love by reciprocally exchanging the gifts with which each person is enriched by grace of the Holy Spirit. To this exchange of gifts older people bring religious and moral values that represent a rich spiritual endowment for the life of Christian communities, families and the world.

The aged women with their rich endowment of faith and of experience they can draw things old and new to the advantage not only of themselves, but also of the whole community. Far from being the passive recipients of the Church's pastoral care, aged women are irreplaceable apostles, they are active in evangelism, especially among their own age group, because no one is more familiar than they with the problems and the feelings of this phase of life. The women encourage one another in relation to all issues be it sickness, family or children issues. Particular importance is being given today, moreover, to the apostolate of older people among people of their own age group in the form of witness of life. As Paul VI wrote in Evangelii Nuntiandi, modern man "listens more willingly to witness than to teachers, and if he/she does listen to teachers, it is because they are witnesses."[19] So it is not of secondary importance to be able to show, in concrete terms, that this season of life, when lived in a Christian way, has a value of its own, enriched by the profound significance that it acquires through the whole course of human existence. Rebecca Friedlander in her book[20] talks of real beauty through God's definition of beautiful and empowering women to shatter rejection, doubt and low self -esteem and celebrate their uniqueness.

As Theology is knowing God and an encounter with God, it addresses and affirms the transformation of the whole person – heart, mind and soul.

---

16 Zalman, *From Ageing to Sage-ing…*, 5.

17 James M. Houston and Michael Parker, *A Vision for the Ageing Church: Renowing Ministry for and by Seniors* (Downers Grove, IL: IVP Academic, 2011), 66.

18 Insegnamenti di Giovanni Paolo II, III, 2 (1980), 539.

19 John Paul IV, "Encyclical Letter Evangelium Vitae," no. 41.

20 Rebecca Friedlander, *Finding Beautiful: Discovering Authentic Beauty Around the World* (London: Baker Books, 2019), 180.

Transformation does not come merely from studying God's word, it comes by engagement with God in everyday practices and experiences. It recognizes the relationship between God and the person who is ageing. As Rebecca Friedlander says we ought to celebrate our uniqueness by accepting the ageing life as a gift from God. This inward acceptance is reflected with an outward expression in relationship, practice and purpose. John Paul II, addressing the participants at the International Forum on Ageing, said: "Older people, with the wisdom and experience which are the fruit of a life-time, have entered upon a time of extraordinary grace which opens to them new opportunities for prayer and union with God. Called to serve others and to offer their lives to the Lord and Giver of Life, new spiritual powers are given to them."[21]

The context in which aged people live are diverse, dynamic and changing. In the recent COVID 19 context the most affected people are the ageing people above 50 years. In few medical institutions they have been even denied medical help in this situation, the worst hit death rate is among this group of people. They have learned to cooperate and in certain places they have volunteered to stay at home to help the younger people affected to get medical aid. While on the other side the "The Hindu" News article on March 24, 2020 in an article, 'No Need to step out' written by Ms. Sweta Akundi brought into prominence the Retirement Homes that make day to day living easier for communities of Senior citizens living together. There were many people helping the elderly people in purchasing the essentials, provisions and medicines. 'Life is difficult,'[22] in this statement M. Scott Peck articulates the inevitable ageing process over time. Peck says, some fully embrace it but some deny the ageing process, both the ways life is difficult. Accepting the difficulties of ageing how can we help ourselves and others to age gracefully.[23] In this process of ageing people must be helped to overcome the indifference and mistrust that hamper their active participation and solidarity in the activities of the society and family.

Mission for the Aged

Women form half of the total population in each community secular or religious. Their importance cannot be denied. Their contributions are valued and regarded, they are often grouped under the category of weaker and marginalised section the subaltern of the society. As they age this is more visible in all the activities. The population of ageing rapidly presents both

---

21 John Paul II, "Encyclical Letter Evangelium Vitae," no. 65.

22 "Ageing and Life Course." Available at: http://www.who.int/ageing (accessed, 20 March 2020).

23 Scott M. Peck, *The Road Less Travelled: A New Psychology of Love, Traditional Values and Spiritual Growth* (New York, Touchstone, 1988), 1.

challenges and opportunities. The context increasingly demands to be made more age-friendly. The World Health Organisation has declared 2020-2030 as the Decade of Healthy Ageing.[24] In this decade it is an opportunity to bring together governments, civil society, international agencies, professionals, academia, the media and the private sector for ten years of concerted, catalytic and collaborative action to improve the lives of ageing people, their families and the communities in which they live.[25] This decade is determined to create age friendly environments in which environments play an important role in determining a person's life which a person experiences at different stages of life.[26]

As we journey with aged people in the prevailing culture of indifference, rampant individualism, competitiveness and utilitarianism which are now threatening all areas of society, and to remove any form of segregation between the generations, a new mentality, a new attitude, a new mode of being, a new culture needs to be developed. A form of prosperity and of social justice needs to be pursued that is compatible with the objective of defending the centrality of the human person and his/her dignity. When each of us recognise and realise we can come together to effect social change. Stanford University Sociologist Doung McAdam calls it cognitive liberation. The next step is collective action. This helps aged people to feel relieved and empowered. Kendig believed that ageism is a contributing factor in determining social treatment of the elderly. "We see them as less capable. In developing countries, seniors stay in work longer which means that, on the one hand, they remain integrated and actively contributing members of society but, on the other hand, they are often exploited."[27] The British writer Anne Karpf says "we all need to change the way we think about ageing. It is time for a major gestalt switch. Each time we see an aged person, we need to imagine them as our future self, and rather than recoil from their wrinkles or infirmities, applaud their resilience. We need to re-humanise aged people."[28] This is *missio hominum* a phrase coined by Gensichen relating to people's activity performed to help and heal

---

24 "Decade of Healthy Ageing: 2020-2030." Available at: http://who.int/ageing decade (accessed, 20 March 2020).

25 "Decade of Healthy Ageing: 2020-2030." Available at: http://who.int/ageing decade (accessed, 20 March 2020).

26 "Age-Friendly Environments." Available at: http://who.int/ageing/age-friendly environments (accessed on 20 March 2020).

27 Caroline, Baum, "We love the elders in our lives and we all hope to grow old, so why does this personal interest not translate to public policy." Available at: https://www.theguardian.com/lifeandstyle/2018/sep/14/the-ugly-truth-about-ageism-its-a-prejudice-targeting-our-future-selves (accessed on 4 June 2020).

28 Cited in Caroline Baum, "We love the elders in our lives and we all hope to grow old, so why does this personal interest not translate to public policy."

other people.[29] The process of ageing years could turn out to be their best and happiest period, especially when they start feeling wanted, loved and cared for by those who are younger than them. In the course of growing old it is possible to console the ageing people by giving them a patient and compassionate hearing to all their problems, grievances and complaints. The need of good listeners and lending of a sympathetic ear trying to lift their heavy burdens from their aching shoulders and thus providing them with heaps of happiness. some of the lives of these people in this process exemplify the virtues of loving kindness and compassion.

The body may break down, but the spirit is still capable of growth, renewal, or even new birth in old age. Those who are "spiritually dead" can find spiritual life through a new or renewed faith commitment in Christ. That is why we find many women after their years of retirement give most of their time to mission and evangelism. The spiritually mature person can keep growing in wisdom, love, joy, and other spiritual gifts. In fact, many of this world's greatest prayer warriors are senior citizens. In most of the churches and Christian institutions we find that many people who pray are the women. In spite of changes, losses, and chronic health conditions, elderly people can continue to cultivate their relationship with God. Too often, however, elderly women encounter obstacles to spiritual support systems such as helping them get to the church, singing and hearing the word of God and to participate in religious activities with other believers. many of the resources of the church—financial support, time, and wisdom—are provided by the older population. The church needs to acknowledge and address the ageing population's contribution, influence, and need. They feel alienated in churches that focus most of their energy on attracting a younger crowd. Failing eyesight can make it hard to read the Bible, and hardness of hearing can make it difficult to hear sermons. Like all Christians, senior women need the fellowship and encouragement of other believers. In God's ministry women's sincerity, nature and performance deserve recognition, acceptance and equal opportunity. They need to be recognized as co-human being at par with men in true partnership which includes the ordination of women.

Mission: Discipleship of Equals

God's mission (*Missio Dei*) which embraces the whole world, cutting across boundaries of race, culture, time and space. Awakening the mission mandate involves awakening the faithful, reaching the lost aged ones in our society as Jesus did in his mission that He became a universal saviour precisely because He was capable of becoming one with each person, each people and each culture

29 J. Verkyul, *Contemporary Missiology: An Introduction* (Michigan: William B Eerdmans Publishing Company, 1978), 4.

in their particular identities. The model of Jesus' mission calls us to discover, in each moment, the call of the Spirit to the churches and to all people of good will. There are no universal models or fixed activities that can fully explain what mission is in each moment. The ultimate norm and source of mission is God who has created a world of great variety and beauty and who is present in the lives of all peoples, birthing, nurturing, encouraging and enabling them to live in hope. Mission is born afresh out of every circumstance of life. Church needs to be awakened by following the two-fold Jesus paradigm of mission: is preferential concern for victims and his self-emptying love for, and openness to, others. Jesus the challenging prophet took the side of the oppressed and marginalized; Jesus the self-emptying servant was ready to embrace and speak with everyone, including the oppressor. What is imperative today is to recapture the universal mission of Jesus in its relation to local concerns. Increasing violence against aged women is a matter of grave concern and raises serious questions. While the Church speaks about the emancipation of aged women, she fails to take cognizance of their condition within the church. Women's struggle for gender equality in the church and in society calls for a reconstruction of the church-in-mission in terms of justice, freedom and the Discipleship of Equals. We need to develop a radical, egalitarian spirituality. In order to rebirth the church as a community of equals and enable women to share responsibilities at all levels the mission of the church must be awakened. For our mission to have credibility and strength it has to proceed from an ecclesia defined as 'a discipleship of equals' that looks at other people and communities not as objects of potential conquest but as true sisters and brothers, as partners in the *Missio Dei*, seeking with us God's rule of justice and equality.

Conclusion

The process of ageing has its own joys, its own triumphs, its own blessings, and its own happiness. In the society where the process of ageing and the aged people are seen as a burden, to confront the challenge of the ageing process we ought to be honest about the issues of ageing which helps us accept and embrace ageing as a part of life's journey. Roselyn Staples, a former pastor of senior adults at Elmbrook church in Brookfield believes that 'Aged people (Ageing people) are a valuable asset and a worthy investment.'[30] This statement is filled with truth because through our ages God is with us and through the biblical characters empowers and inspires women in the process of ageing to unleash their potentials and to keep working for the Kingdom of God. Most of the problems and issues of ageing are age related, understanding helps us to take every step to live creative life.

---

30 "Stories of Faith and growing older with Confidence." Available at: http://www.justbetweenus.org/faith/inspirational–stories (Accessed, 26 March 2020).

10

A Postmodern Missiological Response to the Issue of Ageing

K. Vijayan

Introduction

Ageing is an inevitable part of being alive. Sociologically, we use the word "Ageing" and "old" during all stages of life.[1] In some societies, old age is not sharply defined, but in others, it is specified. One tends to equate old age with idleness, particularly in cases of forced retirement. Because old age has been so tied to the retirement age, it is too early to know if most people will begin to think of age 70 as the start of old age. For now, one will still consider age 65 as an arbitrary point.[2] The age pyramid that existed less than half a century ago has been turned upside down. The number of older people is constantly increasing, while that of the young is constantly decreasing.[3] The attitudes of

1 A child who comes of age is confirmed or pays full price for a ticket. A young person comes of age for voting or driving license. A major league football player is old at the age of 35; at the same time, age 65 or 70 for a worker is deemed old enough to be retired. Cedric W. Tilberg, *The Fullness of Life* (USA: Lutheran Church in America, 1980), 12.

2 Gerald R. Leslie, Richard F. Larson and Benjamin L. Gorman (eds.), *Introductory Sociology: Order and Change in Society*, (Bombay: Oxford University Press, 1994), 157-158.

3 The most recent studies of the United Nations are continuously adjusting the forecasts for population growth in the next few decades downwards. The huge multitude of "young old" (as they are called by the new categories of old age defined by demographers, i.e., those aged between 65 and 70) is added a so-called fourth age, that of the "oldest old" (those over 75), whose ranks are likewise destined to become ever more numerous. It is estimated that over-80 year-olds in the world today are intended to increase to 370 million in 2050, including an estimated 2.2 million centenarians. More recent studies have led to the definition of eighteen United Nations Principles for Older Persons (grouped under five headings: independence, participation, care, self-fulfillment, and dignity). "The Dignity of Older People and their Mission in the Church and in the World" dignita-anziano-eng pdf (accessed on 12/12/2019), 1-18.

society gives meaning to adjectives, such as 'old.' The issue of Ageing is not a new phenomenon as a whole; however, its effect, in reality, is not common thoroughout the ages.

The modern thought is characterized by dichotomies or binaries like mind and matter, soul and body, nature and history, nature and culture, male and female, good and evil, young and old, etc. The binaries are arranged in a hierarchical order in which the first terms in the binaries have primacy over the second terms, which are considered to be inferior. The dichotomy of 'young' and 'old' in a society that exalts youth and undervalues the aged, the people strive to act and appear young. There is no inherent reason why we should not be as proud to be called 'old' as to be called 'young.' By keeping this in mind, it will see the issue of Ageing through the ages, especially, in postmodernity; it will try to bring out some of the postmodern missiological response to the issue of Ageing, and will also draw the conclusion.

THE ISSUE OF AGEING THROUGH THE AGES

According to Duncan, the Professor of Science, the progress of thought in the West in particular, World at large over the centuries has been divided into three main phases-the *Premodern*, the *Modern* and *Postmodern* phase. The *Premodern* phase is that which is embraced by all cultures and civilizations all over the world prior to the seventeenth and Eighteenth centuries in Europe and the West. This Phase may be labelled as the *Age of Faith*, because it allowed for the concept of faith and gave room for the existence of God and the supernatural. The *Modern Period* which is that the Enlightenment in eighteenth century Europe, where human and reason and the scientific approach to the study of natural phenomena predominated in the thinking of man. This phase may therefore be referred to as the *Age of Reason*. The *Postmodern* phase is that the emergence of a new and revolutionary system of thought in the last decades of the twentieth century. This phase may be to call it the *Age of Subjective Relativism*.[4] Therefore, the study of the issue of Ageing in premodern and modernism is very important, in order to have a proper understanding of the ongoing concerns of postmodernism.

Ageing in Premodernity

Ageing was not seen by the early Christians as a "problem" to which some sort of religious solution was required.[5] Though, the Scripture has little to say on the

---

4 R. H. Duncan Lyngdoh, "Postmodernism: Challenges and Prospects," *Indian Theological Journal* 2/2 (July- December 2008): 7-8.

5 Rowan Greer argues that old age in the early church was special, and further explains that since old age was attained only by the few rather than the many in the ancient world. He suggests that we should see old age as representatives of the culmination of both a gift and a burden. The gift in the sense that virtue and wisdom; the burden in the sense that physical

problem of Ageing and the care of older persons, the relative silence of these texts, probably by the very different social and cultural world in which the people who lived to an advanced age, were honored and esteemed within the community.[6] Jesus did not grow old, as he died in the prime of his life, without experiencing old age; does this mean that we are left with no Christologically informed pattern for the Christian practice of growing old? By comparison to the New Testament, the Old Testament tells more stories about characters of considerable age, but here again, the cultural context within which Ageing is understood differs so dramatically from ours that the fit between our concerns and the concerns of the writers is rough. Does this mean that the Bible is of limited usefulness for our theological-missiological reflection on the Christian practice of Ageing? On the contrary, because the scriptural texts provide a different evaluative framework for understanding Ageing, they may cause us to pause and reframe our reflections.

David Aers reveals that in the *Middle Ages*, the time of old age is viewed with uncertainty.[7] The evils of old age were emphasized far more than its potential goods. The former is said to be a weakness, many discomforts, sickness, sorrows, the destruction of the body, the latter is said to be freedom from tyrannical rulers, the end of lust, and the beginning of spiritual joys. By examining the modern view of Ageing, which often takes the form of a fear of Ageing and the aged; To uncover modernity's alienation of ideas from images and attitudes by focusing on the actual lives, in contrast to the cultural representations, of people who are growing older.[8]

---

and mental weakness, but also evils peculiar to the elderly. Rowan A. Greer, "Special Gift and Special Burden: Views of Old Age in the Early Church," in Stanley Hauerwas, et. al., *Growing Old in Christ*, (UK: William B. Eerdmans Publishing Company, 2003), 26.

6 Richard B. Hays and Judith C. Hays, "The Christian Practice of growing Old: The Witness of Scripture," in *Growing Old in Christ* edited by Stanley Hauerwas, et. al., (UK: William B. Eerdmans Publishing Company, 2003), 3.

7 As David quoted from the Bartholomaeus Anglicus, who classified the processes of human life into six stages: (1) The "firste childehode" (the first seven months of life); (2) "another chiledhode" (up to fourteen); (3) "the age of Yonge striplynge" (up to twenty-one or twenty-eight or thirty or thirty-five); (4) "middil age" (up to forty-five or fifty); (5) and (6) are two stages of old age, "elde," which involves "failynga of wittes," culminating in madness; (7) the final stage is "the ende of age and of life." David Aers, "The Christian Practice of Growing Old in the Middle Ages," in *Growing Old in Christ* edited by Stanley Hauerwas, et. al. (UK: William B. Eerdmans Publishing Company, 2003), 38.

8 Carol Bailey Stoneking, "Modernity: The Social Construction of Ageing," in *Growing Old in Christ* edited by Stanley Hauerwas, et. al. (UK: William B. Eerdmans Publishing Company, 2003), 63ff.

Ageing in Modernity

It seems that one of the primary manifestations of *Modernity* is the therapeutic culture of Western civilization. The term 'therapeutic' can be legitimately interpreted as some positive and some negative. However, the dangers of therapeutic optimism, which has been fed by the powers of both modern medical, and psychological therapeutic assumptions that are problematic for Christians growing older in the current cultural context.[9] Whether, this present age is called postmodern, or late modern, or a time of uncertainty, the therapeutic legacy of modernity cannot be denied. The assumptions embedded within that legacy include both psychological and medical claims that from expectations of how we should live as well as how we should die.

The excesses of modernity have frequently perpetuated the self-deception that death can be avoided if we work hard enough and sufficiently trust our rational scientific abilities. Even a superficial reading of theology emerging from many sectors in the Western church is indicative of the fact that we Christians have been charmed into a mess of self-satisfaction, finding ourselves salted and enlightened by the world around us, rather than vice versa. It seems that the church has been a central player in actually writing this story in which we are individual containers of a mind and self that needs therapy, rather than sinners in need of salvation.[10] Many of these shifts have been swallowed whole and fully digested by the majority of us, Christians or not. Even as we entered into the third millennium and stand at the edge of what justly may be called postmodernity, we seem to have at least one foot still planted firmly in the former epoch is all about us, perhaps even about how the entire world, its discoveries, and its God fit or do not fit into our own little personal cosmos.

Modernism categorized center and periphery, superior and inferior, young and old, etc. In modernism, there was no room for the 'other.' The marginalized were excluded or pushed to the periphery. But, postmodernism brought the marginalized and those who were in the periphery to the center. The *deconstructive* postmodernism of the self-resulted in shaking the foundation of the idealism of the Enlightenment. This has resulted in search of the 'other' or 'alterity' and brought to the center. As a result, Iyadurai says, mission in postmodernity is to be *other-cente*red, which identifying with the poor, women, marginalized, and aged to bring into the center of God's reign.[11]

9 Keith G. Medador and Shaun C. Henson, "Growing Old in a Therapeutic Culture," in *Growing Old in Christ* eited by Stanley Hauerwas, et. al., (UK: William B. Eerdmans Publishing Company, 2003), 90.

10 Keith G. Medador and Shaun C. Henson, "Growing Old in a Therapeutic Culture…," 91.

11 Joshua Iyadurai, "Mission in Postmodernity: An Asian Perspective," *Dharma Deepika* 14/2 (July 8 December 2010): 70.

Ageing in Postmodernity

Postmodern voices are looking for people possessing a sense of how theory is suited to the practical matters of everyday living within the moral, as well as industrial, local ecologies of our lives.[12] The potential for the coming era to engage this situation constructively is dependent upon a commitment to the historicity and the particularity of response to the contingencies of life that is offered by such institutions as the church. This engagement will determine the degree to which this humanizing of postmodernity rectifies the excesses of modernity in both our understanding of Ageing itself and in the care of those who are old.[13]

As cited by K. G. Pothen, *deconstruction* by Jacques Derrida shows that when texts are totalized based on the universalizing, and homogenizing frame of modernity, experiences which are different and do not fit this frame are excluded. And he further says, *deconstruction* also shows that Western thought is characterized by dichotomies or binaries like mind and matter, soul and body, nature and history, nature and culture, male and female, good and evil, young and old, etc. The binaries are arranged in a hierarchical order in which the first terms in the binaries have primacy over the second terms, which are considered to be inferior.[14] As modernity considered the body as inferior to mind, the mind is superior, and the body is inferior since the mind is associated with thought and rationality. Further, mind is disembodied, since the body has no role in the activity of the mind. This understanding has been challenged in postmodern thought. In *reconstructive* postmodernism, the body is the locus of experiences. This view recovers the significance of the body for thought. This is also significant in the case of Ageing.

It seems that *reconstruction* is an attempt to explore doing mission with commitment in Christ, to bring about a change in the human relationship through Liberative praxis, and to listen to *other* voices to correct ourselves and also our mistakes in doing mission to the aged. Missiologically, the term

---

12 Three important works are: David Wood, *Philosophy at the Limit* (London: Unwin Hyman, 1990); Leszek Kolakowaki, *Modernity on Endless Trial* (Chicago: The University of Chicago Press, 1990); Giovanni Vattimo, *The End of Modernity:Nihilism and Hermeneutical Culture*, translated by J. R. Snyder (Cambridge: Polity Press, 1998); cited in the footnotes of Johnson J. Puttenpurakal "Transition to the Postmodern-Nietzsche and Heidegger" in Johnson J. Puttenpurakal eds. *The Postmodern: A Siege of the Citadel of Reason,* (Delhi: Media House, 2002), 17; also see in Thomas J. Parayidom "Catholic Spirituality in the context of Postmodernism," in *Indian Journal of Spirituality*, XVIII/2 (April-June 2005): 219.

13 Keith G. Medador and Shaun C. Henson, "Growing Old in a Therapeutic Culture…," 94.

14 K. G. Pothen, "Margins in Conversation: Postmodern Methodologies" in *Margins in Conversation: Methodological Discourses in Theological Disciplines,* edited by Joseph Prabhakar Dayam and P. Mohan Larbeer (Bangalore: BTESSC, 2012), 88.

"reconstruction" means to develop alternative communities in Christ that would share their resources, respect each other's dignities, and work towards justice for all.[15] Therefore, mission to older people, especially if accompanied by a pastoral care alert to the diversity of needs, open to everyone's participation, and aimed at exploiting everyone's capacities, represents an enrichment for the whole community. It is therefore desirable that as many as possible embrace this service, and that they grasp its profound significance as a process of liberation of heart and reciprocal giving between the generations.

A MISSIOLOGICAL RESPONSE TO THE ISSUE OF AGEING

The theological/missiological reflection on the issue of Ageing is intentionally inductive-contextual and experiential. In one of the WCC conferences, put forth some of the challenges to be taken into account in this reflection on *Diakonia* in the Twenty-First Century. These were:

> "the institutionalization of injustice, particularly in the present regime of neo-liberal economic globalization; the reality of climate change and its impact; wars and conflicts and the consequent destruction, trauma and broken relationships; the fragmentation of communities due to aggressive assertion of religious and ethnic identities; the dispossession and displacement of vulnerable people; the violence against many sections of society, especially of women, children, people with disabilities and the aged."[16]

Ageing is ultimately a matter of life and death. To understand what it means to grow older, both for themselves and for others, Christians must be clear in their minds about the theological basis for their thinking and living. Their appreciation of the later years - the opportunities and joys as well as the responsibilities, problems, and suffering - must become one with their conception of God, the church and its mission in the world. To Cedric W. Tilberg, no specific theology of Ageing can be developed in isolation from theology as a whole, just as there are no truly isolated doctrines of any kind.[17]

15 Joshua Raja, "Mission as Creating Common Spaces of Peace," in *Towards a Reconstruction of Mission Stories: Building Communities of Hope and Peace,* edited by Joshua Raja, et al. (New Delhi: ISPCK, 2010), 31.

16 The conference was jointly organized by the Justice and *Diakonia*, Just and Inclusive Communities, and Mission and Evangelism programs of the World Council of Churches in Colombo, Sri Lanka, 2-6 June 2012 on the theme: "Theological Perspectives on *Diakonia* in 21st Century." There were 50 participants involved in various diaconal initiatives in about 25 countries brought with them some hard questions as well as insights on new possibilities arising out of their engagement in the lives of marginalized people. Gerald R. Leslie, Richard F. Larson and Benjamin L. Gorman (eds.), *Introductory Sociology*..., 157.

17 Cedric W. Tilberg, *The Fullness of Life*, 177.

The church's attention and commitment to older people are nothing new. The church has directed it's participation in the mission and pastoral care to older people in the most varied circumstances over the centuries. The church's teaching, far from considering the question as a mere problem of assistance and charity, has always reaffirmed the primary importance of recognizing and fostering the intrinsic value of persons of all ages.[18] However, it has to be recognized that the current situation is unprecedented in many respects. It urges the church to revise her approach to the pastoral care of older people in the third and fourth ages. New forms and methods, more in agreement with the needs and spiritual aspirations of older people need to be sought; new pastoral plans rooted in defense of life, of its meaning and destiny need to be formulated.

These are necessary conditions for encour Ageing older people to make their contribution to the mission of the church and helping them to derive particular spiritual enrichment from their active participation in the life of the ecclesial community. A society for all ages is, therefore, a multigenerational society committed to creating the conditions of being able to fulfill the great potential that older people still have. And also to contribute by making the voice of the church and its mission heard both in the field of reflection and in that of programs of action.

Integration of *both* the Young *and* the Aged

The young members of groups, associations, and movements present in the parishes must be educated to show solidarity towards the elder members of the community. Such inter-generational solidarity is also expressed in the companionship that the young can offer to the old. Young people who have opportunities for involvement with older people will appreciate the value of a formative experience by which they gain in maturity and are helped to develop an awareness of others that remains with them for the whole of their life. In a society in which selfishness, materialism, consumerism are widespread and in which the means of communication serve little to lessen the growing loneliness of man, such values as selflessness, dedication, friendship, acceptance, and respect represent a challenge to those, not least the young, who are striving for the birth of a new humanity.

The aged people should also have a rightful place in *both* society *and* even more so to an honored place within the family. The family is called to be a communion of persons. It needs to be reminded of its special mission to foster, manifest and communicate love, and its duty to provide assistance to its weaker members, not least the elderly, and surround them with affection. The need for the family to be able to benefit from adequate means of material

18 "The Dignity of Older People…, 2.

support should also be emphasized: economic assistance, welfare and health services, and appropriate housing, pension, and social security policies should be available to the needs of the family.[19] It is evident that the decision to dedicate an annual world day to older people, to be celebrated on 1st October each year. The international year of older persons offers a valuable occasion to remember these extraordinary older people-*both* men *and* women-and their silent and heroic witness.[20]

As Vineeta Srivastava assumes that, it must be the reason why India has only recently started taking note of the population of Ageing and the accompanying problems. The aged in traditional societies enjoy a relatively high level of warmth and affection among their kith and kin.[21] In the Indian social scenario of the aged, it is closely knit, and its unique nature and value system has attached a sustained respect for the elders. It seems both the *age* and *experiences* are respected here. The aged have been considered as an *asset* rather than a burden in the Indian society. However, the urbanization and individualization have been more to the disadvantage of the aged.[22] The well-being of older persons also has been mandated in the constitution of India.[23] It

19 "The Dignity of Older People..., 14-15.

20 Women, on average, live longer than men. While this differential varies from years to years, women can expect to live about eight years longer than men. This longer life means that more women must prepare for widowhood in later years than men. As of now, there are approximately 10.1 million widowed women and 1.8 million widowed men.cf. "The Dignity of Older People..., 2.

21 Vineeta Srivastava, *Women Ageing: Social Work Investigation,* (Jaipur: Rawat Publication, 2010), 15.

22 But at the same time, in the present context, aged people have been assigned a negative role by all the societies. They are portrayed as dependent individuals, characterized by a lack of social autonomy, isolation, and neglect. They are considered as if posing a threat to the living standards of younger age groups by being a burden, which only consumes without producing; however, the nature of the problems that the aged face varies in different societies and cultures. The aged in the developed countries face the disheartening experiences of marginalization. In contrast, in a developing country, they are subject to physical Ageing, mainly due to poverty, hard work, dependency, and bed-ridden sickness. cf Vineeta Srivastava, *Women Ageing...*, 16.

23 It is experienced that attitude of youngsters is now becoming more individualistic and has come to disregard the authority of and to disrespect their elders. A division in joint families and landed property, migration of children to far off urban areas in search of new jobs, and change in marital pattern has adversely affected the social security of the aged and their authority in the family. The parents often expect that in their old age they will be taken care of by their children. And, the failure on the children's part easily upsets the aged parents causing them great emotional strain as well as economic trauma. The Article 41, a Directive Principle of State Policy, has directed that the state shall, within the limits of its economic capacity and development, make effective provisions for securing the right to public assistance in cases of old age. Cf. Vineeta Srivastava, *Women Ageing...*, 246.

seems that not only the church, but human civilization is also greatly indebted to them.

Integration of *both* Mission from *and* to the Ageing

The church has looked to Jesus of Nazareth as the definitive model for true humanity, the model for a life lived faithfully. However, Jesus did not live into what we would normally consider 'late-life.' First of all, the manner of Jesus' death stands as a permanent reminder that faithfulness is more important than longevity.[24] Secondly, even though Jesus died young, his suffering both represents and redeems all human experience, all human suffering. This means that Jesus' life and death are to be understood as paradigmatic for all human experience. It does not matter the modern binaries of sealing the people as female or male, illiterate or learned, poor or rich, aged or young. The Christian practice of Ageing requires us to learn the imaginative skill of employing the cross and resurrection as the lens through which we view our Ageing and dying. The Christian practice of Ageing as interpreted for us by the New Testament is the pattern of self-giving (*kenosis*) for the sake of others, which is shaped by the example of Jesus, who emptied himself and became obedient, even to the point of death, for our sake (see Phil. 2:1-13).[25]

The Christian mission from the Ageing is to lead, to teach, to counsel as their gifts allow, and as opportunities arise. In late life, Christians remain subject to the possibility that God will act decisively in history and their lives in such a way as to turn their lives upside down. They may be called to a new ministry, receive new revelation, see the fulfillment of a long-awaited hope. In this, they do not differ from younger Christians. Above all, in old age as in youth, Christians are to take the Lord Jesus Christ as the model for their daily lives and interactions with others. Therefore, Christian mission from the Ageing is a lifelong habit of believing God's witness in the scriptures and acting on it, for as long as God gives life.

An important role in promoting the active participation of older people in the work of mission and evangelization is now played by the church-based associations and the ecclesial movements, "one of the gifts of the Spirit [to the church] of our time."[26] Many older people have already found an extremely fertile field for their formation, commitment, and apostolate in the various associations present in our parishes. They have become real protagonists within the Christian community. Nor is there any lack of other groups, communities,

24 The way of discipleship, as Jesus repeatedly taught his followers, leads to the cross (e.g., Mark 8:34-38; Luke 14:25-27). Jesus models for us a resolute trust in God that empowers us to act freely and to bear witness to the truth, even if such witness-bearing may lead to death.

25 Cf. Richard B. Hays and Judith C. Hays, "The Christian Practice of growing Old...," 13.

26 "The Dignity of Older People...," 11.

and movements working more specifically in the world of the third age. Thanks to the associations, they create an environment in which communion can thrive between the various generations and a spiritual climate that helps older people to maintain their spiritual vitality and youthfulness.

Mission to the aged involves the need to train pastors, Christian leaders, and volunteers-young people, adults, older people themselves-for service to older people. Pastoral workers who are imbued with humanity and spirituality, and who can enter into a rapport with people in the third and fourth ages, and to respond to their often very individualized human, social, cultural and spiritual needs. The needs of older people must also be addressed by the various branches of specialized pastoral care. These include the family apostolate, which cannot ignore the bonds between older people and their family, not only at the level of social services but also at that of religious life; the various forms of social ministry; and the apostolate of health-care workers.

Therefore, mission *from* and *to* the aged, as Paul puts it, is "to know Christ and the power of his resurrection and sharing (*koinonia*) of his sufferings, becoming like him in his death" (Phil. 3:10). As we grow old, we should seek to discern how to give our lives for others. Old age is not a time simply to relax, nor is it a time only to reminiscence about the past; instead, as throughout our lives, we must continue to pursue the way of service, conforming our own lives to the self-giving pattern of Jesus.[27] This postmodern Christological pattern for the years of 'late-life' challenges and overthrows many of the modern conservative models for Ageing that we see around us: old people as helpless, useless, burdens on society or old age as a time to sit back and reap the rewards we have earned through a lifetime of work:

From Vulnerable to Venerable

The factors that many older people from the center of the human community and civil life to the fringes are many: avoidance of responsibility at the institutional level and consequent social inadequacies; poverty or a drastic reduction of income and of the necessary financial resources to secure a decent standard of living and appropriate levels of care; and the progressive removal of older people from their own family and social environment. However, the most painful dimension of this marginalization is the lack of human relations. Older people suffer not only by being deprived of human contact but also from abandonment, loneliness, and isolation. And as their interpersonal and social contacts are diminished, so their lives are correspondingly impoverished; they are deprived of the intellectual and cultural stimulus and enrichment they need. Older people experience a sense of impotence at being unable to change their situation, due to their inability to participate in the decision-making processes

27 Richard B. Hays and Judith C. Hays, "The Christian Practice of growing Old...," 13.

that concern them both as persons and as citizens. The net result is that they lose any sense of belonging to the community of which they are members.[28]

According to the data of the Health Ministry of India, while the elderly are said to be the most vulnerable to the COVID-19 pandemic, people above 60 years account for only 17% of total cases in the country till now gives comfort.[29] However, as per the statistics of the World Health Organization, the violence against older people, who are already bearing the brunt of this pandemic, has risen sharply since the beginning of the COVID-19 pandemic and imposition of lockdown measures.[30] The problem concerns the whole of society at its various institutional levels that needs to intervene to ensure adequate protection, including jurisdical protection, for that, not negligible part of the population that lives in a situation of extreme social, economic and cultural deprivation.

From Exclusion to Inclusion

Exclusion from the world of work and everything related to it occurs in the life of aged people today in an over abrupt and stubborn manner. Only rarely does it coincide with the needs, opportunities, and preferred choices of the older people concerned. Many older people seek in vain a form of employment; they frequently do so to compensate for inadequate or non-existent pensions. This need for financial security must be satisfied: older people must be given a chance to do something. They must be enabled to express their creativity and to develop the spiritual dimension of their lives. That compulsory retirement can trigger off a process of premature Ageing now seems demonstrated.

Conversely, the pursuit of some form of employment beyond retirement age would have a beneficial effect on the quality of life of older people. The spare time that they have on their hands is, therefore, the first resource that needs to be addressed. An active role needs to be restored to them. Their access to the new technologies, and employment in socially useful forms of work, need to be promoted; and opportunities of eng Ageing in forms of volunteer work and services of benefit to the community, opened up to them.

From Minimal to Full Participation

It is a fact that older people, that the lack of representation of older people, and to remove the prejudices and misconceptions that have damaged their image

---

28 "The Dignity of Older People...," 7.

29 The greatest risk for severe illness from COVID-19 is among those aged 85 or older. There are also other factors that can risk their severe illness, such as having underlying medical conditions. http://timesofindia.indiatimes.com/articleshow/74988310.cms?utm_source=contentofinterest&utm_medium=text&utm_campaign=cppst (07/08/2020).

30 https://www.who.int/publications/m/item/covid-19-and-violence-against-older-people pdf, (07/08/2020).

in our time. If they are given the opportunity, to participate actively in the life of the community, both at the civil and the cultural and associational levels. This is confirmed by the numerous positions of responsibility held by older persons, for example, in the field of the volunteer services, and by their far from negligible political influence.[31] Steps must be taken to stop the culture of indifference, rampant individualism, competitiveness and utilitarianism which are now threatening all areas of society, and to remove any form of segregation between the generations, a new mentality, a new attitude, a new mode of being, a new culture needs to be developed. A form of prosperity and social justice needs to be pursued that is compatible with defending the centrality of the human person and dignity.

Conclusion

Reconstructive postmodern mission is to enable people to imagine, dream or share a vision of new alternative relationships where *both* centre *and* periphery; *both* male *and* female; *both* young *and* old; *both* liberation *and* salvation; *both* physical *and* spiritual; *both* reflection *and* praxis, etc. While critically reviewing the existing attitude of the churches towards its mission to and from the aged, it recognizes the search of the integration of *both* the young *and* the aged at various levels within the churches and outside, for relevant patterns of Christian witness in today's postmodern context. It reconstructs such binaries in today's context to make it relevant and being closer to these two relationships (*both* with God *and* with Others) so that one nourishes the other. It is also an attempt to reconstruct the Reign of God through the lives of aged people who are influenced and challenged by the message of Jesus Christ that many older people from the fringes of the human community and civil life to the center, from vulnerable to venerable, from exclusion to inclusion, from minimal to full participation.

31 "The Dignity of Older People…," 9.

11

Vānapratha-sannyāsa Schemes of Life as Gerotranscendence An Appraisal of a Hindu Perspective of Ageing

Giri Krishnan

Introduction

The process of growing old is called ageing, which reflects on the changes occurring in individuals in the course of life. Everyone goes through this natural process and phase of life at one's own time and pace. Ageing is viewed from different perspectives according to each culture and the experiences of the aged, either optimistically or pessimistically. On the one hand, "ageing has been defined as the collection of changes that render human beings progressively more likely to die."[1] Ageing is also defined as a progressive functional decline or a gradual deterioration of physiological function with age, including a decrease in fecundity, or the intrinsic, inevitable, and irreversible age-related process of loss of viability and increase in vulnerability.[2] On the other hand, according to a Hindu view of life, ageing is an opportunity for spiritual development to fulfill the ultimate goal of life; and the aged are offered *seva* or service by the society.[3] The *vānaprastha-sannyāsāśrama* discourse is one of the ancient religious views of the aged in the Indian context. The current trend on gerontology as the science of old age that deals with the problems faced by the elderly, however, is 'positive ageing', centered on the theory of gerotranscendence.

---

1 Joao Pedro de Magalhaes, *Gerontology Information*, (June 16, 2013), available at: https://www.senescence.info/gerontology. pdf, 3 (accessed on 17/08/2020).

2 Magalhaes, *Gerontology Information*..., 5.

3 Sarah Lamb, "Hinduism Teaching and Aging," *Encyclopaedia of Gerontology and Population Aging*, ed. by Danan Gu and Mathew E. Dupre, https://doi.org/10.1007/978-3-319-69892-2_144-1 (accessed on 17/08/2020).

Hence, the problem involved in this study is to investigate various aspects of ageing in *āśrama* scheme of life, and to analyze if the notion of positive ageing is present in it in view of gerotranscendence. The study raises the following research questions: What is the perspective of ageing in *vānaprastha-sannyāsa* scheme of life in Hindu tradition? Is *āśrama* concept of ageing relevant today in the light of gerotranscendence? Taking into account the issues raised, this paper begins with an overview of ageing in the Hindu view of life. Secondly, it elaborates the ageing in *āśrama*[4] scheme of life. Having traced the origins of *āśrama* scheme from Śruti-Smṛti tradition, it brings out the views of ageing in both *vānaprastha* and *sannyāsa āśramas* separately. Thirdly, an attempt is made in the paper to locate *āśrama* scheme in the theory of gerotranscendence that advocate 'positive ageing.'[5] A brief explanation of the theory along with its various dimensions is brought out and *vānaprastha-sannyāsāśramas* are analyzed in the light of gerotranscendence in this section. Fourthly, contemporary appropriation of the ancient views of *āśrama* scheme is explained. Finally, the paper attempts for an appraisal of ageing in *āśrama* scheme with its positive ideals and limitations, besides delineating some implications and possible Christian adaptation of the views of ageing from *āśrama* scheme of life. This study is therefore an effort to explore a Hindu view of ageing based on the *vānaprastha-sannyāsa* stages of life from a gerontological perspective.

Ageing in Hindu View of Life[6]

As the Hindu view of life considers ageing as a natural process of human being, it is important to deliberate on this natural phenomenon in gerontological discourse in an Indian context. Hindu view of life is believed to be holistic, all embracing, all encompassing and it takes into account 'from the womb to tomb and beyond' of an individual. Undoubtedly, Hindu view affirms the *saṁsāric*[7] life but nevertheless it negates the world. World negation and affirmation are like two sides of the same coin in Hindu thought and, thereby, making it a more complex view of life. In Hindu tradition renunciation is the higher view of life and old age is considered as an 'opportunity for cultivating renunciation.'[8]

4 The term *āśrama* has two different meanings: (i) Stage of Life, referring to the four stages of life; (ii) Hermitage. The former meaning is the consideration of the study.

5 'Positive ageing' refers to the process of maintaining a positive attitude with 'feel good factors' of oneself, keeping fit and healthy, and engaging in life.

6 Hindu view of life here would mean the view of life based on the *Sruti* and *Smrti* texts of Hindu religious tradition.

7 It refers to the life in the material world.

8 Chakravarthi Ram-Prasad, "A Classical Indian Philosophical Perspective on Ageing and the Meaning of Life," *Ageing and Society* 15/1 (1995): 1–36.

Hindu view of life on ageing in this study, however, is limited to the *āśrama* scheme of Hindu tradition.

Ageing in *Āśrama* Scheme

Varṇāśrama scheme of life is one of the essential features of Hindu tradition. While *varṇa* scheme supplies the normative paradigm for the different caste or races with stipulation of duties and responsibilities attached for each *varṇa*, the *āśrama* system directs the individual of each *varṇa* in different phases of life from childhood to old age with its own sets of obligatory functions. While *varṇa* is on the social aspect of an individual in relation with different social groups, *āśrama* is related to the personal aspect of individual's development through various stages. *Varṇa* is fixed at birth, whereas *āśrama* as the order of life is a connected institution, moving from one *āśrama* to another at different stages within a life time.[9]

There are four *āśramas* or stages of life as in the case of four *varṇas*. As per the *āśrama* scheme an individual from upper *varṇa* sails through these four stages of life such as student stage (*Brahmachārya*) – a period of training; householder stage (*Gṛhastha*) – a period of work for the household and society; hermit or forest dwelling stage (*Vānaprastha*) – the period of withdrawal; and renunciation or ascetic stage (*Sannyāsa*) – the period of renunciation. These four stages of life are oriented towards one's ultimate goal, *mokṣa*. S. C. Tiwari and Nisha M. Pandey comment, "*Ashram* scheme is devised as an instrument of life, as the best means towards the fulfillment of what was conceived to be the fullest and the most efficient management of individual, social and economic orders as a whole."[10] The ultimate purpose of *āśrama* schemes, i.e., *mokṣa*, is pursued through two paths – *pravṛttimārga* (path of activism) and *nivṛttimārga* (path of detachment). One who follows the former path goes through *gṛhastha* and *vānaprastha*, and finally reach *sannyāsa* stage, whereas one who follows the latter embraces *sannyāsa* without going through the former states of life in the *āśrama* scheme.[11]

Origins of *Āśrama* Scheme

The concept of *āśrama* scheme of life began to appear in Upaniṣadic period which is evident from Śvetāśvatara Upaniṣad VI. 210 and Chāndogya

9 T. R. Venkatarama Sastri, "The Smṛtis: Their Outlook and Character," *The Cultural Heritage of India* vol. II (Calcutta: The Ramakrishna Mission Institute of Culture, 2001), 330.

10 S. C. Tiwari and Nisha M. Pandey, "The Indian Concepts of Lifestyle and Mental Health in Old Age," in *Indian Journal of Psychiatry* 55/6 (2013): 288-292. Available at: www.indianjpsychiatry.org/text.asp?2013/55/6/288/105553, (accessed on 10/09/2020).

11 Swami Harshananda, *A Concise Encyclopaedia of Hinduism* vol. 2 (Bangalore: Ramakrishna Math, 2012 (first edition 2009), 328.

Upaniṣad II.23.1 or even in the Aitareya Brāhmaṇa 32.10. Often there is no clear distinction between the 3rd and 4th stages of *āśramas* as seen in the case of Chāndogya.[12] These four *āśramas* explained in the Dharma Sūtras are known as *Ācārya-kula*, *Gṛhastha*, *Bhikṣu* and *Vaikhana*. Āpastambha speaks of them as *brahmacāri*, *gṛhastha*, *vānaprasthin* and *parivrajaka*.[13] Most probably the early Vedic society followed only the first two *āśramas* and the asceticism that has gained importance in Upaniṣadic period seems to be due to the influence of the heterodox doctrine of asceticism taught by both Buddha and Mahavira. The prescriptions of actions or *dharma* of *varṇāśrama* are given in sutra literatures such as Srauta and Gṛhya.[14]

In *āśrama* scheme, *vānaprastha* and *sannyāsa* are directly related to old age. Both are renunciatory stages with an attitude of non-attachment meant for a *dvija* (the twice-born). *Vānaprasthāśrama* is said to have developed in opposition to the teachings of Buddha and Mahavira who promulgated complete renunciation and celibacy, which threatened the family life and the existence of a healthy society. The *āśrama* scheme was said to have been introduced in order to stabilize the very existence of family and society that was otherwise jeopardized by the influence of Buddhism and Jainism that searched for freedom in the forest.[15] The institution of *sannyāsa* is said to be against the very tenet of Hindu way of life but of *śramaṇa*[16] origin. However, later on Brahmaṇical sages developed four stages of life and adopted 'homelessness' as the last stage of life although their preferences were the conditions of *gṛhastha*, not of *sannyāsa*.[17]

Vānaprasthāśrama Scheme

The *Vānaprasthāśrama* is traditionally considered in India as the stage of the aged. During *vānaprastha* an individual slowly withdraws oneself from the active life in society. Having fulfilled all the obligatory duties of *gṛhastha* as

12 K.V. Saoundara Rajan, *Concise Classified Dictionary of Hinduism* vol. I (New Delhi: Concept Publishing Company, 2001), 36.

13 *Parivṛajaka* is referred to a wandering ascetics or mendicant. In the later Vedic period the fourth asrama was known as *parivrajaka* who survive on the food only by *bhikṣa*. Cf. K. V. Saoundara Rajan, *Concise Classified Dictionary of Hinduism* vol. 2 (New Delhi: Concept Publishing Company, 2001), 129.

14 Rajan, *Concise Classified Dictionary of Hinduism* vol. I..., 36-37.

15 P. Victor Premsagar, "*Vanaprasthasrama Dharma* – A programme of Renewal and Religion as Realisation for Retired People," *Bangalore Theological Forum* XXVI/3&4 (September & December, 1994): 16.

16 *Śramaṇa* movement, which gave birth to Jainism and Buddhism, was an ancient religious development existed parallel to, but separate from, Vedic Hindu tradition.

17 Sukumar Datta, "Monasticism in India," *The Cultural Heritage of India* vol. II (Calcutta: The Ramakrishna Mission Institute of Culture, 2001), 583.

given in the Gṛahya Sutras, a married person begins to exercise detachment from the affairs of the world. *Vānaprastha* is the period of retreat in order to loosen the social bonds.[18] Regarding *vānaprastha* stage Manu Smṛti describes: "When so ever a householder gets to see wrinkles on his body, white hair on his head, and has his grandchildren, he should resort to the forest."[19] "He should be engaged in regular study, control his senses, maintain a friendly behavior with everyone, and have a tranquil mind. He must give charity, should not accept gifts from others, and have mercy on all living beings."[20] Citing Manu, Radhakrishnan notes, "one must enter the third stage when one becomes a grandfather.... When one's bodily powers wane, it is time to depart to the forest and prepare oneself for the true life of the spirit."[21] However, those who suffer from hardship of old-age ailments or contagious diseases embrace *mahāprasthāna* (walking unto death; literally, the great/final departure/ journey) by entering a river or fire, a religious suicide.[22]

In *vānaprastha* (forest hermit) stage one is expected to handover one's family responsibilities to the children. Having given up household tasks, husband goes to the forest accompanied by his wife. The term *vānaprastha* is the composite form of two words: *vana* meaning forest and *prasthāna* meaning going, implying a forest going person. A *vānaprastha*, a resident of forest, chastise his body with the aim of purifying his soul. Confining oneself to the forest without entering a village or even refraining from stepping on a ploughed land, *avānaprastha* build a hut in the forest and lead a life of chastity although lives with his wife. Dress materials such as animal skin and *kuśa* grass are obtained from the forest itself. His bed is the bear ground. He lives an austere life with unshaven hair and beard, and survives on forest produce such as roots, herbs, vegetables and fruits or by begging from other hermits once a day. One is prohibited to hoard the food items for more than a year but only for a short period.[23]

A *gṛhastha* carries either *Śrauta* (the Vedic) fires or *Gṛhya* (domestic) fire while retiring to the *vana* or forest and offer fire oblation to gods. He continues to perform *pañcamahāyajñas* (five daily sacrifices) and offer regular

18 S. Radhakrishnan, *The Hindu View of Life* (New Delhi: Harper Collins Publishers and The India Today Group, 2009 [1927]), 57.

19 Buhler G, ed., *Manu Smriti: The Laws of Manu*, Chapter 6 Hymn 2.

20 Buhler G, ed., *Manu Smriti: The Laws of Manu*, Chapter 6 Hymn 8.

21 Radhakrishnan, *The Hindu View of Life*..., 63.

22 Harshananda, *A Concise Encyclopaedia of Hinduism* vol. 3..., 97.

23 C. S. Venkateswaran, "The Ethics of the Puraṇas," *The Cultural Heritage of India* vol. II (Calcutta: The Ramakrishna Mission Institute of Culture, 2001), 295; H. C. Chakladar, "Some Aspects of Social Life in Ancient India," *The Cultural Heritage of India* vol. II (Calcutta: The Ramakrishna Mission Institute of Culture, 2001), 560-561; Swami Harshananda, *A Concise Encyclopaedia of Hinduism* vol. 3, 496-97.

sacrifices such as *darśapūrṇamāsa* and *cāturmāsyas*.[24] He regularly recites Vedas, extends hospitality by receiving all guests irrespective of their *varṇas* and feed also other beings.[25]

Sannyāsāśrama Scheme

Sannyāsa, the life of a recluse or a monk, is the final stage of an individual in the *āśrama* scheme, culminating in spiritual perfection that one seeks, i.e., *mokṣa*. Manu Smṛti states, "After spending the third portion of one's life in the forest, the fourth portion of life should be spent as a *sannyāsi*, by surrendering all attachments (for the world)…. Delighting in meditation on the Supreme, independence from others, giving up all desires, with only the Self as companion, seeking supreme bliss, shall live like *sannyāsi*."[26] As it is a stage of sublimation and a state of great excellence and beauty, an individual "renounces all possessions and distinctions of caste and practice of formal rituals."[27] As Radhakrishnan points out, "Renunciation is the feeling of detachment from the finite as finite and attachment to the finite as the embodiment of the infinite."[28] The Padma Purāṇa[29] speaks of three types of *sannyāsins*: *karma-sannyāsin* who devotes in performing oblation of sacred fire to God, *veda-sannyāsin* who practices the Vedas and *jñāna-sannyāsin* who is rooted in the knowledge of the *Ātman*. The last one is considered as superior to others.[30]

Sannyāsa stage in *āśrama* scheme, however, was restricted only to the Brahmins while it is denied to all other *varṇas* including other *dvijas*, the twice born upper *varṇas*.[31] As *vānaprastha*, the recluse, gains adequate inner strength for a complete renunciation, he sends his wife to be taken care of by the children and adapts *sannyāsa* or monastic way of life. A *sannyāsin* is constantly on the move without a permanent dwelling, observing self-control and detachments.[32] It is said, "The *sannyāsi* becomes fit to achieve immortality by not possessing any materialistic thing, by restraining his senses, by casting out the love and hatred from him, and by living a life of harmlessness to living beings."[33] He is said to relinquish even his own former name and caste.[34]

24 Harshananda, *A Concise Encyclopaedia of Hinduism* vol. 3…, 496-97.

25 H. C. Chakladar, "Some Aspects of Social Life in Ancient India…, 561.

26 Buhler G, ed., *Manu Smriti: The Laws of Manu*, Chapter 6 Hymn 49.

27 S. Arulsamy, *Religion for a New Society* (Delhi: ISPCK, 2000), 10.

28 Radhakrishnan, *The Hindu View of Life*…, 55.

29 Padma Purāṇa is one of the eighteen Major Purāṇas, a *Smṛti* text, in Hindu tradition.

30 Venkateswaran, "The Ethics of the Purāṇas…, 295.

31 Harshananda, *A Concise Encyclopaedia of Hinduism* vol. 3…, 497.

32 Harshananda, *A Concise Encyclopaedia of Hinduism* vol. 1…, 179.

33 Tiwari and Pandey, "The Indian Concepts of Lifestyle…, 288-292.

34 Rajan, *Concise Classified Dictionary*…, 37.

Sannyāsin is a solitary soul who 'dwells in love and walks in righteousness', yet he is known as a 'parasite' as he neither contributes to society nor cares for national egoism or patriotism. For him, all are equal (*samatā-sarvasmin*).[35] At this stage, everyone is embodiment of the soul; the name and form (*nāma-rūpa*) do not matter for a *sannyāsin*.

Locating *Vānaprastha-Sannyāsa* Scheme of Life in 'Gerotranscendence'

Theory of Gerotranscendence

The theory of gerotranscendence that focuses on 'positive ageing' is said to have developed over a period of two decades by Lars Tornstam, a Swedish Gerontologist. It emphasizes on the many vital components which are otherwise overlooked in the understanding of ageing. According to Tornstam, ageing involves developmental changes related to increased life satisfaction. He asserts:

> "The gerotranscendent individual... typically experiences a redefinition of the self and of relationships to others and a new understanding of fundamental, existential questions. The individual becomes... less self-occupied and... more selective in the choice of social and other activities. There is an increased feeling of affinity with past generations and a decrease in interest in material things and a greater need for solitary "meditation." Positive solitude becomes more important. There is also often a feeling of cosmic communion with the spirit of the universe, and a redefinition of time, space, life, and death."[36]

Tornstam further clarifies that gerotranscendence does not refer to 'a state of withdrawal or disengagement' but it goes beyond the old dualism of activity and disengagement view of life.[37] There is a gradual shift in meta-paradigm of an ageing person, "...from a materialistic and rational view of the world to a more cosmic and transcendent one, normally followed by an increase in life satisfaction."[38] The gerotranscendence occurs in the final stage of natural ageing process and it is argued that older adults become increasingly connected to the mysterious and spiritual realms of the universe. Tornstam

---

35 Radhakrishnan, *The Hindu View of Life*..., 64.

36 Lars Tornstam, *Gerotranscendence: A Developmental Theory of Positive Aging* (New York: Springer Publishing Company, 2005), 3-4.

37 Tornstam, *Gerotranscendence: A Developmental Theory of Positive Aging*..., 4.

38 Feheen Rajani and Hena Jawaid, "Theory of Geotranscendence: An Analysis," *Austin Journal of Psychiatry and Behavioral Sciences* 2/1 (April 21, 2015): 1; Arjan Bram, "Gerotranscendence," Longitudinal Aging Study Amsterdam, Available at https://www.lasa-vu.nl/themes/emotional/gerotranscendence.htm# (accessed on 02/09/2020).

noted that "although older adults tended to withdraw, it was a reorientation to a different perspective and experience, to a more reflective and satisfying state of being and thinking."[39] Such a view of ageing is a shift from the negative view of ageing to a positive view, called 'positive ageing,' which is also called by some others as 'successful ageing.'[40]

Dimensions of Gerotranscendence

Allyson R. Rempel identifies the following three dimensions[41] of gerotranscendence in Tornstam's view:

(i) The Self Dimension: In older adults the view of the self changes and they become less self-centered. They appreciate the life they lived and discover new aspects of self by connecting themselves with the earlier generations which is expressed in increased religiosity or spirituality. Although care for the body is still present, they pay less attention to the physical body, having no bodily obsession.

(ii) The Social and Relationship Dimension: The older adults increasingly break away from their expected roles – separating self from roles, and become less judgmental. They relate meaningfully with a select few and the solitude is viewed more positively. Increased asceticism is common among the older adults as they reject cultural norms.

(iii) The Cosmic Dimension: The older adults see their lives as a 'connected whole' as they tend to increase attachment to the earlier generations. The perceptions about life and death are changed – death is less feared and life is viewed in different perspectives, having meaning and purpose. Spirituality plays a larger role, mystery becomes more accepted and time is viewed unimportant or unlimited. Allyson asserts, "older adults who identify themselves as spiritual have been found to have increased will-being compared with people who do not."[42] Thus there is a growing connection with spirituality in old age, which is the cosmic dimension of gerotranscendence.

---

39 Allyson R. Rempel, "Gerotranscendence and Successful Aging: The Lived Experience," *Sophia* (2013): 11. Available at https://sophia.stkate.edu/msw_papers/253 (accessed on 10/09/2020).

40 Cf. Rowe J. W. and Kahn R. L., *Successful Aging* (New York: Pantheon Books, 1998).

41 Rempel, "Gerotranscendence and Successful Aging: The Lived Experience..., 12-15.

42 Rempel, "Gerotranscendence and Successful Aging: The Lived Experience..., 15.

Vānaprastha-Sannyāsa Āśramas in View of Gerotranscendence

Many characteristics and the essence of gerotranscendence find its expression in the *vānaprastha-sannyāsa āśrama* scheme of Hindu tradition. Samta P. Pandya states: "Lars Tomstam's concept of gerotranscendence share core components with the last two stages of the four-stage of Hindu model of the life span…."[43] All the three dimensions – Self, social and cosmic, are evident in one way or the other in the last two stages of life in *āśrama* scheme. While *gṛhastha* leads a materialistic life, a *vānaprastha* or *sannyāsa* embraces a cosmic and transcendent view of life as perceived in gerotranscendence. The solitude longed by the individual in gerotranscendence is fulfilled in *vānaprastha-sannyāsa* stages in the *āśrama* scheme. The solitude of the forest in *vānaprasthāśrama* helps a person to escape from the flutter of mundane life to meditate on higher values. Thus one ceases to be the active member of the family and community thereby one's affiliation and association terminates. Ideally, this stage has greater significance as it is close to the final stage and *mokṣa*. *Vānaprastha* stage points to the fact that one's stature cannot be reduced to the demands of society; and human being is neither a mere custodian of the culture of a society nor a mere producer of its wealth.[44] The purpose of *sannyāsa* life is to achieve the state of spiritual freedom. As Arulsamy states, "This stage indicates that human life has a deeper significance, that it is not over in merely being born, growing up, marrying, earning a livelihood, founding a family, supporting it and passing away…. He spends the time in searching to realize the true being in himself."[45] Radhakrishnan views that although the sole purpose of a *sannyāsin* is to attain spiritual freedom, it is not mere freedom from the attachment of the world. On the one hand an individual is free from craving of riches or glory and on the other one is not elated by success or disappointed by failure.[46]

According to Samta P. Pandya, since the Indian context provides rich spiritual heritage and spiritual worldview on ageing it promotes the idea of gerotranscendence.[47] In the *āśrama* scheme of life as the physical abilities decline due to old age the obligations of *āśrama* become more spiritual[48] or transcendental. According to Shrinivas Tilak, the old age is not a period of total disengagement but a period of differential as one has to practice whatever

43 Pandya, "Aging Spiritually…, 2.

44 Radhakrishnan, *The Hindu View of Life*…, 63.

45 S. Arulsamy, *Religion for a New Society* (Delhi: ISPCK, 2000), 10.

46 Radhakrishnan, *The Hindu View of Life*…, 64.

47 Pandya, "Aging Spiritually…, 2.

48 Tiwari and Pandey, "The Indian Concepts of Lifestyle…, 288-292.

enables oneself for the liberation, though one gives up the affairs of the world.[49] Thus *āśrama* scheme of Hinduism is considered as the most self-sustaining method for "leading a meaningful life, and knowing the art of leaving the world graciously at the end."[50] It is said that in order to live in dignity, an old person requires 'new goals or new patterns of life.'[51] The *vānaprastha-sannyāsa āśrama* scheme of life seems to suggest a purposeful stage of the elderly in *Śruti-Smṛti* tradition in India and it is ideally akin to the notions of 'satisfaction with life', 'successful ageing' and 'positive ageing', enshrined in gerotranscendence.

Contemporary Appropriation of *Āśrama* Scheme

Āśrama scheme has ideally placed the entire life of an individual in more organized manner in the *Śruti-Smṛti* tradition of ancient India. However, due to the change of socio-political context, religious beliefs and lifestyle, old age was perceived as decline and decay of bodily functions that are associated with illness and death. Buddha viewed the life as full of suffering and condition of the old age as in distress and turmoil. Although, hospitals were set up for the care for society by Aśoka, no specific steps were taken to improve the conditions of the elderly during Maurya or subsequent Mughal dynasty periods. The structure of Indian society underwent drastic changes during British era and joint family system has been gradually replaced by nuclear families. The support system built up for the elderly through three or four generations in the joint family is found wanting. The traditional living patterns are further eroded by industrialization and modernization besides the emergence of nuclear family. The conditions of elderly became more deplorable as their needs were ignored as they were left to fend for themselves.[52]

A question arises, hence, whether the *āśrama* scheme of life is merely a thing of the past? One of the major characteristics of Hindu religious tradition is the spirit of accommodation and adaptability. The modernism and contemporary living as part of social changes is absorbed and adapted especially by the renascent Hinduism of the present period. The contemporary cosmopolitan middle class adherents of Hindu tradition are said to participate in new social forms in relation with ageing. Life in old-age-home is perceived as *vānaprasthāśrama* for the elderly. According to Sarah Lamb, "…many in India expressly perceive old-age-home living as akin to the "forest-dwelling"

---

49 Shrinivas Tilak, *Religion and Aging in the Indian Tradition* (Albany: State University of New York Press, 1989).

50 Rajan, *Concise Classified Dictionary of Hinduism* Vol. I…, 9.

51 C. Margaret Hall, "Religion and Aging", in *Journal of Religion and Health* 24/1 (Spring, 1985): 70.

52 Tiwari and Pandey, "The Indian Concepts of Lifestyle…, 288-292.

or *vānaprastha* life phase long presented in Hindu texts as appropriate for old age, where one purposefully loosens ties to family and the world in order to pursue spiritual realization."[53]

In an ethnographic research conducted on twenty nine homes of the older adults in Kolkata, Sarah Lamb claims that majority of the homes adopted in their name and mission statements the concept of 'spiritual forest dwelling' and *seva* or service. The mission of one of the homes of elderly stated: "to provide "a life away from the din of family, spent in solidarity religious practices," a site to pursue *vānaprastha āśrama* or "forest dwelling" phase of the Hindu householder's life."[54]As per the changing world, many such homes give a new identity and personhood especially for women different from the intergenerational family where dependency and gendered relations are maintained. These homes often cultivate independent and egalitarian way of living for the aged; thereby transcend the limitations of the traditional care in the joint families.[55]

In yet another sociological study carried out by Samta P. Pandya, reveals that spirituality and religion contribute to the positive ageing. The study concludes that for the majority of the residents of Pitamaha Sadans, the old age home run by the Chimmaya Mission, a Hindu based spiritual organization, "ageing was a state of mind, something that could be modified with…, and death was a process that led to God proximity."[56]*Āśrama* scheme of life is thereby accepted and adapted by the Hindu mind in accordance with the evolving and changing life of our times.

Appraisal and Implications of *Vānaprastha-Sannyāsāśramas*

Positive Ideals

Although, the whole *āśrama* scheme of life is not seen in the contemporary mass society, this ideal dominates a Hindu mind. A select few still hold and follow this fourfold plan of life, representing the soul of the society, and the entire members of community draw their paradigm in such ideal individuals. It is appropriate to state the words of Radhakrishnan in this connection, "When the wick is ablaze at its tip, the whole lamp is said to be burning."[57] This is essentially true for the *āśrama* scheme of life for the Hindu society as well.

53 Sarah Lamb, "Lives Outside the Family: Gender and the Rise of Elderly Residences in India," in *International Journal of Sociology of the Family* 33/1 (Spring, 2007): 57.

54 Lamb, "Lives Outside the Family…, 57.

55 Lamb, "Lives Outside the Family…, 46-48, 57.

56 Pandya, "Aging Spiritually: *Pitamahasadans* in India", *Cogent Social Sciences* 2/1 (2016): 1, available at https://www.tandfonline.com/action/journalInformation?journalCode=oass20 (accessed on 01/09/2020).

57 Radhakrishnan, *The Hindu View of Life…*, 65.

Although, there is continuity of the past there has been progress in all Hindu ideals. Hence there is no unalterable or uniform stationary Hinduism at any point of its history.[58] Hinduism accepts all stages of life as equal and significant as Radhakrishnan comments: "The blossom does not deny the leaf and the leaf does not deny the stalk or the stalk the root."[59] Hinduism appreciates the *sannyāsin* but abstain from disapproving *gṛhastha* as each one has to pass through these stages one after the other. Renunciation is not perceived in relation with the work associated with scripture that are aimed at the welfare of society, rather one renounces all that of 'I' and the 'mine' along with attachment with the family and the world.[60] Hence, such renunciation model of *āśrama* scheme opens up an ideal life, which transcends all hierarchical, discriminative, divisive casteism and gender binary that fragmentize the society, thereby ultimately leading to oneness of humanity.

Limitations

Āśrama scheme of life is not without limitations as one may analyze this ancient pattern of life that had limited outlook from contemporary multiple worldviews. Firstly, *vānaprastha* is viewed as the stage of life traditionally to loosen the social bonds. In the contemporary context, however, majority of the aged people are depended on their children or others, rather than being reclusive in the forest. Some even engage in begging and quite often lead a deplorable life. Welfare of *vānaprastha* stage of life today depends on how they have spent their lives as *brahmacārin* and *gṛhastha*. The life of *vānaprastha* sometimes seems to be 'useless' and a burden to society as it demands a lot of dependency, care, assistance and protection.[61]

Secondly, Ascetic and householder stages in *āśrama* scheme divide the views of individuals in a society into separate and opposed realities. *Āśrama* scheme is hierarchical and it is against equality of individuals in a society. Householder stage involves social duties and responsibilities but the ascetic stage is free from such obligations. When the entire *āśrama* scheme is permitted only for the Brahmins and other *varṇas* are prohibited from completely practicing them, it turns out to be discriminatory on caste ground to benefit a select few. The *Kṣatriyas* embracing *vānaprastha* stage was common as many kings withdrew to the forest after enthroning their sons, but

58 Radhakrishnan, *The Hindu View of Life…*, 94-95.

59 Radhakrishnan, *The Hindu View of Life…*, 65.

60 Arulsamy, *Religion for a New Society…*, 10.

61 J. Chellappa Packiaraj, "Process of Ageing in Hindu-Asramic System", in *Gurukul Journal of Theological Studies* IX/1&2 (1999): 73-76.

there is no much evidence for them to become the *sannyāsins*.[62] In the same manner a *Vaiśya* becoming either *vānaprastha* or *sannyāsa* has been a distant possibility. Hence, it is argued, "… the rejection of renunciation is tantamount to a rejection of equality and anti-structural dissent. This follows from the … hierarchy."[63] Equality is achievable only in the world of the renouncer and abolition of differences and hierarchy is a spiritual possibility for a renouncer. So *āśrama* implies that equality is 'otherworldly' and non-hierarchy doesn't make any sense for ordinary people during *gṛhastha*.[64]

Thirdly, *āśrama* scheme of Old age in Hinduism is viewed from a male perspective. Old people lived in India in 'perilous circumstances.'[65] If the wife shares the higher values of the husband, she accompanies her husband to the forest during *vānaprastha* stage of life.[66] The great women like Anasuya and Lopamudra are said to accompany their husbands to the forest.[67] However, *sannyāsa* is meant only for the male of Brahmins alone. Thus old age in *āśrama* scheme may find wanting from a gender perspective as it excludes women in the higher spiritual stage.

Implications

Notwithstanding the limitations it bears, *āśrama* scheme that deals with the affairs of the elderly may be viewed as one of the ancient views on the contentment of life even in old age, designed on a spiritual frame work for a purposeful life, yielding to gerotranscendence.

Although, the *āśrama* scheme expects individuals to live without the support of others and maintain one's own life till the end thereby to keep a balance of welfare and social harmony, it is the responsibility of the society to extend help to the ageing community irrespective of the caste or *varṇa*. These responsibilities need to be taught in the *brahmacārya* or student stage. It is the *dharma* or debt of the *gṛhastha* individuals to look after those who are in *vānaprastha* and *sannyāsa* stages of life. Gradual withdrawal from the worldly affairs is essential for all. But how far they will be able to spend the time

---

62 T. R. Venkatarama Sastri, "The Smrtis: Their Outlook and Character", *The Cultural Heritage of India* vol. II (Calcutta: The Ramakrishna Mission Institute of Culture, 2001), 332.

63 Joseph Chittooparampil, *A Cultural Hermeneusis on Caste Culture, its Discontents and Politics of Culture* (Delhi: ISPCK, 2005, 125-126, Quoted from S. M. Parish, *Hierarchy and its Discontents* (Delhi: Oxford, 1997), 49-50.

64 Chittooparampil, *A Cultural Hermeneusis on Caste Culture…,* 126.

65 Usha Menon, "Old Age and Hinduism," *Oxford Bibliographies*, Available at https://www.oxfordbibliographies.com/view/document/obo-9780195399318/obo-9780195399318-0211.xml#obo-9780195399318-0211-div1-0004 (accessed on 25/08/2020).

66 Radhakrishnan, *The Hindu View of Life…*, 63.

67 Sastri, "The Smrtis: Their Outlook and Character…, 332.

gracefully in meditation, study of scripture and worship to embrace the *mokṣa* in dignity depend on the society in which the main actors are the *gṛhasthas*.[68]

Many Hindu organizations today engage to help the aged to meet the challenges of both physiological and psycho-moral problems of the aged. Although the intergenerational joint family still remains as the major place of residence and care for the elderly in India, the state and private institutions and many individuals increasingly own responsibility of looking after the aged.[69] Caring for the aged is perceived as "a fundamental part of a reciprocal intergenerational cycle and form of moral religious duty or *dharma*."[70] However, in contemporary India one witnesses a sudden leap in the number of 'non-traditional-joint-family based ageing' in the form of the old age homes offering care for the aged. Sarah Lamb observes, "Many old-age homes position themselves as modern sites for offering *seva* (respectful care) and forest-dwelling lifestyle to today's older people."[71]

Christian Adaptation

In the light of gerotranscendence, the old age in *āśrama* scheme may be perceived as a period of preparation towards the ultimate goal of life that can result in graceful ageing. This spiritual ideal may be utilized as a common property of humanity by all, irrespective of religious affinity, for the cause of the aged. The main concerns of life during *vānaprastha* are *dharma* and *mokṣa*. One devotes oneself to intellectual activities and meditation besides leading a life of self-control and friendliness.[72] Both husband and wife dedicate themselves in *tapas* and try to find the answer to the question on the mystery of life. It is the period of freedom, experimentation of spirituality and yogic discipline. "It is the continuation of *Grihasta* [*sic.*] but with mature relationship between husband and wife, both seeking salvation through non-attachment, meditation and *yoga*."[73] Considering it as a period of retirement, Chenchiah, one of the renowned members of the 'Madras Rethinking Group', is said to suggest that a new purpose in life can be experienced by the retired people by embracing *vānaprasthāśramadharma*. If *vānaprastha-sannyāsāśramas* can be viewed from gerotranscendence perspective, Indian Christians may be able to

---

68 Packiaraj, "Process of Ageing in Hindu-Asramic System…, 73-76.

69 Sarah Lamb, "Cultural and Moral Values Surrounding Care and (In) Dependence in Late Life: Reflections from India in an Era of Global Modernity," *Care Management Journals* 6/2 (Summer, 2005), 80.

70 Sarah Lamb, "Hinduism Teaching and Aging", *Encyclopaedia of Gerontology and Population Aging*, ed. by Danan Gu and Mathew E. Dupre, 1, Available at https://doi.org/10.1007/978-3-319-69892-2_144-1 (accessed on 25/08/2020).

71 Sarah Lamb, "Hinduism Teaching and Aging…., 2.

72 Tiwari and Pandey, "The Indian Concepts of Lifestyle…, 288-292.

73 P. Victor Premsagar, "Vanaprasthasrama Dharma…, 17.

adapt and imply the essence of these schemes of life for the welfare and well being of the aged in the Christian church and appropriate them for her mission to the elderly for a positive ageing.

Conclusion

Hinduism considers old age as a 'life phase.' Spirituality of ageing as seen in *āśrama* scheme and in gerotranscendence can be taken into account to deal with the issues of the aged. It is true that religion has "both a palliative and a preventative effect for older adults."[74] As India is known for its richness of religiosity and spirituality, utilizing the spiritual resources like *vānaprastha-sannyāsa* scheme of life may be vital to instill graceful ageing. As gerotranscendence is aptly defined as "a shift from a materialistic and pragmatic world view to a more cosmic and transcendent one,"[75] *āśrama* scheme of life can be made known for a better conception of the aged in Indian contexts. In *āśrama* scheme, old age and death are neither the end nor opposed to life, rather part of the reality of soul, the life, the whole. Hence, perceiving *vānaprastha-sannyāsāśramas* as gerotranscendence is a viable option for a purposeful or graceful ageing approach in the Indian context.

---

74 Melvin A. Kimble, et.al. (eds.), *Aging, Spirituality and Religion: A Handbook* (Minneapolis: Fortress Press,1995), 5.

75 Arjan W. Braam, et.al., "Cosmic Transcendence and Framework of Meaning in Life: Patterns Among Older Adults in The Netherlands," in *The Journals of Gerontology: Series B* 61/3 (May, 2006): S121.

12

Familial and Community Care in *Vṛddhāvastha*[1] Socio-religious *Jarā-śāstra*[2] from Classical Hinduism

Wilson Paluri

Introduction

'Healthy ageing', 'Active Ageing', 'Ageing with Confidence', and 'Happy Ageing are some concepts popularized today that shows the paradox regarding how we view old age and how we actually age. Age is not just a biological function of the number of years that one lives, or the physiological changes the body goes through during the life course. It is also a product of the social norms and expectations that apply to each stage of life. Ageing, hence, represents the wealth of life experiences that shapes one's life in society. Each culture has a certain set of expectations and assumptions about ageing, which are part of socialization. The varied dimensions of ageing (*jarā*) in India can sociologically be understood as a series of transition from one set of social roles to another, and such roles are structured by the socio-religious system.[3]

Social gerontology[4] suggests that *jarā* not just reflects the physiological process of growing older, but also our attitude towards and belief about the

---

1 *Vṛddhāvastha* is a Sanskrit compound consisting of the terms *vṛddha* (old) and *avastha* (state). It refers to the state of 'old age'. https://www.wisdomlib.org/definition/vriddhavastha (accessed on 25/08/2020).

2 In this paper the term *Jarā-śāstra* is used for gerontology. Here *Jarā* means 'ageing' and *śāstra* means 'scientific treatment of the subject.'

3 Lekshmi Nair, "Aging in India – A Conceptual Clarification in the Background of Globalization" in *European Scientific Journal*, 10.2 (Jan. 2014), 379.

4 Social gerontology refers to a specialized field of gerontology that examines the sociological aspects of ageing. It focuses on developing a broad understanding of the experiences of

ageing process. The attitude towards the elderly has not just been affected by our religious worldview but also by large societal changes that have happened over the past century. Researchers recognize that urbanization and modernization have contributed greatly to lower the influence and prestige that elderly people once held. Older people are not as essential to the economic survival of their families today as they were in the past. The advancement of medical sciences and high-quality medical care has prolonged human life and has provided a new meaning to *vṛddhāvastha* in the society. Yet, there are other aspects of the ageing experience depending on class, caste, gender and other social factors, which needs greater attention today. It is necessary that in addition to the physical, the psychological and social significance is also taken into account.

The socio-religious *jarā-śāstra* is an exploration into a religious dimension of this social phenomenon to help us to understand *vṛddhāvastha* and *jarā* from the perspective of religion and from the viewpoint of the elderly in a given community. Certain pertinent questions to be addressed in this regard are: What do we learn from the socio-religious gerontology about ageing process and the situation of elderly in an Indian family and society? What does scripture and tradition teach us about *vṛddhāvastha* and *jarā*? How does the understanding of ageing help us in the change of our attitude towards our elders?

Elderly in an Indian Family

The studies show that the growing concern related to the problem of ageing in India today is the changing family and kinship bonds. Close family ties that offered social security and care to the elderly have gradually weakened over the past decades under the pressure of urbanization, modernization and value change.[5] In traditional Indian culture, elders were revered and respected in society and old age was not at all a problem. There were strong social supporting systems and observances with regard to elder care in Indian culture and society. The elderly actively participated in religious and social activities. Their counsel was highly valued in familial and community matters. Their status in the family and society was reinforced by their rights over the finances and property. But the rapid social changes in society are showing the complete

---

people at specific ages, like mental and physical well-being, and also age-specific concerns like the process of dying.

5 T. M. Dak, "Changing kinship and family patterns and vulnerability of aged in India" in: *Life in Twilight Years*, ed. by Indirani Chakravarti (Calcutta: Kwality Book Company, 1997), 91.

disintegration of traditional family system and loss of familial care for the elderly.[6]

The growing tendency towards urbanization and modernization is promoting individualism and commercialization of the value patterns among younger generations, which rates the significance of the elderly in the family on the basis of their usefulness. Most of the weak, unemployed, uneducated older people are seen as useless and are abandoned by the family. Laura Spinney observes that at large religious festivals like Maha Kumbh Mela, families ditch their older family members in the crowd. People go to the religious places like Allahabad during such mega festivity to wash their sins in the sacred river Ganges. But 'there is also a darker side to such large religious gatherings, as some take advantage of the swirling crowds to abandon elderly relatives.'[7] Such deliberate abandoning happens more often to the elderly widows who end up in government-run shelter. Conditions are notoriously bad in these homes, however, and many prefer to remain on the streets begging. There is another group that has predominantly women, whose families no longer want to support them, and they are brought to the holy cities like Varanasi and Vrindavan, because, in Hindu religion, to die in these holy places is to achieve *mokṣa*.[8]

With the advancing age, most elders lose their family headship roles and as a result there is a corresponding decline in their status and power in the family. This change results in serious shrinkage of quality care for the elderly and makes them vulnerable.[9] Jean Dreze, who is a strong advocate of social security pension for the elderly, states that, apart from the abandoned elderly men and women, there are thousands of women who are living with their sons and are as good as abandoned, literally kept on a starvation diet. 'The comfort of the elderly often takes the back seat' even in relatively well-off families. Hence, he says, "in the harsh lives of the elderly, the pension is a chance to enjoy small comforts – relieving their pain with some medicine, winning the affection of grandchildren or simply avoiding hunger."[10]

In most Indian families, looking after aged parents is considered as the duty of the son (eldest son in particular). According to the Hindu ideal derived

---

6 P. K. Nayar, "Changing Role of the Family in the Care of the Elderly" in: *Ageing in India*, ed. by S. D. Gokhale et.al. (Bombay: Somaiya Publications Pvt. Ltd., 1999), 170.

7 Laura Spinney, "At Largest Religious Festival, some Abandon Elderly" https://www.nationalgeographic.com/news/2013/2/130223-culture-travel-religion-india-maha-kumbh-mela-world-women-widow-hindu-festival/ (accessed on 19/09/2020).

8 Laura Spinney, "At Largest Religious Festival, Some Abandon Elderly."

9 D. Jamuna, "Elder Care in India: Conflicting Tradition and Modernization" in *Aging Societies in a New Millennium* (Honolulu: Proceedings of 3rd International Conference of IAHSA, 1999), 34.

10 Jean Dreze, "Beyond Small Mercies" in: *The Hindu (eNewspaper)*, 10th July 2016.

from *Manusmriti*, a woman should be looked after by the male relatives until the end of her life, with responsibility shifting from her father to her husband and then to her son. But, the reality is often very different. Such care has become difficult due to the host of the changes taking place in the family and society. Migration of children in search of occupational opportunities and economic burden has drawn them away from their aged parents.

In the light of these and many other key issues related to elderly in Indian society, it is important to evolve an indigenous elder care model which would suggest incorporation of positive elements into an overall family and community care system. An exploration into religious traditions to understand the ageing process and to bring changes in our attitude towards the elderly would be a step towards this goal.

Vṛddhāvastha and *Jarā* in Religious Texts

The Sanskrit term *jarā* or *jaras* is commonly used to refer to 'becoming old', 'worn out', 'producing decay', 'consuming', 'and general debility consequent on old age' and others. The term *jarā* is derived from the Sanskrit root *jṛsvayōhana* which is defined as *vaya kṛta śḷathā māṁsādayā* according to the Vācaspathyam,[11] which means that the muscles and the other tissues get loosened under the influence of ageing. Hence, the term *jarā* indicates the decline of *dhātus* (fundamental elements in the body), *indriyas* (sense organs), mental faculties, and virility in the later period of an individual.[12] It indicates the physiological aspect of ageing.

Jarā is mentioned in a couple of passages in Bhagvad Gītā indicating varied implications. In BG. 2.13, *jarā* is mentioned in reference to the embodied soul that goes through childhood, youth and old age (*jarā*) without undergoing any change. In BG. 7.29 Krishna advises Arjuna to take refuge under him in order to attain liberation from old age and death (*jarā-maraṇa*). BG. 13.8-12 encourages one to reflect upon the evils and miseries produced due to birth, old age (*jarā*), sickness and death. Such reflections would cause indifference towards sense-pleasure, which eventually will lead to immortality. Similarly BG. 14.20 suggests that a person could be freed from birth, death, decay (*jarā*) and pain, and would attain immortality if he/she goes beyond the influence of three *guṇas* (*sattva, rajas* and *tamas*). These passages indicate that body decays and perishes as a person approaches old age, but the soul in its spiritual pursuit attains immortality. In Bhagvad Gītā, '*jarā*' is used to indicate both 'old age' and 'ageing processes. Where *jarā* is mentioned in Bhagvad Gītā and Dharmaśāstras in connection to socio-religious aspects and spiritual

11 *Vachaspatyam (Brihat Sanskritabhidhanam)*, compiled by Sri Taranatha Tarkavachaspati (Varanasi: The Chowkhamba Sanskrit Series Office, 1962), 3058.

12 Sujit K. Dalai and Laxmikant Dwivedi, "The Concept of Jarā in Ayurveda," *Aryavaidyan* 18/4 (May-July 2005), 203-4.

experiences, it is used to indicate biological and physiological changes of *vṛddhāvastha* in Ayurveda literature.

The term *jarā* has a reference in Ayurveda[13] (science of life) and Rasaśāstra[14] (chemistry and alchemy) in connection with senility and ageing process. Ayurveda indicates that *jarā* (senility) is a natural process (*svābhāvika vyādhi*). It suggests that *Rasāyana* or *Vayassthāpana* (longevity promoters) drugs should be introduced during young and middle age to prevent premature senility.[15]

Caraka-samhita[16] states that *jarāvastha* or *vṛddhāvastha* begins from 60 years marked by diminishing strength of *dhātus* (fundamental elements in the body), *indriyas* (sense organs), and mental faculties. Suśruta-samhita[17] classifies *jarā* as *kālajā* (timely, i.e., around 70 years) and *akālajā* (untimely).[18] *Kālajā* appears at proper time even after protection and *akālajā* appears before proper time due to improper care and prevention.[19]

Ayurveda contemplates *jarā* as a natural and inexorable process that ultimately ends in death. Some aspects of the aetiology of *jarā* could be drawn from Ayurveda such as *swabhāvoparamavada* (theory of natural destruction),[20]

---

13 Āyurveda is a branch of Indian science dealing with medicine, herbalism, taxology, anatomy, surgery, alchemy are related topics. Traditional practice of Āyurveda in ancient India dates back to nearly first millennium BC. https://www.wisdomlib.org/ayurveda (accessed on 28/08/2020).

14 Rasaśāstra is an important branch of Ayurveda, specialising in chemical interactions with herbs, metals and minerals. Some texts combine yogic and tantric practices with various alchemical operations. The goal of Rasaśāstra is not only to preserve and prolong life, but also to bestow wealth upon humankind. https://www.wisdomlib.org/rasashastra (accessed on 28/08/2020).

15 "Jara" https://www.wisdomlib.org/definition/jara (accessed on 28/08/2020).

16 Caraka-samhita is an ancient Indian Ayurvedic text on internal medicine written by Acharya Charak. It is believed to have arisen around 400-200 BCE. It not only provides knowledge about Ayurveda in its totality but also explains the logic and philosophy on which this system of medicine is based.

17 Sushruta-samhita is written almost at the same time period as the Caraka-samhita, and refers to the field of Ayurvedic surgery (shalya). Even as it deals with the practice and theory of surgery, it is an important source of Ayurvedic aphorisms.

18 There are different causative factors in our day-to-day life that accelerates our ageing process – changes in environment; consumption of food cultivated with chemical fertilizers and modern technology; accumulation of toxin in the body; psychological stress and other.

19 Keshari Bipin Bihari and Goswami P. K., "Conceptual Study of Jara (aging) and its Management in Ayurveda w.s.r. to Triphala Rasayana," *Unique Journal of Ayurvedic and Herbal Medicines* 2/2 (March-April 2014): 15.

20 This theory suggests that the process of deterioration occurs naturally. This is nature's unique process.

kāla (time factor),[21] *śarīra vriddhikarabhava-abhava* (depletion of growth factor),[22] role of *tridosha* (three biological energies)[23] and role of *agni*,[24] *dhātus*[25] and *srotas*[26] in ageing. Apart from the knowledge of these causes of ageing, Ayurveda prescribes *Rasāyana* (*rasa* means 'nutrition' and *āyana* means 'promotion') *Tantra* for the geriatric health care. *Rasāyana* therapy is a specialized procedure practiced in the form of rejuvenative measures, dietary regimen and health promoting methods. A person who goes through this therapy attains longevity, improved memory, intelligence, freedom from diseases, optimum strength of physique and senses.[27] There is enough attention given to make the ageing process and old age efficient and productive in Ayurveda and Rasaśāstra.

Hence, *jarā* in scriptures is seen as the anatomical, physiological, biochemical and functional changes that occur in a person as per the time. Ageing is not a disease, but the risk of developing disease is increased as part of ageing. The ancient sages developed a system of Ayurveda to overcome the physical and emotional distress and suffering attached to ageing. The texts such as Bhagvad Gītā, on the other, suggest spiritual pursuit and immortality as part of the ageing process.

Alternative Elderly Care Model: Re-visiting Socio-religious Principles

Hindu society is governed by social factors like classes, castes (*varna*) and different stages of life (*āśrama*) that directs a person's life and determines the moral imperative for him/her. *Jarā* doesn't happen in isolation, but is a shared feeling of the socially organized groups namely family, peer group and society. A study of important socio-religious concepts like *saṁskāras* (sacraments),

21 According to this theory, modification is the characteristic feature of time. *Jarā* is a phase of life that occurs by the effect of time.

22 It means that the absence of favourable conditions for growth may lead to ageing process.

23 *Tridosha* (*vata, pitta and kapha*) is the most important factor in maintaining good health and production of diseases. *Doshas* exists in the body all the time, but it varies as per the age, day or night period and after taking meals. *Vata-dosha* dominates during old age. *Vata-dosha* by nature decreases luster of skin, lessens body strength, dries and decays the body and hastens ageing process.

24 Body tissues are regularly nourished by dietary substances and *agni* is said to be responsible for the conversion of dietary substances into tissue elements. In the old age, *vishamagni* affects the digestion and creates under nourishment of the tissues.

25 During the old age, quantity as well as quality of *dhatu* (body energy) decreases causing the aging process and diseases in old age.

26 The main function of *srotas* (channels of body) is to transfer the body fluids, which is affected in the old age due to various reasons.

27 Keshari Bipin Bihari and P. K. Goswami, "Conceptual Study of Jara (aging) and its Management in: Ayurveda w.s.r. to Triphala Rasayana", 15-17.

varṇāśrama (different castes and stages of life), *puruṣārtha* (goals of life), *panch-mahā-yajñas* (five great sacred duties), *karma* (action) and *saṁsāra* (rebirth) helps in understanding the societal norms for *vṛddhāvastha* and *jarā*. These norms were set in highly Brahminical patriarchal context applicable to the men of high caste. Klaus Klostermaier states that the Vedic religion became increasingly patriarchal and later Hinduism clearly disadvantaged women in many respects.[28] Theoretically, these principles may not be directly applicable to women or a person from a low caste, nonetheless, we consider reflecting upon them, as society is generally governed by these norms.

The task, here, would be to rediscover these principles in modern context from the perspective of elderly care to reclaim the perceptible space and respect for elderly in the family and society.

Caring for Spiritual Fulfilment

Hinduism places utmost importance to *mokṣa* (attainment of spiritual liberation) as the ultimate goal or end sought through human endeavour. *Dharma* (righteous living/discharge of duties), *artha* (acquisition of wealth and property), *kāma* (gratification of desires) are the other three *puruṣārthas* (goals of life). N. K. Devaraja observes that *sannyāsa āśrama* and *mokṣa* were not part of original Vedic ideal. *Sannyāsa* was part of the śramaṇa[29] tradition and was resisted by the Brāhmins initially. It was ultimately accepted by 'later Hinduism as formulated by Manu', and this acceptance must have been facilitated by the emphasis on *mokṣa* as the final goal of life.[30] In the course of time, however, all the six orthodox philosophical schools as well as Buddhism and Jainism accepted *mokṣa* as the supreme goal.

Among the *puruṣārtha*, *dharma* and *mokṣa* are considered to have spiritual values and *artha* and *kāma* as having material values. *Dharma*, *artha* and *kāma* pertain to *pravṛtti* (engagement) with its goal of *abhyudaya* (material well-being) and *mokṣa* belongs to *nivṛtti* (disengagement) with its goal of *niḥśreyasa* (greatest good).[31] It is generally understood that *artha* and *kāma* could be the goals achievable during the adulthood, and *dharma* and *mokṣa* are to be pursued throughout especially during *vṛddhāvastha*.

Louis Renou provides another theoretical classification 'based on the phases of human activity: *dharma* as moral activity; *artha* as interested activity; and *kāma* as playful activity. These three ends (*puruṣārtha*) reflect the three

28 Klaus K. Klostermaier, *Hinduism: A Short Introduction* (Oxford: Oneworld Publications, 2006), 27.

29 The term śramaṇa is used to refer to non-Brahminical tradition or ascetic tradition.

30 N. K. Devaraja, *Hinduism and the Modern Age* (New Delhi: Islam and the Modern Age Society, 1975), 16-17.

31 *Sanatana-Dharma* (Madras: The Theosophical Publishing House, 1966), 233.

functions that are subordinate to a fourth end: *mokṣa* or liberation.'[32] *Mokṣa* being the spiritual activity draws greater attention during the ageing process. The activity theory of social gerontology suggests that for individuals to enjoy their *vṛddhāvastha* and feel satisfied, they must maintain activities and find a replacement for the statuses and associated roles they have left behind as they aged.[33] Hinduism offers the morals of *dharma* and *mokṣa* to such older people who are seeking meaning and purpose of life in their *vṛddhāvastha*. It is obvious that even such spiritual activities could be enjoyed by only those elderly people who have the financial security and who enjoy filial piety in their *vṛddhāvastha*. In today's modernized India most of the elderly struggle to meet their daily needs and don't have such pleasure of renouncing all physical activities to just pursue spiritual life.

Spiritual activity is seen as a journey towards maturing (2 Cor. 4:16-17) and bearing fruits of righteousness (Ps. 92:12-14) in the Bible. Proverbs (16:31; 20:29) indicates that experience is the splendour of *vṛddhāvastha* that is obtained by following *dharma* (righteous path). Psalmist (Ps. 73:26) praises God for being the strength as body keeps failing in the *vṛddhāvastha*. Creating a space for such spiritual fulfilment, for the older people in the family and society, needs greater attention today.

Hindu scriptures prescribe certain *saṁskāras* (sacraments) as ritualistic tools for the attainment of physical and spiritual purity as a person grows older. The series of *saṁskāras* are ritual presentation of various stages of life from the pre-natal to the post-mortem existence of an individual.[34] *Saṁskāras* helped in the "purification of human life, facilitated the development of personality, imparted sanctity and importance to human body, consecrated all material and spiritual aspirations of human and ultimately prepared an individual for an easy and happy exit from this world of complexities and problems."[35] The *jarā* combined with such religious beliefs, social customs and rules regarding health and hygiene brings stability and happiness to the person who is ageing.

Saṁskāra ceremony invites many persons including spiritual gurus, learned persons, elderly ones and others, which provides a great opportunity for younger generation to learn cultural and social values of a family.[36]

32 Louis Renou, *Hinduism* (New York: George Braziller, 1962), 54.

33 R. Havinghurst, B. Neugarten and S. Tobin, "Patterns of Aging," in *Middle Age and Aging*, ed. by B. Neugarten (Chicago: University of Chicago Press, 1968), 169.

34 Samarendra Saraf, *Hindu Caste System and the Ritual Idiom* (Delhi: Mittal Publications, 1986), 130-31.

35 Rajbali Pandey, *Hindu Samskaras: Socio-religious Study of the Hindu Sacraments* (Delhi: Motilal Banarsidass, 1882), 277-78.

36 Anukriti Guar, "Critical Analysis of *BalaSamskara* w.s.r. to Developmental Milestones in Children: A Review Study," *Journal of Ayurveda and Integrated Medical Sciences* 3/2 (Mar-Apr. 2018): 89.

Unfortunately, the urbanization and migration of young couples to other places has reduced the importance of *saṁskāra* ceremonies and deprived the elderly of participating in such auspicious family programs. There is no time for such rituals in the busy materialistic life of a person, which equally affects his/her social life and spiritual growth. There is growing evidence that social participation protects against morbidity and mortality. On the contrary, in many traditional families, elderly, especially widows are asked to abstain from such family *saṁskāra* celebrations altogether.

In both Old Testament and New Testament, the community leaders emerged from a larger set of older people. The Pastoral Epistles (1 and 2 Timothy, Titus) supports the fact that older people were to exercise leadership in their respective communities by their lifestyle, teaching and counsel. Carter notes the active participation of older people of faith in relation to their communities, where *vṛddhāvastha* was not a time to be cast off or retired.[37] The continuity theory of gerontology suggests that older people try to preserve and maintain internal and external characteristics such as values, personality, preferences and behaviour patterns, throughout life, despite changes in their health or life circumstances.[38] After establishing religious and cultural values older people continue to provide on-going models for future generations, which need to be recognized and appreciated.

Caring through Community Participation

Hinduism is distinguished from other religions on the basis of two important social institutions – *varṇa* (the system of caste)[39] and *āśrama* (the stages of life).[40] They operate in terms of *pravṛtti* (engagement) and *nivṛtti* (disengagement) from worldly life. In the process of ageing, 'the first two

---

37 W. Carter, "New Testament and Aging: Survey and suggestions for Future Research," *Journal of Religion, Spirituality and Aging* 21/1-2 (2009): 65.

38 Kara Rogers, "Aging: Life Process" Available at: https://www.britannica.com/science/aging-life-process (accessed on 22/08/2020).

39 The ancient Indian sources make a sharp distinction between the two terms – *Varna* or class and *jati* or caste proper. However, the later sociologists have connected *varna* with caste, and it is used to explain that the Hindu society is divided into watertight compartments to which one belongs by birth. These commensal and endogamous units called castes are arranged within an overarching fourfold hierarchy of *varṇas* – Brāhmin, Kṣatriya, Vaiśya and Śūdra. Cf. A. L. Basham, *The Wonder That Was India* (London: Sidgwick & Jackson, 1988), 148.

40 Based on the early scriptures such as Aitareya Brāhmaṇa 33.11 and Chāndogya Upaniṣad 2.23.1, the different stages of life of a person are divided into *brahmacharya* (life as a celibate student until one turns twenty-five), *gṛhastha* (life of a householder until one reaches the age if fifty), *vānaprastha* (life of retirement in a hermitage) and *sannyāsa* (life of a wandering ascetic till one dies). Cf. P. V. Kane, *History of Dharmasastra*, vol. 2, part 1, (Poona: Bhandarkar Oriental Research Institute, 1974), 420.

stages of life, those of the student (*brahmacharya*) and of the householder (*gṛhastha*), represent the phase of participation in worldly activities, and those of the hermit (*vānaprastha*) and the renunciant (*sannyāsa*) represent the phase of withdrawal from them."[41] Śaṅkara in his commentary on the Bhagvad Gīta states that "it is the twofold Vedic Religion of *Works* and *Renunciation* that maintains order in the universe."[42] The two ways of life – one of action (*pravṛtti*) and the other of renunciation (*nivṛtti*) have come to be recognized as the different phases of ageing. More or less the same practice is found in Buddhism and Jainism, for there too one could disengage from the worldly activity in the later age. The disengagement theory, an earliest gerontological theory, suggests that withdrawing from society and social relationships is a natural part of growing old.[43] Such 'disengagement', however, should be a 'voluntary act' by the concerned person, which in no way indicates his/her *isolation* and *alienation* by the family and society.

In India, even when a family is composed of four or five generations, the family system functioned in such a way that nobody was neglected and respectful relationships existed on a hierarchical basis; the older the person, the greater the respect. The effect of the global economic reorientation has changed this scenario and has shifted the focus of elderly from being part of social unit to economic unit,[44] which has left them alienated and abandoned. Those who run old-age homes say that children have no time to visit their elderly parents after they dump them in these homes.[45] It is completely opposite of what *nivṛttimarga* proposes – disengagement/ renunciation of the world for spiritual pursuit. The spiritual aspect of *nivṛtti* needs to be rediscovered to provide a new meaning to the detached life of an elderly in the community.

Arvind Sharma makes interesting observations by interpreting *varṇa* and *āśrama* in modern terms. He looks at *all* of *varṇa* (*brāhmin, kṣatriya, vaiśya and śūdra*) as contained in *every* individual (*sārvavārṇikatā*) instead of every individual being comprised within one particular *varṇa* at a given time.[46] Similarly, *āśrama* could also be viewed as an internal aspect of a

41 Arvind Sharma, *Classical Hindu Thought: An Introduction* (New Delhi: Oxford University Press, 2000), 184.

42 *The Bhagvadgita with the Commentary of Sri Sankaracharya*, trans. by Alladi Mahadeva Sastry (Madras: Samata Books, 1985), 2.

43 W.A. Achenbaum and V. L. Bengtson, "Re-engaging the Disengagement Theory of Aging: On the History and Assessment of Theory," *Development in Gerontology* 34/6 (1994): 760.

44 Lekshmi Nair, "Aging in India – A Conceptual Clarification in the Background of Globalization," 385.

45 Laura Spinney, "At Largest Religious Festival, some Abandon Elderly."

46 Arvind Sharma argues that doctrine of *sārvavārṇikatā* imposes fourfold obligation on every Hindu: 1) As a Brāhmin every Hindu must have minimal familiarity with the Hindu scriptures and rituals; 2) As a Kṣatriya every Hindu must undergo compulsory military

person's daily life in his/her engagement (*pravṛtti*) in the world during the day and disengagement (*nivṛtti*) from such activity during the night.[47] All the *varṇas* and *āśramas* converge and merge in the individual making him/her accountable in terms of all at the most basic level. Socially, however, it is understood that individuals should belong to different vocations irrespective of birth and stages of life.[48] Bhagvad Gītā informs that though there is an emphasis on the renunciated life, the abandonment of active social life is not estimated at any stage of life (including *sannyāsa*).[49] An active productive life should be throughout pursued by everyone including an older person, but in a spirit of absolute detachment (*niṣkāma-karma*). The activity theory of gerontology proposes that the participation in informal activities is most effective in the later life satisfaction. Activity levels and social involvement is the key to the ageing process and happiness.[50] One way of changing society's negative attitude towards ageing and the aged is to motivate the elderly to participate in more activities at all levels and in all areas of the society.

There is a need to develop strong intergenerational relationship to give equal importance to the well-being of all in a family. *Pitṛ yajña*, one of the five *yajñas* (sacred duties), directs us to one such principle.[51]*Pitṛ yajña* is the

---

training as well as experience political empowerment by participating in the political process; 3) As a Vaiśya every Hindu must undergo required vocational preparation and pursue a vocation; and 4) As a Śūdra every Hindu must perform some form of manual labour or service. Cf. Arvind Sharma, *Hinduism For Our Times*, 46.

47 Arvind Sharma explains this minisculization or interiorization of the *āśrama* in terms of treating each day as encapsulating a lifetime. In the morning a person is in the stage of brahmacharya spending time in the matutinal study of the scriptures; the forenoon and afternoon are spent as a gṛhastha earning a livelihood to run the house; in the evening one spends time in quiet contemplation with one's wife an in vānaprastha; and finally before retiring for the night one meditates on the highest truth divesting oneself completely of the distractions of daily life to accomplish the sanyāsa stage. Cf. Arvind Sharma, *Hinduism For Our Times*, 48.

48 Arvind Sharma, *Hinduism For Our Times*, 57.

49 M. Hiniyana, *The Essentials of Indian Philosophy* (London: George Allen & Unwin, 1948), 52.

50 B. Lemon, V. Bengtson and J. Petersen, "An Exploration of the Activity Theory of Aging: Activity Types and Life Expectation among In-movers to a Retirement Community" in *Journal of Gerontology*, 27 (1972), 511-23.

51 The Hindu scriptures teach that in the ordinary course of life, a person does many actions that cause harm to other beings. To atone for such actions, five *yajñas* (sacred duties) have been prescribed, which are: *deva yajña* (duty towards gods), *pitṛ yajña* (duty towards our parents and ancestors), *bhūta yajña* (duty towards other living beings), *manushya yajña* (duty towards human beings) and *rishi yajña* (duty towards sages and gurus). All these five duties are considered equally important and performing more of one *yajña* cannot compensate for the non-performance of the other duties. Cf. Klaus K. Klostermaier, *Hinduism: A Short Introduction*, 29-30.

reverential bonding with parents, elders and the fostering of family values for the unity and well-being of the family. Caring for parents and elderly is an important aspect of family life. Compulsory ceremonies like *shrāddha* and prayers to the ancestors during the time of special occasions are prescribed in the scriptures to encourage the filial piety among the family members. Both as a virtue and duty one is expected to respect and care for the elderly in the family. *Matrdevo bhavah, pitṛdevo bhavah*...(may mother be a god to you; may father be a god to you..) is the ideal to be promoted to show honour and respect towards the older people.

Harris notes that honour for parents "is equated with worship and awe" in the Bible.[52] Respect for the elderly arises out of concerns rooted in the nature of God. This pairing of an older person's authority alongside God's own authority is repeated when Pentateuchal law commands that "You shall rise before the aged, and defer to the old; and you shall fear your God" (Lev. 19:32).[53] Scripture equates old age with maturity and wisdom (Pro. 16:31; Prov. 20:29). Age brings wisdom, which itself deserves honour. The symbolic interactionist theory developed by Lars Tornstam proposes the idea that as people age they transcend the limited views of life they held in earlier periods. They become less self-centred and feel more peaceful and connected to the natural world.[54] Older people must be regarded as the repositories of knowledge in the community "with them being the natural reference point for transmission of accrued religious knowledge, experiential wisdom, and conceptions of corporate identity."[55]

Conclusion

Among common people, *vṛddhāvastha* and *jarā* is associated with the expectation of suffering and the negative feelings of fear and unpleasantness, rather than the expectation of joy and positive feeling of comfort and blessedness. A Comparative Christian feels assured of the place in heaven after death, whether he/she deserves it or not. The possibility that God in Christ has outplayed suffering and death, by experiencing and negating them, relativizes our suffering and reframes our death as transient and not permanent. Such hope gives new meaning to life, especially to the older people. But an ordinary

52 V. G. Harris, *Biblical Perspectives on Aging: God and the Elderly* (New York: The Haworth Press, 2008), 108.

53 V. G. Harris, *Biblical Perspectives on Aging: God and the Elderly*, 102.

54 Lars Tornstam, *Gerotranscendence: A Developmental Theory of Positive Aging* (New York: Springer Publishing Company, 2005), 17.

55 Elizabeth MacKinlay, "Biblical Perspectives on Aging," in *Encyclopaedia of Gerontology and Population Aging*, ed. by Danan Gu and Matthew Dupre, (2019) Available at: https://link.springer.com/referenceworkentry/10.1007%2F978-3-319-69892-2_139-1 (accessed on 15/09/2020).

Hindu, even if he/she has accumulated enough merit in life through pious deeds or devotion to God, is not sure how his/her *karma* would work out eventually. As they approach old age, they begin to experience fear and anxiety about their afterlife. Death is a mysterious and serious aspect for many Hindus, which they prefer to avoid thinking about, rather than confronting it. In such a context, biblical understanding of renewed form of maturity, restoration to community life, honouring elders, and a capacity to challenge anxiety with trust in God would help the elderly end their life journey with comfort and joy.

Modern concerns around physical and cognitive decline, coupled with our perception of dignity as dependent upon productivity and independence, are profoundly challenged by the *elderly care model*, which offers communities new conception of care. A revisit to certain social-religious principles like *puruṣārtha*, *saṁskāras*, *pitṛ yajña*, *varṇa* and *āśrama* within the framework of elderly care provides constructive insights for families that have become more modernized and lost the family values. Such socio-religious gerontology based on the lessons derived from the scripture provides several alternatives in our approach to later life that deserves our respectful enquiry and implementation.

13

New Media
A Caregiver for the Aged

D. Samuel Sounderaraj Singh

Introduction

Access to New Media is becoming much prevalent in today's present scenario especially during the time of COVID-19. Here New Media refers to the combining of computer and Communication Technologies for example smart phones. Communication Technologies describes any electronic devices that help to produce, manipulate, store, communicate and/or disseminate information. This New Media helps even the *have-nots*[*] to catch up and plug in to this increasingly globalized and accessible system. This New Media is in largely used by people of all age group. Use of New Media becomes part and parcel of people's everyday life because it informs, instructs and becomes the own message makers of their life in the world. Human beings are born to learn till they leave this world. Age is no barrier and the greatest thing in life is to learn something new and for this any type of media can definitely help all the ages. Whether it is Television, radio, news paper or new media all are purely dedicated to educate people of all ages about every topic one is interested in or thinks of from science through to history, theology and current events. Hence, when one uses the media, his/her everyday life becomes a media-life. Apart from children, youth and adults, little is known about how ageing population use the new media in their daily lives and their familiarity with the technology and adaptability with such technologies. This paper attempts to focus on the methodological process of user-centered system design[1] in the daily lives of the aged, secondly in what ways does this new media help to prevent and alleviate

1 D. A. Norman, "Cognitive Engineering," in *User-Centered Systems Design*, edited by D. Norman and S. Draper (Hillsdale, NJ: Lawrence Erlbaum, 1986).

isolation and loneliness and finally how to create an interest to develop and retain socially-connected to live their best in this interactive era.

Definition of New Media

New Media is a comprehensive term in the academic field and termed in the beginning of the 21st century. This term New Media is a taken-for-granted concept when social-apps encompass the amalgamation of Mass Media such as film, images, music, spoken and written word, distributed with the power of computer technology. Any **media** content that is designed by the users and consumed by end-users on the Internet and can be accessed on multiple digital platforms is termed as New Media.

Key Principles of User-Centered System Design for the Aged

User-centered systems design (UCSD) is a process focusing on usability throughout the entire development process and further throughout the system life cycle.[2] Some of the key principles of User-centered design for the aged are:

- **a) Catch the User attention**–the area of action the aged are interested in or the context of use, the users' aim, tasks and needs should be a guide for early progress.
- **b) Create user participation**–individual users should actively partake, involve primarily and continuously throughout the entire process and throughout the lifecycle.
- **c) Make Simple design representations**–the design must be represented in such ways that it can be easily understood by users and all other stakeholders.
- **d) Use Prototyping**–begins with the prototypes and continuously should be used to visualize and evaluate ideas and find solutions in cooperation with the end users.
- **e) Methods customization**–the user-centered systems design process must be specified, adapted and/or implemented locally for the each individual.
- **f) A user-centered attitude**–should always be established.

Media and Ageing

Studies on ageing were done on the concept of age in relation to a variety of human developments. But communication research on media and ageing has been recognized only a little by several researchers. Kaluger and Kaluger for example, argue that biological processes of ageing are often tempered

2 Jan Gulliksen & Bengt Göransson, "Key principles for user-centered Systems Design," (2003). Available at: http://www.it.uu.se/research/hci/acsd/KeyPrinciplesPoster-v.1.2en.pdf (accessed, 10/10/2020).

by individual, social, economic and environmental differences.[3] Hurlock adds the possible effects of health, living conditions, social and marital status, education level, and gender on the ageing process.[4] The above quotes emphasis on life-position indicators of ageing that has received attention in the communication literature as well. Graney and Graney suggest that use of the mass media performs an important function in the lives of the elderly, when social contacts with others diminish in later life; the media are used to maintain social psychological satisfaction.[5] Schramm[6] and Cassata[7] support this notion that increased media use functionally counteracts the sense of alienation often experienced in later years.

Involving in social structure, standard of living, health conscious, economic and educational background as sociological and biographical factors affecting media use has been viewed as additional attention in the literature. Wenner[8] proposed that television viewing patterns are linked to elements of life-position. His factor-analytic study identified three types of viewers. Type-1 viewers were discriminating; they were socially mobile, oriented toward information programming, and married. Type-2 viewers used television for companionship and preferred not to watch alone. Type-3 viewers used television for companionship, as a time-killer, and as a topic for conversation; they lived alone or in retirement homes. The sudden causes of social isolation are varied and depend on individual circumstances such as a scattered family, the death of a partner, a chronic health condition, dishing sight or hearing are only some of the factors that can leave older people feeling alone. But for a decade, an array of technologies has changed the way many of us interact. Internet communication systems such as email and social networking sites like facebook and twitter have revolutionized personal communication for younger people not for the aged especially above 65s, many studies show that they have been largely excluded from this revolution and most have never used the internet.

---

3 G. Kaluger and M. F. Kaluger, *Human Development* (St. Louis: C.V. Mosby, 1979).

4 E. B. Hurlock, *Developmental Psychology* (New York: McGraw-Hill, 1975).

5 M. J. Graney, and E. E. Graney, "Communications Activity Substitutions in Aging," *Journal of Communication*, 24/4 (1974): 88-96.

6 W. Shramm, "Aging and Mass Communication," in *Aging and Society* (New York: Russell Sage, 1969).

7 M. Cassata, "A Study of the Mass Communication Behavior and the Social Disengagement of 177 members of the Age Center of New England," Unpublished Doctoral Dissertation, Indiana University, 1967.

8 L. Wenner, "Functional Analysis of TV viewing for Older Adults," *Journal of Broadcasting*, 20 (1976): 77-88.

Aged and the Barriers in New Media

New Media in common relies on computer-mediated communication and creates a platform with the purpose to inform the users, to create messages by the users, to share and to modify the content that the users receive. Moreover, this platform can be used to interact with other users via blogs, content communities, social networking sites or social worlds.[9] Considering the newness of the concept of New Media a considerable number of older adults suffer from functional limitations, such as limited cognitive and perceptual abilities[10] which hinder Elderly people from using New Media. Lee describes that the elderly people perceived four types of barriers such as intrapersonal, i.e., think that they (elders) are too old for it, functional barriers, i.e., think that they decline in memory, structural barriers, i.e., they think that the cost of a device is too much and interpersonal barriers, i.e., think that they need someone to teach them.[11] Also many think that they perceive a lack of code of social conduct in the online platform. These entire barriers make the elderly population to un-adopt and to un-use the New Media.

Aged Attitude towards the New Media

Elders think that online social norms differ from offline social contact and hesitate to access the New Media or to connect with others. In offline platforms, when connected the behavior of others will be quite formal except between friends, relatives and close acquaintances, whereas in the online platform, most contacts will be in informal behavior to communicate with them. Secondly, the elders think that the forms of self-disclosure and self-representation are different in offline and online in the New Media. Offline behavior is expected to be modest and polite. But in the online platform, it is widely acceptable to upload pictures of oneself as self-centered and embarrassing, and even as silly and empty-headed.[12]

Need for the Usability and Sociability for the Aged

How to draw the aged to a community? The reasons vary. Some want information or support, to interact with others, have fun, meet new people or

9 A. M. Kaplan and M. Haenlein, "Users of the world, Unite: The Challenges and Opportunities of social media," *Bus Horiz*, 53 (2009): 59-68.

10 N. Charness and W. R. Boot, "Aging and Information Technology Use," *Curr Dir Psychol Sci*, 18 (2009): 253-258.

11 P. Lee, *The Democratizations of Communication* (Cardiff: University of Wales Press, 1995).

12 V. Lehtinen, J. Nasanen and R. Sarvas, *A Little Silly and Empty-Headed: Older Adults Understandings of Social Networking Sites*, 23rd British HCI Group Annual Conference on People and Computers: Celebrating People and Technology (Cambridge: British Computer Society, 2009), 45-54.

voice their own ideas. Even religious participants come for some reason. Aged with attitude and goals appear to attract other aged people with similar goals and who are often like each other; this creates a stable community in which there is less aggression. Software to support the aged often lacks suitable functionality and usability because of three technical problem areas such as design, security and scalability to produce systems that can handle the aged. Jenny Preece[13] suggests when we talk about *design,* theories about culture and social activity in the *New Media* we lay the foundation for software design. But for the aged, identifying the best software in their local language to record histories of behavior, store communication and knowledge, explore the nature of interpersonal and mass communication and accurately track the number of people participating and with who is still to appear. About the *Security,* aged communities will be strong by how secure they are. Personal information of all kinds must be made secure, which means not only the device they use also the users remarks of them should be secured. *Scalability* refers to research priority, for the significant technical challenges and implications for sociability and usability for the aged. The research should include: How should we structure conversations for the aged? How to restrict online crowds and develop social protocols for the aged? What kind of online governance is needed to control inappropriate behaviors and to ensure fair practices of all kinds of information for the aged? These are the basic software supports largely for the aged populations to participate and to access New Media.

New Media A Caregiver for the Aged

There is a wide range of online platforms to access, some of which have special needs that influence the aged to use them and how they carry out their tasks. Identifying tasks and their sub-tasks helps the aged to ensure that New Media will provide appropriate usability. There are special requirements for health when one wants to identify the tasks for the aged. The fact that aged people differ from each other physically and mentally, but these differences are not taken into account in online UCSD when using the New Media. It is the responsibility of the care-takers at home to identify which online platforms influence the aged to user interfaces and behavior in the online system. At the same time those who give Home-care for elders is also called non-medical care at home. It is always good to allow the aged to remain in the comfort and security of themselves. New Media offers elders the opportunity to live life with more freedom flexibility, independence and comfort to consume a vast amount of information. Spending their ideal time with new media widens their universe, enabling them to interact with people who share their cares

13 Jenny Preece, *Online Communities Designing Usability, Supporting Sociability* (Chichester: John Wiley and Sons, 2000), 387-391.

and concerns. Socialization as always shares anything and everything with one another such as stories, experiences, gossip, recipes etc. interacting with others is like vitamin C and keeps the elders young and healthy. Vicki Rackner, author of "*Caregiving without Regrets: Three Steps to Avoid Burnout and Manage Disappointment, Guilt and Age*" describes that social media is a great way for caregivers to remedy from isolation and disconnected from their closest confidants. Social networking sites can help a caregiver to maintain their relationships with their family and friends, while forging new alliances with their peers who are taking care of elderly loved ones of their own. A strong support is unique; it can be comforting to know that there are times when elders have stress, confusion and to not cope with the situation. New media gives the opportunity to ask family and friends for help with handling such tasks.

Evaluation

According to the World Health Organization humans are living longer than ever before and there will be more than 2 billion elders over the age of 66+ by 2050, i.e., 22 percent of the global population. Bible says, "Even to your Old age and gray hairs I am he, I am he who will sustain you. I have made you, and I will carry you, I will sustain you and I will rescue you" – Isaiah 46:4. Hear sustain means "to give support or relief" and to provide nourishment for old age and allow them to lean on them. Throughout the scripture we read and also noticed in all the Summer Institute papers that we have a God who is with the aged all their days. This verse from Isaiah 46:4 gives us a picture of a God who walks with the aged from the moment they feel weak, lonely and when their hair becomes gray and their legs become weak. He never leaves them or forsakes the aged. He is with the aged especially at the time of stress, confusion and in difficult situations.

The recent lockdown also proved how this new media helped the churches to carry out her mission when there was fear on our physiological and psychological status of living, lack of social mingling, going out and to do the routine work. People of all ages across the globe shared motivational posts on the new media to help the aged to remain positive and inspired during the pandemic. It's an advantage for the elders to use of new media which significantly increase to provide sustenance on physiological and psychological conditions of living. Access to new media, keep in close contact with busy and/or distant family members, socializing with friends and community members by sharing through text, audio and pictures.

Conclusion

As in real life, aged people when they start to access the New Media it will bring different goals, based on their needs. This is because, isolation is one of the thwarts for the aged and it varies according to individual circumstances such as scattered family, death of a partner, a chronic health condition etc., which make the older people to feel alone. Aged need motivation and support, as do care-takers in the home, but the question of how the aged will use the New Media is needed, both at the social level and at the individual level. In practice, sociability and usability are closely integrated. Knowledge of social interaction directly informs sociability planning and indirectly influences much usability designs. User-centered design focuses on users rather than on technology.[14] Consequently, empirical research will help to know better about the aged user's interaction in New Media for the software developers to design ideas and to test and refine the new system.

Therefore, those who take care of the aged in their home have to spend time to describe about the new media and its importance. Elders always enjoy looking at the photo albums of their relatives and recollect about the past. Ageing is and will continue to be an important factor in determining the use of technologies. It is the responsibilities of the caretakers in the family to help the aged to get connected with the new media. Caretakers have to follow a number of steps to ensure their elders enjoy the benefits of new media: 1) find out which device is the best (smartphone or tab) to start with. 2) Arrange online access, the best is cell phone provider for the elders 3) teach them clearly the desired social networks 4) configure privacy settings and practices 5) caretakers should communicate with them on a regular basis, so they get familiar with using the technology because, memory is a very important thing for the aged. Above 85 years one never knows what to remember and what to forget. New media especially for the elders is a great way to laugh, learn, and share and be connected. The New Media also helps to form his/her old-age personality with a principle by adding ideas from a world-view and developing social conduct.

14 D. A. Norman, "Cognitive Engineering," in *User-Centered Systems Design*, edited by D. Norman and S. Draper (Hillsdale, NJ: Lawrence Erlbaum, 1986).

14

Gerontological Hermeneutics An Ethical Deconstruction

Mervin Shinoj Boas

Constructing theology for the other is a colonial error.
Placing an enemy in front to construct theology is a postcolonial error.
Constructing theology for own existence based on own reality
without the sense of otherness and without placing
any enemy is a postmodern position.
Gero-theology consists of everyone.
It is a collective and inclusive theology.
Ageing is a reality of life with all living beings.
It is an ongoing process from the beginning to end of life.
It goes beyond all the human made boundaries.
It is a universal theology based on contextual particularities.

Prescript

Ageing[1] is a reality of life not on the basis of certain scientific notions. It is a practice of day to day reality with a sense of inquiry based on the inherently **subjective nature** of knowledge. Ageing cannot be reduced to the realm of being purely scientific or theoretical for those are supposed to be beyond the hazards of scientific reductionism in order to reach out to the experiential realities of Ageing.

Epistemic horizons for constructing theories without acknowledging its practicability, as per modernity, have been changed to a different pattern of realistic attitude in the field of Gerontology.[2] Modernity authenticates theory on its own unique pillars. Practicability of theory is not considered seriously

1 The terms Ageing and Gerontology are used interchangeably in this essay.

2 Gerontology is a scientific study of being aged of human beings, animals and fungi.

by arguing that theories have an authentic ground of its own notions whether it is practiced or not because theory is constructed out of scientific knowledge[3] which is understood as of the most powerful faculties for a dynamic society or to make the society dynamic. The authenticity of scientific knowledge is based on reliability and validity[4] that claim to be beyond the borders of biased observations. This authenticity constructs solid foundations for theory. Thus, theory gets authority that does not need the support of praxis. In this way theory is set apart from praxis and vice-versa. With the emergence of the hermeneutical frames of Critical Theory in association with the epistemic frame of Frankfurt School with the vibrant theoretical currents of Hebermas, positivism was crucially questioned and began to search for scientific natural laws as a **principle source of knowledge.** Epistemic attempt had been there to construct gerontological hermeneutics with this principle source of knowledge in order to make gerontology as a scientific method supported by scientific theories with subjective hermeneutical frames.

On this ground Hebermas constructed the concept of **hermetic knowledge** which brought out a wider realm of **understandings of meanings** beyond the borders of gerontological hermeneutical foundationalism. It deconstructed and reconstructed the forever prefixed or pre-formulated or pre-constructed and pre-occupied meanings of gerontological phenomena. The possibility for constructing new meanings on the basis of new understandings has found its own space. This hermeneutical crossroad encourages to acknowledge gerontology from different interdisciplinary as well as multidisciplinary academic discourses not only theoretically but practically also by considering ageing as a reality of **all living beings.** Here gerontological hermeneutics go beyond the borders of anthropocentrism. The point to be noted here is that gerontological hermeneutics transcends anthropocentism and bio-centrism in order to reach out to the realm of Eco-centrism.[5] When it is acknowledged as a new significant epistemic horizon of hermeneutical knowledge along with the Hebermasian notion of thought of **critical knowledge**. Both hermetic and critical knowledge should be considered with equal importance on **objective knowledge.** Further, both are accepted as postmodern intellectual discourses, which are unavoidable factors for understanding ageing on ethical realities. Here is a hermeneutical notion from the subjective knowledge to the objective knowledge and vice-versa within the methodological frame of gerontology. It reached out to the postmodern epistemic frame of gerontological hermeneutics.

3 Allen W. Wood, *Kant's Ethical Thought* (Cambridge: University of Cambridge, 1999), 215-25.

4 Peter Singer, ed., *Ethics* (New York: Oxford University Press, 1994), 113-176.

5 Tayongtemjen, *Introduction to Christian Ethics* (Kolkata: Espace, 2013), 205-212.

In this context postmodernist criticism has to be taken into consideration due to its power to question the theories on the realm of its inherent relativity of observed phenomena and at the same time due to the inescapable subjectivity of the authors who construct and establish theories. The fact to be noted here is that ageing has been liberated from the captivity of theories based on subjectivity into the ground of praxis depended upon objectivity. This paradigm shift brings the practical realities of ageing which transcends the hermeneutic blocs of the scientific theoretical knowledge of gerontology.

At the same time, it should be acknowledged that without theories nothing can be practiced. Praxis is in need of theory and at the same time without praxis theory is insignificant. This postmodern epistemic understanding justifies the relationship between theory and praxis. Therefore, ethical understandings of ageing should be a combination of theory and praxis. Theory is about explanations of phenomena that provide significant lenses that help to view and review for having knowledge and understandings. Therefore, there is a need of theory as well as praxis on ageing for a holistic approach. In this process, Kuhn states, new epistemology of methods, research questions, interpretations, and explanations are the ingredients which is described as **scientific revolution** through which ageing can be revisited ethically.

Hermeneutics of Metaphors: Gerontological Ethics Re-conceptualized

Faith Forming Space: Re-realized as Beyond the Borders

Wealth is a common cause for cheating each other even in the name of God. This may be the reason for Jesus who advised us not to have investments of wealth or property at any cost on earth. Inherited property is one of the reasons for which and by which the aged, even parents, have been ill-treated and cheated even in the name of God and with the support of so-called faith (Gen. 27:20). One of the spiritual fathers Isaac was cheated by his own son in his old age for capturing the family property with the support of his own wife and the entire cheating story is placed in the name of God by mentioning that God helped. Even faith in God is being utilized for cheating the aged. The old man Isaac is cheated by his own son and his own wife. This brings out a reality that old age can be a time for to be cheated easily even by own blood relatives. Wife cheated the old husband; son cheated the old father. The story of Isaac portraits the reality that the entire family got together to cheat the aged for capturing the possessions.The unethical vision of the text is that the one who cheated the aged has been considered as the spiritual father later. Is it an inspirational text to cheat the aged for having wealth unethically with the support and guidance of a gang who appear as faithful personalities on faith and spirituality? The text makes the reader to be ethically conscious to bother about the cheating events that occur even in the faith forming spaces where the aged has been victimized and the cheating persons are considered as the role models of faith in the name of God.

The text makes the readers to be vigilant on the cheating process in the life of the aged even by the friendly behaviour and pretence of own community members and friends. Cheating the weak is the worst event that cannot be tolerated ethically. Permission is granted by the text to cheat the aged without commenting that it should not have happened. It is a question of biblical gerontological ethics that demand to respond to the issue by relocating faith with a dynamic ethical norm. But irrespective of all the matters of cheating, the text portraits Isaac the aged as a good person who does not have any revenge towards the cheater and remains for blessing the cheater. Old age is a time of blessing others who may be the cheaters. Beyond the tension between the wife and the husband and the son and the father, and the elder brother and the younger brother, the aged remain as the source of blessing, source of forgiveness, source of kindness, source of love, source of sharing, without any revenge or enmity even towards the cheater. Family is supposed to be a faith forming space. When it is changed to an evil place the aged tries to re-redeem the atmosphere of faith without any revenge or enmity. What an amazing image of the aged. Even though others create a problematic situation, the aged save the context without affecting its impact badly. The role of the redeemer is well established for the aged here. Here **ageing is an experience of being beyond the borders.** It means that ageing transcends the prejudiced expectations, formulae, methods, interpretations and responses which are the globally accepted foundations of scientific revolutions. Therefore, ageing is a tool that can be used for deconstructing the foundations of relationship for restructuring the context ethically beyond the unethical boundaries.

Body as Temple of God: Body-centered Hermeneutics Re-visualized

One of the well-established metaphors of the New Testament authenticates that the body is the temple of God (1 Cori. 3:16) It is with a good ethical vision to keep the body pure without committing any evil[6] or immoral[7] activities. Further, to keep the body holy is conceptualized as the wise worship. Maintaining holiness of the body by imagining it as a temple of God where God dwells with the presence of the Holy Spirit is a vision that does not allow the body to be victimized, demoralized, exploited, oppressed, and abused. This vision of body is a counter-conceptualization towards the Greek philosophical insight that argues that body (flesh) is evil and weak. The analogy of body as temple of God does not allow to disrespect or abuse the body of the aged.

6 Alasdair Mac Intyre, *A Short History of Ethics* (New York: Macmillan Publishing Company, 1976), 5-13.

7 Morality is a social construct. Tom L. Beauchamp, *Philosophical Ethics* (New York: McGraw-Hill Book Company, 1982), 5-11.

Acknowledging the dwelling presence of God in the aged body motivates to take care of the aged body responsibly and respectfully with honor and privilege.

Abusing the aged body is a reality of contemporary context. Old Age Homes are the examples of the same. Increasing the number of Old Age Homes cannot be a matter of prestige of religion but it shows the exact face of an irresponsible or unjust society. A responsible society will not give up the aged or throw them away into the old age homes which most probably do not have a homily atmosphere. Giving shelter to the aged in an old age home is not a matter of charity service of religion for its mental satisfaction but a reality of a society which is not yet ethically transformed.

The metaphor of body as the temple of God connotes that the body of the aged is pure, qualified for a dwelling place of God, and with the presence of the Holy Spirit in order to be respected and honored instead of treating as an unwanted or unnecessary or invalid expensive, unproductive and also a time-consuming thing. The metaphor is powerful enough to demand that those who are as inmates of the old age homes or on the street should be treated as the temple of God. This ethical value of this metaphor brings out the glory of the aged body. Further, I Cor 3:17 states that God's temple is sacred and the human body is that temple. Therefore, the aged body is sacred. That is why the Holy Spirit dwells in it. Sacredness of the aged body is a wonderful motivation to take care of the same with reverence.

Again, I Cor 12:27 establish that the body of a human being is the body of Christ. It reminds us that body of the aged should be considered as a body of Christ. How should we deal with the body of Christ? The same way the body of the aged should be treated. When I see the aged I should feel like seeing the body of Christ. The body of Christ is broken. My body is a body of Christ which is broken. The aged body is a body of Christ which is broken. Both bodies are broken for the sake of each other. The communion of the broken bodies is the reality between the aged body and me. This is what Holy Communion is about. The *koinonia* with the body of the aged is a holy fellowship. I am not supposed to avoid the same at any cost in my spirituality. The body of the aged is broken for me and at the same time I break my body for the aged.

This is what is the **cruciform fellowship or humanity** as per M. M. Thomas. Still the body of the aged is broken and demands us to break our body. What a powerful metaphor that demanding us to be with the broken body of Christ. How can I neglect or avoid or negate the body of the aged since it is the temple of God, sacred, dwelling place of God, with the presence of the Holy Spirit, body of Christ which is broken for others? Our attitude towards the body of the aged should be transformed into that realm.

Body-centered epistemology is a construct of gerontological hermeneutics. Body is the realm of the experiences and expressions.

Explorations and expositions of ageing take place by focusing on the body. Thus, the body is a powerful medium to acknowledge the features and significance of ageing. An aged body is therefore, an unavoidable source of experiences, feelings, emotions and expressions that construct the ethical hermeneutics[8] of gerontology.

Gerontological Body[9]: An Ethical Hermeneutical Deconstruction[10]

Gerontology is a knowledge of Body. All the issues related to the ageing take place in the body and are revealed in the body or experienced by the body. Expressions of ageing take place within the body. The phenomenon of ageing is in relation with the body. All the issues related to ageing are bounded with the body. Memories of the aged live within the body. Thus, the bodies of the aged remain as the norm of gerontological ethics. Existential reality of ageing is grounded within the body. Body is a practical reality more than scientific theoretical explorations. Here euro-centrism is deconstructed to make a paradigm shift in the realm of *from theory to praxis* to *praxis and theory together* to construct new hermeneutical epistemic notions of thought.

Constructing theories on the basis of experiential praxis and praxis on the basis of existential theories of body are the notions here. It is a mutual move without centralizing on any of these. This gerontological ethics consists of theoretical value that are authenticated by the experiential praxis and ethics of praxis is validated by the existential theory of the body. This notion of mutual move brings out *epi-foundationalism* which is considered as one of the patterns of postmodernism. Gerontological body thus remains as a de-constructive force against foundationalism. Thus, a gerontological body is identified as a postmodern body due to its epi-foundational nature. Epi-foundationalism is a school of thought against the concentration of any power-centralized dynamics. Therefore, an aged body becomes an ethical norm for decentralization. Here the postcolonial task of destructing the center in order to make the margin as center does not take place because in this process the center remains as a reality but only the location is changed or shifted. In this process the location of the margin becomes the center. Without the power-concentrated center dynamics of notions take place that is considered as social existence. Becoming a centerasa margin and margin as acenter has the same impact. It is negated by the gerontological praxis-oriented theory and theory-oriented praxis. Thus, an aged body reaches out to the realm of being beyond

8 Emmanuel E. James, *Ethics: A Biblical Perspective* (Bangalore: Theological Book Trust, 2001), 13-26.

9 The body which is with the process of being aged.

10 Oliver A. Johnson, *Ethics: Selection from Classical and Contemporary Writers* (New York: Holt, Rinehart and Winston, 1958).

the borders of center as well as margin. This paradigm shift of gerontological hermeneutical ethics plays a vital role to acknowledge the significance of the aged body in the theological epistemology and remains as a normative factor for deconstructing the existing theological hermeneutics for the sake of the gerontological body.

Gerontological Body: Hermeneutics of Contextuality Reconstructed

The body is one of the main formative factors for almost all the contextual theologies since the body is an existential reality within that ontological phenomenon that exists. Body is the medium to define the context; explore the context; experience the context not on the basis of any prefixed universal theories but on the basis of contextually-valued ontological existence. For dalit, feminist, womanist, adivasi, and tribal theologies body is the powerful factor for constructing developmental insights but in this construction the vital role of pre-formulated and preoccupied universally accepted theoretical notions can be identified. For instance, Dalit methodological frame of *methodological exclusivism* which is constructed with the notion of exclusivism. Exclusivism is identified as a product of modernity and has been utilized to construct a classical traditional theological frame.

In this context gerontological body is a norm to save this kind of theoretical subjectivity into not the realm of praxis-oriented objectivity but to the ground of mutual notions between subjectivity and objectivity of existential reality for an ontological exploration. Context is acknowledged without any centralization of subjectivity or objectivity but with the support of equal importance of both. Notion of objectivity within the hermeneutical frame of subjectivity and vice-versa should be a reality of gerontological body which defines the features of the context. Thus, an aged body becomes a norm for the realization of the context. For example, in the story of Isaac the self consists of the other by finding out that the other exists within the self and vice-versa. This ontological reality helps to overcome the conflict situations. That is why Isaac remains as a force to reestablish the relationships within the family context. In short, the aged body is acknowledged as hermeneutical ground of ethics to realize the context in order to reconstructing the context.

Gerontological Voice: Hermeneutics of Voice Restructured

Restructuring the context to acknowledge the gerontological voice to be heard which has been almost silenced is a task of the Gerontological hermeneutics of voice. Gerontological voice may not be academic enough. It may not be authenticated by the dominant voice in the field of academics. This is a postcolonial issue. The silenced voice needs to be validated by the approved and accepted dominant academic professional voices to consider as academically approved voice. The voice of the silenced has been captured by the so-called epistemic ground of academics. The subaltern voice may not have the access to get approved by the professionally skilled so-called globally and locally accepted academic voices.[11] Therefore, the silenced subaltern voices are being heard only through the dominant voices which are almost the sources for silencing the subaltern voices. The possibility for the local voices for *being heard* without the approval of the dominant or professionally approved skilled voices should be an agenda of the contemporary context of the subaltern. If it is diluted by the familiar hegemonic voices of the professional power class the voices of the subaltern will be silenced and it will be a further ground of echoing the dominant voices that already exist as approved monopoly voices of the so-called academic monsters. The voice of the gerontology should be considered as the genuine voice in the field of academy without the authentication or validation of any academically hegemonic voices.

Postscript

Gerontological body is a norm to analyze the nature and features of society or community. The aged body speaks out about the morality of the context, ethical norms of the context, responsible attitude of the context, and organic presence of the context. It means that when the aged body is observed and analyzed the nature, character, behavior, attitude, responsibility, and ethics of a community or society can be understood. Thus, the aged body remains as a source of ethical understandings that has reliability. It is through a scientific method of knowledge. Thus, scientific theoretical epistemic notions remain within the practical ground of gerontology and these theoretical fractions are the ground for acknowledging further praxis-oriented fragments. Aged body remains as a bridge between theory and praxis and as an ethical norm for understanding the features of community. An unacknowledged neglected and forgotten factor, ie., gerontological body, is significantly identified as an ethical norm to analyze the community as well as in the realm of theory

11 The real subaltern voices such as dalit, woman, adivasi, tribal voices are there but not being heard because their voices are not authenticated or validated by the academically approved professional voices. The subaltern may not have access to reach out the academically professional and approved voices to consider as academic voice. Therefore, the real voice of the subaltern remains an un-academic voice without the approval of the academic disciplines. The subaltern may not be familiar with the technicality of the academic voice and its languages colonial languages. Authentication of the downtrodden voices is an ethical issue. In order to hear the silenced subaltern voices, the context should be restructured to liberate the same from the bondage of the so-called academics. The voice of the subaltern to be heard without any approval of the so-called accepted hegemonic voices of the world of professional. If I want to make my voice, my voice should be authenticated by the accepted dominant voices of the skilled professionals even in the field of theology. Otherwise it would remain as un-academic voice and will be rejected or not approved and therefore, it will not be heard. This happens in the ground of Gerontological voices.

and praxis. Further, gerontological body remains as a significant constructive factor in the ground of spirituality too by realizing the gerontological body as scared, God dwelling place, the presence of the Holy Spirit, as body of Christ which is broken for others. The aged body, in short, should be considered as a hermeneutical tool of Christian social ethics.

15

Indian Feminist Theo-gerontology Towards Growing Positively

Nelavala Gnana Prasuna

Introduction

Old age is an ever-present worldwide phenomenon. Every culture has arrived at its definition or understanding of the last stage of human life over the centuries. Certain cultures greatly value the later stage of life, while others do not. Due to factors such as biological, social, religious and cultural influences, ageing can affect women and men differently. Ageing is often looked upon as being a disaster by many, despite it being a natural and unstoppable event. However, my mother, a retired teacher, aged 80, who has such a positive outlook on life, makes us, her children, think that she has no age limits. When she was 45 years old, she used to ask for a lift to school in a nearby village, as my father, also a teacher, worked at another school in a different location. She would stop any vehicle enroute and ask for a lift sometimes even truck drivers would oblige! And now in her 80s, in March 2020, and just before the lockdown was announced as a response to Covid-19, she asked for a lift to church so that she could participate in the Lenten service and met with a minor accident. Of course, she has recovered. I also recall an assertion made by Dr. Satyavani, on YouTube when she said: "People are saying Corona virus attacks aged people and aged people are dying. I am 65 years old. I am strong, and I have enough immunity power even to the extent of killing this virus. If Corona virus enters my body, it will die but I will not die due to this virus. So don't say old people will die due to corona virus."[1] She continued to give examples how elderly are maintaining very good health in some of the homes for senior citizens and how the elderly practice yoga in the parks in Chennai. Another person

1 *Dr. Satyavani's Herbal Medicines to fight Corona Virus*, https://youtu.be/V9A-EJQ_ct0 (accessed on 30 March, 2020).

who has made me think differently and positively about the old age is Mother Teresa. Mother Teresa called "Messiah of the poor" well disciplined, led a life of compassion and listening to the people in need even at the later stage with wrinkles on her face. She died at 87 leaving an extraordinary image as an old age woman.[2]

So what do we understand about ageing? How do we define it? How do we understand it? My mother, Dr. Satyavani and St Mother Teresa have led me to look at "old age" from a particular viewpoint to propose "grow positively." We have numerous examples of how the elderly resist the "old age" image. At the same time, we are aware of familiar questions such as "Why am I still alive as a weak older woman?" "Why do I have to continue to live when I am no longer accepted?" "Why should I lead a life of dependency?" "What does it mean to say that God created women in God's image?" "Does God's image disappear when women transit into later life?" "What does it mean to grow positively?" These questions need urgent attention in the Indian theologies. Hence, an attempt is made here to explore an Indian Feminist Theo-gerontology from older women's perspectives.

Methodological Departures

Methodologies of traditional, social and biological sciences have taught much about ageing and old age. But their methodologies addressed only limited problems and asked limited questions. Accordingly the kind of knowledge they produced has also been limited. For example, traditional methodologies explain what causes wrinkles but do not explain what those wrinkles mean to older people, especially women. They document the income and income-related inequalities that exist in society but they do not explain what these inequalities mean to older people and especially older women. According to Linda Gannon, traditional gerontological research has three basic defects: Androcentrism that makes men's lives the standard for measurement and so men have the power to define. For example, The Baltimore Longitudinal Study of Ageing began in 1958 and carried on for 20 years without women. In other words, initially, the research was based on men, and women were added to the research later on; biological determinism, the primary purpose of women is reproduction and thus menopause is looked upon as a "deficiency disease," rather than a normal life transition; Dualism creates binaries and makes one superior and the other inferior such as female and male, public and private, body and mind and so on.[3] The traditional methodologies fail to identify what

2 See for more details, B. K. Chaturvedi, *Mother Teresa: Messiah of the Poor* (New Delhi: Diamond Books: 2016).

3 Margaret Cruikshank, *Learning to be Old: Gender, Culture, and Aging* (Third Edition) (Maryland, Rowman& Littlefield Publishers: 2013), 195.

it means to live as aged people and specifically as aged women, in the midst of intersections.

Even feminist theories initially excluded older people - both in their choice of research questions and in their theoretical approaches.[4] Martha Holstein calls the exclusion of older women from feminist work as a symbolic of the "gerontophobia."[5] However, J. Diane Gamer says that there is an increasing interest in feminist gerontology, and one of the main reasons is that the ageing of feminists themselves who confront the combination of the myths, stereotypes, and discrimination based on age and gender.[6] My intention in this essay is to propose the concept of "growing positively" and offer some recommendations to the ageing, to the church and to the theological institutions. In this work the experiences of older women are the main source in constructing Indian Feminist Theo-gerontology. Although the essay focuses on older women, the debate in this work includes older men as the issues of aged in common are not given adequate attention in the theological debates.

Method of Research

Older women in India face violence at various levels although they are skillful.[7] To test this theoretical understanding, I chose 25 women, aged 60 to 95, from the South Andhra Lutheran Church, the India Evangelical Lutheran Church and the Church of South India to do ground research as I have connections with these women. Respondents are from Dalit middle class group. The lockdown period (due to COVID-19), June – August was used to carry out the research. A semi-structured interview schedule was used to elicit information from the respondents. The ground research was conducted over the telephone. One of the disadvantages of this survey was that there was no eye to eye contact between the researcher and the respondents. But, I could listen to their stories and evaluate their emotions. The objectives of the study are as follows:

- To understand the living arrangements and the needs of elderly women
- To discover the contributions of the elderly women
- To gather recommendations from them for them

4 Toni M. Calasanti & Kathleen F. Slevin, "Introduction: Age Matters," in *Age Matters: Re-Aligning Feminist Thinking*, edited by Toni M. Calasanti & Kathleen F. Slevin (New York, Routledge: 2006), 3.

5 Martha B. Holstein, "On Being an Aging Woman" in *Age Matters:* Age Matters," in *Age Matters: Re-Aligning Feminist Thinking* Edited by Toni M. Calasanti & Kathleen F. Slevin (New York, Routledge: 2006), 324.

6 J. Diane Garner, DSW: "Feminism and Feminist Gerontology," in *Fundamentals of Feminist Gerontology* Edited by J, Dianne Garner, DSW (New York, Routledge: 1999), 6.

7 See for further details, Nitmal Ruprail, *Silver Generation in India: A Bibliographical Study (1889-2000)* (New Delhi: Anamika Publishers & Distributors (P) LTD: 2002).

- To examine the role of church and spirituality in the lives of older women.

Defining the Terms

While developing Indian Feminist Theo-gerontology, I feel it is necessary to clarify the undertone of the terms and why I use these terms.

Use of the term Feminist: Feminism as a term stirs up different reactions. The term has many connotations and definitions. Feminism is often branded as anti-national, anti-cultural and anti-religious and blamed as a product of western colonialism. Many preferred to replace or displace the term 'feminism.' Feminism has paved the way for women to raise their voice. I employ the term feminism as I find the term is potential with its prophetic and critical edge in taking up my own different identities: as a woman, as a Dalit, as a Christian, as a Lutheran, as a theologian and as a growing person.[8]

Theo-gerontology: The term *Theo* refers to God and gerontology is the study of ageing people. Theo-gerontology is a study of older people and their connection and relationship with God.

Feminist gerontology is a theory that gives priority to both gender and age, critiques and raises a voice against the unjust ways of treating the older women by the traditional structures of society; and by its new interpretations revises the experience of ageing and promotes "growing positively."

Feminist Theo-gerontology in this work is a study of older women from God's point of view. It offers new ageing friendly interpretations of the scriptures and the spiritual experience. Feminist Theo-gerontology attempts to work for and work with ageing people and strives to find deeper connections between God and the later life and promotes "growing positively."

Ageing and Gender Dynamics

Technically, human beings age and grow at every stage of life. For example, "she attained age" is often celebrated in India. Ageing doesn't simply happen at retirement. When I was 10 years old, teenagers were seniors (old) to me. When I was in my teens, the twenties were seniors (old) to me. In my fifties, the 60s are seniors (old) to me. So "old age" –is in other words "growing" and it is a process from the day we are born. Ageing is not just a biological process but also a psychological, intellectual, social, cultural and spiritual process.

As women age, their life experiences are shaped by their respective race, caste, class, culture, religion and ethnic identities. Gender relations are dynamic and they create different pressures and restrictions as women grow. All 25 respondents responded to the question, "Do you experience

---

8 Nelavala Gnana Prasuna, *Engendering the Divine Image: Conversations with Dalit Women's Experience* (Delhi: Christian World Imprints, 2020), 9-10.

discrimination because you are a woman at this age? Responded, "Men at old age certainly enjoy privileges whereas women are overburdened." The church and society reinforce traditional roles of women making them more vulnerable at the later stage. The Second World Assembly on Ageing, held in Madrid, Spain, in 2002 recognized a need to challenge stereotype images of ageing and later life, particularly those related to older women. The Assembly also stated, "Older women face greater risk of physical and psychological abuse due to discriminatory social attitudes and non-realization of the human rights of women and addresses increasing disadvantages for women in society and harmful stereotypes."[9]Ageing is not experienced equally by men and women. For example, in India, graying hair is regarded as a sign of maturity and it is an honour to men but gray hair in a woman is regarded as negative and a diminishing sign of her body. 15 respondents mentioned that the hierarchical system gave privilege to men. Women even at the later stage are overburdened. They are discriminated against because they are both old and female and in the case of widows the volume of discrimination is higher.

Issues of Older Women

Signs of ageing and experiences of ageing are different and deeply connected. Some of the experiences of older women those who have shared in a random survey are: Denial of old age and physical appearance, poverty and dependency, loneliness, care giving and care taking, discrimination, attachment to God and the church, and spiritual life. I am conscious that there is a gap between women who are fortunate enough to be financially independent and those who are dependent.

My respondents were mainly retired teachers and were conscious of their appearance. Although physical ageing signs become prominent, most of them expressed that they were young in spirit and more active than young people. 10 respondents confirmed they attended church well dressed; 5 women said they were at a social disadvantage in terms of their physical appearance; 10 responded that they didn't care about their appearance as they were too old to concern themselves with such things. Kamla Khetarpal says, "Unless there is a physical reminder like a gradual onset of arthritis, a heart attack or a disability, one does not want to accept the fact that one is old."[10] In India, many parents are not prepared for the beginning of old age, and this is something theologians should address.

---

9 Tina Maschi & George S. Leibowitz, eds. *Forensic Social Work: Psychosocial and Legal Issues Across Diverse Populations and Settings* (Second Edition) edited by (New York: Springer Publishing Company: 2018), 252.

10 Kamla Khetrarpal, "Ageing: A Blessing," in *India's Elderly: A Multidisciplinary Dimension*, edited by A. K. Kapoor, & Satwanti Kapoor (New Delhi: Mittal Publications, 2004), 3.

The poverty threshold is higher for old people than the rest of the population. One of the respondents, recalling her experience of poverty and dependency of older women, said, "At Tirupati, one young man tied his mother up, gave her a plate and a bed sheet and left her on the street, at a bus stop. She started begging for food." When I was listening to this story, I could sense her emotions and her weeping tone as solidarity. Another woman expressed that she is devalued by her own son, even though her son's family lives with her in her own house. She feels lonely and dishonored. She broke into tears as she expressed that, "my son never speaks to me." This is the plight of many older women in India. Housing is an important living arrangement for older people to live in peace. Among the respondents, 10 had no house of their own but lived with their children. 15 women had their own house, and children live with them. However, 20 women have expressed loneliness as one of their biggest struggles - often on a daily basis. Women with limited, or no income, are doubly invisible, being regarded as "poor" women. 5 respondents struggled to manage to get their daily food: they felt distressed, being deprived of their basic needs. Either the family, or the church or society did not pay attention to their needs and they are deprived of their basic rights.

In many cultures across the world, women are the "default" long-term caregivers within a family system. This role of care-giving almost invariably has an adverse effect on women's ageing over time.[11] 20 were the care-givers at home. They help in the kitchen, take care of children, drop off and collect children from schools and so on. One respondent aged 95 was sweeping the house, when I called her on the telephone. When asked, "At this age, how is it you are so active and involved in cleaning and washing, etc.?" She replied, "I am so happy to do these jobs by myself and I have been doing these activities for such a long time, and I am very healthy and very active." Moreover, she was a guest at her son's house as she came to visit them. The voluntary help given by older women is priceless. There were also older men who contribute to the family in taking care of their wives. One respondent shared that she was almost bed ridden for a number of years, as her legs have become disabled due to sickness. But her husband is a caregiver. Her two sons and daughters-in-law and four grandchildren share the same house with three apartments. But her husband does the nursing, cooking and all other activities related to her. She said, "I am so lucky to have him as my husband and he is more than a father."Another woman shared that she is fortunate to have a husband who takes care of her who does all cooking at home as she can't see properly due to problems in the eye. It was encouraging to listen to such stories of warmth in the lives of older women during my conversations.

---

11 Christina R. Victor, *Old Age in Modern Society:* (New York: Springer, 1994), 150-151.

To the question about their spiritual life, respondents answered that, "Devotion to God, praying, reading the Bible, singing, participating in Bible quiz, attending the church programs, and watching Christian channels on the TV" are the primary functions which make them feel satisfied and active. Spirituality gives emotional support in their old age. My respondents expressed that God answers their prayers and relieves tension and gives them peace and satisfaction. For example, one respondent said: "one day I had nothing to eat and no money to buy. I was only praying to God and God heard my prayers and God sent Rs. 2000/- through one sister."

To the question, "What do you expect from the Church as an older person? The responses are:

1. Networks and fellowships for the older women and men.
2. Homes for the aged and especially for aged women.
3. Special events like retreats, workshops and Bible studies especially designed for the elderly.
4. Regular financial assistance to the poor older women.

Feminist Gerontology: A Brief Overview

Feminist scholarship has largely ignored older women, and gerontologists have overlooked feminism. However, Susan Sontag's *The Double Standard of Ageing* came up in 1978 and De Beauvoir's *Old Age* in 1972 and Barbara McDonald's work *The Women's Movement* in 1980s' and these works urged that old age should be recognized in feminist scholarship. Feminist scholars of ageing began to question the issues relating to ageing women. As a result, feminist gerontology emerged in the 1990s. The first important works in feminist gerontology are *Women, Feminism, and Ageing* by Collette Brown in 1998 in which she outlines a new vision for understanding older women and their place in society; J. Diane Garner's work *Fundamentals of Feminist Gerontology* in 2014 explores feminist ideals and advocacy for ageing women in health care, home life, work and retirement.[12] For Feminist gerontology gender is an interpretative tool to analyze social life across the life span that alters the experience of ageing. It recognizes that the experiences of both women and men are structured by gender relations: dynamic, constructed, and institutionalized. People are oriented to behave in the ideals of womanhood and manhood through these processes. Feminist theories regard traditional theories and models of ageing as insufficient because they failed to address differences in power and privilege in gender relations: the experience of women in the

12 Virginia E. Richardson & Amanda S. Barusch, *Gerontological Practice for the Twenty-First Century: A Social Work Perspective* (New York: Columbia University Press: 2006), 45.

context of ageing, civic engagement, and care-giving demands, and issues of race, ethnicity, and class and caste.[13]

Feminist gerontology pressurizes organizations, religions and governments to respond to the needs of older women; works towards elimination of stereotypes; committed to change double standard attitudes and promote social and economic justice; broadens the range of roles available to ageing women; Incorporates gender, as well as race, class, age, and caste and sexual preference and works at the intersection of ageing; Utilizes theories and methods that accurately depict life experiences; Concerned with emancipation and liberation of the aged people from all kinds of oppression and domination.[14]

Constructing Indian Feminist Theo-Gerontology

The problems of aged people especially women are not given adequate attention by Indian Christian theology. The essay underscores the urgent need of theological explorations from aged people's perspectives and women in particular. Ageing is a natural process set within the context of life, but gender relations which are socially and religiously constructed have consequences in the life of aged women either leading to privileged or underprivileged status. Feminist Theo-gerontology is a study of older women from the perspective of God and finds out the deeper connections between God and the older women. The study is concerned with the life of older women and men and committed to promote life in abundance towards growing positively. The study has brought out different experiences of older women in different contexts.

To the question "What do you mean to live a life in abundance?" They expressed that often they feel deprived, and felt lonely which added to their health issues and made them feel as though they were being suffocated. On many occasions, they felt that they had no voice and that their duty was to only listen and obey. After leading a life of many decades of contributing life in developing the family, investing in human capital, contributing to the church in various ways, and to society at large, at their later stage of life they felt depressed and discriminated against. All 25 respondents gave a strong recommendation for church, "to establish home for senior citizens and that would help many to live in peace."

15 respondents are living together with their husbands. 10 respondents are widows and 5 of them were staying with their children and they confirmed that they feel loss of freedom. And 5 of them confirmed that children were staying with them in their house, and that had left them with a freedom of

13 Vern L. Bengtson and Marguerite DeLiema, "Theories of Aging and Social Gerontology: Explaining How Social Factors Influence Well-Being in Later Life," in *Gerontology: Changes, Challenges, and Solutions*, volume 1, edited by Mafonna Harrington Meyer & Elizabeth A. Daniele (ABC-CLIO: 2016), 43.

14 J. Diane Garner, DSW: "Feminism and Feminist Gerontology," 10.

choice. Occasionally, one aged couple spends few months in their son's house as they are requested to take care of their grandchild. The grandmother burst into tears as she was asked to do many domestic activities in their son's house. This is the kind of struggle that grandparents are facing at their old age.

With regard to their spiritual life, 15 respondents said that their devotional life gives them peace. They spend most of the time in reading the Bible, praying and attending the church gatherings. To the question, "What is your position in the church?" All 25 responded that the churches recognized them and honoured them and especially so on Women's Sunday. The Respondents also shared the fact that the congregations prayed for them, and some congregations even granted a pension for the poor, older women. The question that springs to my mind and the respondents' as well is, "Is that enough?" The older women are seeking an identity as matured human beings; they want to be affirmed as a blessing of God. This work draws strength form Jesus' words, "I have come that they (older people) may have life and life in abundance?"

Re-reading the Biblical Narratives: Jesus' View on Older Women

In life stages from birth to death, in the experiences of growth and in the development of senses people believe that God is the source of life and helps life to grow. Life is God's image and it is a God's gift to everyone. Children are born with God's image and it will remain in them until their death. Reassurance of this fact is a source of strength for older women to draw on - to accept and delight in - in the knowledge that they are continuing to be God's gift of life to their families, to the Church and society - and that they have the right to live a life in abundance. Older women need to be empowered to reclaim Life the image of God within them.

The church regards Jesus of Nazareth as the ultimate model for true humanity, the model of a life lived faithfully. Jesus died at a very young age, without experiencing old age. Luke tells us that "Jesus was about thirty years when he began his work" (Lk. 3:23), and after three years he was killed. So he would have been around thirty three and half years old at the time of his death. On what terms can the figure of Jesus have implications for the elderly? What strengths can we draw from Jesus affirmation, "I have come that they may have life and life in abundance" in constructing Indian Feminist theo-gerontology?

Although Jesus died young, his attention towards and the compassion for the elderly becomes the major source in developing theology from the perspectives of the older women. In his experiences of sufferings, death and victorious resurrection everyone is included. His experience as an advocate on behalf of the vulnerable, his attention to the least, his attacks on systems of injustice and his compassion to the needy becomes the key in constructing Feminist Theo-gerontology. We are familiar with some stories which tell us the way Jesus treated older women and became a powerful advocate on behalf of the lives of older women and men. Rereading of the two stories the poor widow who offered two coins and the persistent widow from Luke's gospel have stronger implications in the context of older women.

Poor Widow and her Offering (Luke 21:1-4): An Agency for the Visibility of Older Women

The story of a poor widow who offered two coins has a significant relevance to Indian church in the context of older women. Older women in India often feel invisible and lonely. Especially widows face triple disadvantages by being woman, aged, and widow. They are labeled as evil and misfortune beings in India.[15] Martha Holstein while discussing on the embodied experiences of older women says that the culture does damage to the ageing women by "devaluing" the older woman's body "while rendering it invisible."[16] Older women make themselves invisible due to their visible indicators of gray hair, wrinkles, and sagging skin.20 respondents expressed that they felt often excluded socially, and they themselves wanted to be invisible due to their ageing appearances. It is even disturbing that 5 widows among the respondents were invisible even at the time of their children's wedding. They were invisible because they were branded as misfortune or evil in the eyes of society and also because of their internalization of the evilness within them. Luke's story of the poor widow who offered two coins becomes the powerful model for the visibility of aged women, and aged widowed women.

The woman in the story is poor and a widow and some sources say that she is aged.[17] She does not seem to be a privileged woman nor have a high status. But she offered two coins and Jesus affirms that "the poor widow has put in more than all the others." Jesus' affirmation sounds that she sets aside her own requirements and needs and gave all that she had. Feminist interpretation of the poor widow's offering of two coins focuses on recovering the poor widow's agency. This woman represents double vulnerability; she is both widowed and poor and even aged. But she acts not as an invisible victim but as a self-liberator with intention, conviction, and clear vision. The woman's presence in the temple among the rich people is a sign of liberation from the social stigma of poverty and widowhood. It is also, a sign of reclaiming her identity as the image of God. Her offering in spite of her impoverishment signals her continuing conviction that, despite unfaithful leadership, the temple

15 Rekha Pande, "The Forgotten Widows of Vrindavan in India," in *Handbook of Research on Multicultural Perspectives on Gender and Aging*, edited by Rekha Pande & Theo van der Weide (Hershey PA: IGI Global, 2018), 200.

16 Martha Holstein: "On Being An Aging Woman," 325 & 330.

17 Sharon Jaynes, *What God Really Thinks about Women: Finding Your Significance Through the Women Jesus Encountered* (Eugene: Harvest House Publishers, 2010), 202.

remains an epicenter of God's restoring activity to people like her. Feminist interpretation asserts that she is a model not of giving, but of her agency even in her vulnerability.[18]

Even in the church, older women are the major fundraisers and contributors to the church and they do it with enthusiasm. Yet they feel distressed about themselves. During the conversations, respondents shared that they give to church thinking that they are giving to God, even if they encounter issues of corruption in the church, they leave those issues to God's judgment. One respondent said, "I feel ashamed to give very little offering, as others give more to the church, and this leads to conflicts in my family." But the woman in the text refused to feel bad about her little contribution, but she did it from her heart in spite of her impoverishment. The woman comes into public, into the midst of the rich and into the temple setting aside her devalued body, poverty and widowhood status. Her devotion, self-determination and self-identity become a powerful model to the older women who internalize devalued status to themselves. Jesus notices the poor woman and affirms her contribution as the worthiest offering of all and calls others to recognize and value her determined faith in action. Jesus makes the woman visible in the midst of the rich, in the midst of the oppressive structures. He calls others to give attention to this woman. Jesus' act of affirmation has greater implications for the church and older women in India. The contributions of older women to their families, church, and society are countless. The poor widow's self-determination calls older women and especially widows to come out of the attached stigma and affirm their identity as the image of God. Jesus' affirmative action challenges the church to give attention to the older women and who are invisible after making all contributions and appreciate their contributions.

The Savvy Widow's Might (Luke 18:1-8): Towards Justice for Older Women

Luke's story of an aged widow who is persistent to get justice has stronger implications for older women who live like dry bones in India. Gender and age discrimination make the life of the older women more difficult, as their rights are often violated. They have no access to land, and they are restricted due to discriminatory inheritance laws and practices, resulting in their increased poverty and financial dependence on the family or the state.[19] During Jesus' time, especially in ancient times, widows were people who had lost not only

18 Cynthia A. Jarvis & E. Elizabeth Johnson Eds. *A Feasting on the Word Commentary: Feasting on the Gospels,* (Luke Vol. 2) (Louisville, Westminster: John Knox Press, 2014), 219-223.

19 Tattwamasi Paltasingh and Renu Tyagi, "Gender-sensitive Intervention for Elderly Women," in *Caring for the Elderly: Social Gerontology in the Indian Context,* edited by Tattwasmasi Paltasing & Renu Tyagi (New Delhi: Sage Publications, 2015).

their husbands but their social standing and their own life. In contrast to such status, the widow in the story is a savvy victory. The choice of a widow to fight for justice is a stunning model and exhibits her boldness, and persistence.[20] This woman in the story is vulnerable due to her age and by being a widow and a victim of injustice at the hands of an unjust judge. But her persistence and boldness changes unjust judge's mind granting justice.

There are two ways of reading this story and both ways are significant in the context of older women in India. One way of reading the story of persistent widow is to see the unjust judge as the protagonist bearing the lesson for the reader. If an unjust judge grants a request, how much more will a loving God grant the wishes of God's children? The judge in the story is not soft towards the woman's request. But somehow he wants to get rid of her. He thought to himself, "Though I have no fear of God and no respect for anyone, yet because this widow keeps bothering me, I will grant her justice, so that she may not wear me out by continually coming (4-5)." Out of self-interest, he though it is easier to grant justice than to keep dealing with the widow.[21] The woman with her daring and dashing persistence changed the unjust judge's mind. Jesus compares God to unjust judge, saying, the unjust judge grants justice because she was persistent, how much more loving God would grant the requests of God's children. No doubt, Jesus' story reinforces the practice of importance of prayer and the faithful commitment of God to "grant justice" on earth to those who pray to God day and night (Lk. 18:1, 6-8).[22] There are many powerless aged women especially widows in our church and society in the midst of unjust systems and unjust people. The story exhorts the older women and church to pray and act in bringing a change in the unjust systems towards granting rights of the older women.

Another way of reading the story is to see the woman as the protagonist and thereof bears the lesson. The woman in the story, in her vulnerability, becomes the Christ figure who fights evil and injustice on behalf of the poor and neglected. She in her determination to get justice makes the unjust judge, the symbol of oppression to do justice. An analogy that bears lesson here: As a widow is persistent to secure her rights, so is God in securing the rights

---

20 Robert Farrar Capon, *Kingdom, Grace, Judgment: Paradox, Outrage, and Vindication in the Parables of Jesus* (Grand Rapids: William B. Eerdmans Publishing Company, 2002), 329; Denise George, *Tilling the Soul: Prayer Penetrates Your Pain* (Grand Rapids: Zondervan, 2004), 136.

21 Mary Ann Beavis, *The Lost Coin: Parables of Women, Work, and Wisdom* (London: Sheffield Academic Press, 2002), 58.

22 F Scott Spencer, *Salty Wives, Spirited Mothers, and Savvy Widows: Capable Women of Purpose* (Grand Rapids: William B. Eerdmans Publishing Company), 264.

of those pleading God.[23] This story has greater implications for the older women's context in India. Older women feel that they have no rights, and they have no voice. The woman in the story calls older women to be bold, strong and to get justice by persisting. Jesus affirms that God grants the requests of their children. This affirmation is a boost to older women to pray and fight for their own rights and for the rights of others. Rereading the scriptures with the older women from the perspective of older women would provide the boost to the older women to reaffirm themselves as Christ like figures to fight evil and become mighty in changing the unjust structures and people.

Both the poor widow who offered two coins (all that she has) and the persistent widow represent boldness, ability, victory, agency, faith, self-determination, giving, persistence and confidence. They are the symbols of liberation from the ascribed stereotyped social status as widows, poor and aged women. Jesus affirms their being and calls others to recognize their identity and give attention and to do justice. Jesus affirms that God is on the side of the least in society and grants their requests. Experiences of my mother, Dr. Satyavani, and St Mother Teresa and my respondents extend a call for attention of theologians and churches to break the stereotyped images of the aged; reclaim the images of the aged women and men as the image of God; provide space for them to "grow positively."

Conclusion

As far back as I can remember, my grandparents have played a central and unique role in my life. As I was writing this essay I remembered my maternal grandparents who showered me with unconditional love, care and faithful availability, especially in the absence of my father. In the life of my children, the contributions of my parents are enormous. Personally, I have benefited immensely from love and acceptance of several older women and men. Their contributions in my life and to the church and society are enormous. My own experience with the older women and men, my own experience as growing and the experiences of my respondents have provided the source for me to construct Indian Feminist Theo-gerontology. It critiques the social structures that dehumanize the older people; argues that older women's lives are profoundly situated, because age, like gender, is a social category that affects women's status and their everyday interactions with others and at the intersection of caste, gender and class; emphasizes on deconstruction of the stereotyped understanding and myths about old age; emphasizes on reconstruction of the later stage of life that continues to grow in God's image that is in them; On recovering the biblical images of older people in reaffirming

23 O. S. B. Daniel Durken, ed., *New Collegeville Bible Commentary: New Testament* (Collegeville: Liturgical Press: 2008), 283.

God's image in them; on becoming an advocate towards the rights of the older women and men; on using the resources of older people to prepare the older community to "grow positively." However, further research is needed to develop Indian Feminist Theo-gerontology. This essay strongly recommends that the theological institutions should introduce a curriculum related to the aged people and offer courses at BD and M.Th. levels.

16

Theological Culture of Ageing Together

Daniel Kirubaraj

Introduction

Trinitarian Community Cultural Action embedded in human beings can be implicit through Theological Culture of Ageing Together (TCAT). For Theology, Culture and Community Life has an organic relationship among them. Obviously, people in our world today grieve ageism.[1] As such, God, Nature participatory 'Ageing Together' from a theological perspective as an aspect of larger issues of ageing; frames the main goal of this study. The pursuit of this goal necessarily relates to the question of theology embedded cultural practices in ageing together than that of the technologically promoted virtual culture.

Anthropologists largely focus gerontology[2] on ageing and Ageism. Gerontology, a 'branch of biomedical sciences pursues ageing'[3] from various

1 Butler coined the word 'Ageism' 'in 1969, redefined it in 1975. It is, "a process of systematic stereotyping and discrimination against people because they are old, just as racism and sexism accomplish this with skin color and gender…Ageism allows the younger generations to see older people as different from themselves; thus they subtly cease to identify with their elders as human beings." Robert Neil Butler, *Why Survive? Being Old in America* (New York: Harper & Row, 1975).

2 "…mainstream gerontology – with its highly technical and instrumental, avowedly objective, value neutral and specialised discourses – lacks an appropriate language for addressing the basic moral and spiritual issues of our ageing society … and the fundamental questions of human existence… [around] what it means to be old." Thomas R. Cole and Ruth Ray, "Introduction: The humanistic study of aging past, present or why gerontology still needs interpretative inquiry," in *Guide to Humanistic Studies of Aging: What does it mean to Grow Old?* Edited by T. R. Cole, R. E. Ray and R. Kasterbaum (Baltimore: John Hopkins Press, 2010), 1-29.

3 The three concepts it relates to are: *Life expectancy* - 'how long, on average, an organism can be expected to live.' *Longevity*- 'the period of time an organism is expected to live under ideal circumstances' *Lifespan*- 'the period of time for life events of a species or sub-

anthropocentric perspectives.[4] Joao Pedro de Magalhaes sees ageing as 'growing older in a deleterious sense and progressively more likely to die.'[5] *Senesciencia*', an electronic journal reports ageing as an inevitable process not necessarily negative; but being matured physically and mentally.[6]

TCAT refers to the communion of God Nature and Humans. Particularly, all people - in the image of God and especially, the older in a 'wider sense.' International Longevity Centre of UK suggests, 'Ageing Together' as 'a communion of human beings', without 'us and them' divides.'[7] Since the Creation, the Trinitarian God Community is in communication[8] with certain God Culture[9] and in the context of Nature. However, rationalistic temper of technology and bureaucracy questions any non-scientific and supernatural vision. Social sciences provide modernity and postmodernity the scales of explanations, which was once with theology and philosophy.

Social Sciences like anthropology, psychology illumined modern life and analysed the crisis of authority of religious thought; but it was not a solution. Nevertheless, instead of capitulating to social sciences, Mosely suggests, "we can learn what they can teach about the religious dimensions of our cultural situation without abandoning the proper work of theology."[10] Also social sciences reveal, 'all human societies require a culturally cohesive religion.' Yet,

---

species typically occur; the maximum longevity of humans is 122 years'. Michel Allard, et al., *From Van Gogh's Time to Ours: 122 Extraordinary Years* (New York: W. H. Freeman & Co., 1998).

4 Postmodern and poststructuralist impacts changed the theoretical academic culture into 'humanistic gerontology' relating to 'arts and humanities': literature, autobiography, theatre, film, music and philosophy etc. – created new transdisciplinary and transcend disciplinary divisions of academic forms like gender and queer studies. Julia Twigg and Wendy Martin, "The Challenge of Cultural Gerontology," *The Gerontologist*, 53/3 (2014): 1-7. Available at: http://gerontologist.oxfordjournals.org (accessed, 01.07.2014).

5 Joao Pedro de Magalhaes, "What is Aging?" Available at: What%20Is%20Aging_%20 Definitions%20an… (accessed: 15.09.2020).

6 Ub.edu/senesciencia/noticia/what-is-ageing (accessed, 14.09.2020).

7 AT is beyond the older couples living as spouses or the single elders living in Homes for Senior Citizens. https://ilcuk.org.uk/what-happens-next/(accessed, 19.09.2020).

8 "Communication is one of the foundations of any culture, and God culture is certainly no exception." John A. Naphor, *God Culture: Book One of the Understanding the Almighty Series* (Morgan James Faith; Illustrated edition, 2014), 76.

9 "God, as primary cause, creates the intersex person through the free interplay of secondary causes, in the same way and to the same extent that God acts in the creation of every other person." Elyse J. Raby, "You knit me together in my mother's womb": A Theology of Creation and Divine Action in Light of Intersex," *Theology and Sexuality*, 24/2 (2018): 98-109. DOI: 10.1080/13558358.2018.1463637.

10 James G. Moseley, "Culture, Religion, and Theology," *Theology Today*, 37/ 3 (1980): 315-322.

not much work has been convincingly done on social and spiritual coherence. Hence, the concept and perspective inherent in the newly introduced neologism – *theo-gerontology*[11] which adheres to cultural awareness, conceptual adequacy and worshipfulness is employed in this study. The significance of the study is based on equal and independent interaction of God, Nature and the Humans. In that process, it hypothesises TCAT as an ongoing practical, holistic and participatory God + Nature + Human Culture (GNHC).

With this understanding, the study first highlights cultural issues and concerns related to 'Ageing Together.' Secondly, certain theo-gerontological approaches to TCAT. Thirdly, why and how TCAT can be meaningfully implied in the present context? Limitations of the study are the vast area of each of the three concepts: 'Theology', 'Culture' and 'Ageing Together' and their processes cannot be focused in their length and breadth. Further, the issues dealt with are centred more on Western experiences than those of the East.

TCAT: Cultural Issues and Concerns

Socially, ageing is a lifelong process of a person[12] growing older. Plato viewed ageing as 'a unique and fortunate experience of good life achieved through the best used gifts and time of the past.' Aristotle despises ageing as 'a natural process' of physical and moral decline.[13] Ageing, positively posits individuals of old age being wise, kind, dependable and happy. Negatively, ageing is being old, ill, useless, isolated, depressed and grumpy.

Current theories of ageing include both positive and negative approaches. There is always a choice of approach in gerontology.[14] Theories of both Ageing and Ageism posit older adults as being 'incompetent but warm'. Social and psychological theories approach ageing from individual, interpersonal, evolutionary and socio-cultural levels. They provide us a deeper understanding of Ageing. Three such theories are 'Terror Management Theory,'[15] 'Stereotype

11 Songram Basumatary newly introduces this terms to connect theology to gerontology and explore possibility of theological alternative to address the socio-culturally created horrifying negative image of Ageing. For details, see the last essay in this volume.

12 James Birren, "Theories of *Ageing*," in *Handbook of Theories of Ageing*, edited by Vern L. Bengtson, et.al. (New York: Springer Publishing Company, 1999), 467.

13 On Youth, Old Age, life and Death, on Breathing, by Aristotle, Written in 350 BCE, Translated by G.R.T. Ross. Available at: http://classics .mit.edu/Aristotle/youth_old.mb.txt (accessed, 20.09.2010).

14 Johnson, "Cultural Influences of Ageing and Ageism," Available at: https://us.sagepub.com/sites/default/files/upm-assets/90251_book_item_90251.pdf (accessed, 27.10.2020).

15 Terror Management Theory provides us the roots and motives of 'ageism towards old age groups among young and middle aged groups and among the young-old age group. Jeff Greenberg, Tom Pyszczynski and Sheldon Solomon, "The Causes and Consequences of a

Embodiment Theory'[16] and 'Social Identity Theory.'[17] These include the role of the culture and social norms and their values and highlight how cultural messages are subtly maintained at individual levels; and ways they can get challenged.

Daniel Bell writes: "the real problem of modernity is the problem of belief... a spiritual crisis since the old anchorages have proved illusory and the new ones have become submerged."[18] While Daniel claims a new religion to bring a new unity to modern life; he also seeks a realm of culture, a theory of 'the public household.' Yet, he wants the social fruits of religion and not its theological roots. Max Weber, Karl Marx, and Ferdinand Toennies too, criticise modernity for alienating men and women from authentic human society. They concede the idea of institutionalised religious functions and not its substance.[19] This shows how religious orders require social and cultural coherence. Referring to Paul Tillich's warning 'religions tend to make ultimate claims for them', Moseley suggests that "Tillich's Protestant principle is the critique of religion in the name of religion – when we hear calls for a renewal of the unifying function of religion.[20] Further he writes; in this sense, theology is a culturally vital enterprise... Much as we have to learn from it, more and better social science cannot take the place of theology."[21] This claim encourages this study to claim an authentic 'Theological Culture.'

Need for Self-Esteem: A Terror Management Theory, in *Public Self and Private Self*, edited by Roy F. Baumeister (New York: Springer, 1986), 189-212.

16 Stereotype Embodiment Theory defines 'ageism among the young-old and old-old age group. For more details refer Becca Levy, "Stereotype Embodiment a Psychosocial Approach to Ageing,"*Current Directions in Psychological Science*, 18/6 (2009): 332-336.

17 Social Identity Theory provides, 'an overview of the manifestation of ageism among different groups. Henri Tajfel, and John C. Turner, "An Integrative Theory of Intergroup Conflict," *The Social Psychology of Intergroup Relations*, 33/47 (1979): 74.

18 Daniel Bell, *The Cultural Contradictions of Capitalism* (New York: Basic Books, 1976), 10-14.

19 Gregory Baum, *Religion and Alienation: A Theological Reading of Sociology* (New York: Paulist Press, 1975).

20 Paul Tillich, *Systematic Theology* (Chicago: University of Chicago Press, 1967). Cited in James G. Moseley, Culture, Religion, and Theology."

21 James G. Moseley, Culture, Religion, and Theology."

TCAT: Postmodern Approach

'Postmodern approach'[22] demands a new theological reflection on Christian understanding of reality based on the Bible. G. J. Rossouw,[23] a theologian from Rand Afrikaans University, suggests following ten opportunities for theologians to revisit theology in the postmodern cultural context:

- To see it as 'an opportunity to understand the reality without which any discourse remains impoverished.
- To involve moral discourses on contemporary cultures with ethical analysis curtailed by modern science, politics and economics; and with new style of communication and leadership.
- To maintain a spirituality of wholeness with a bigger picture of personal and social life without set of 'do's and don'ts rules.'
- To imply a narrative theology wherein the Bible spirituality of wholeness for socialising of people with a commitment that evokes ownership of the world.
- To involve human subjectivity centred church communication with cognitive, emotive, and conative dimensions both from clergies and laities.
- To correct the imbalance of the character formation and inverse the order of two questions 'what we believe?' and 'who we are?' It makes theological culture identity and characters not a mere intellectual process but a comprehensive socialisation of community of believers.
- To draw a theology of God from the scripture which bestows unconditional dignity and value to all human beings – the widows, poor, orphans, tax collectors, Samaritans and not only elite experts.
- To imply the postmodern culture of 'from being right to doing right.' It is not to be anti-human or orthodoxy but to be complemented with orthopraxy.
- To reject Christian belief due to comparison of other religions warrant either to privatize Christianity from the social sphere or to make it relevant to others who differ and live the life meaningfully

22 Tyron Inbody, a theologian claims that postmodern is both a reaction to and result of modern culture. He compares it to 'Intellectual Velcro dragged across culture which characterizes almost anything one approves or disapproves.' Tyron Inbody, "Postmodernism: Intellectual Velcro Dragged Across the Culture?" *Theology Today*, 51/04 (1995): 524-538.

23 G. J. Rossouw, "Theology in Postmodern Culture: Ten Challenges," *HTS Theological Studies*, 49/4 (1993): 894-907. Available at: https://doin.org/10.4102/hts.v49i4.2528 (accessed, 03.11.2020).

in its fullness; on the basis of complete Christian understanding of reality.

- To practice a religious pluralism with cultural harmony in our global village. For, those differences of religions are in fact, differences in cultural claims.

These theoretical approaches urge to address a definite TCAT.[24] It is also a demand to go a step further beyond the 'theologies of, and with certain cultural and practical vision of God;[25] and a culture of humans itself as worship of God.[26] This is attempted below within the 'theo-gerontology' as TCAT.

TCAT: Theo-gerontology Approach

This section highlights three main concerns which relate to TCAT within the purview theo-gerontology. They are: theological interventions of Trinitarian Community God, the 'Nature' which embeds and serves the context of culture and the Humans' adventures of TCAT. In that process, references are made to the Bible.[27]

TACT and Theos God

TCAT comprehends that the *Theos-God*, 'in the beginning', entered into an irrevocable, *YAWEH*-borne and 'God Womb' cultural relationships.[28] This claims that TCAT is God's own property, and that it is God's interactive scheme

---

24 "The approach of experiential realism could indicate where science and faith deal with the same reality, where science questions faith assumptions, and where faith goes beyond the mandate and method of science. Although prescientific, Martin Luther's theology is the classical prototype of an experiential theology. We experience God's creative power in all of reality. We discern its regularities through observation and reason. So faith opens up all the space needed by science." https://www.researchgate.net/publication/229865054_Martin_Luther's_experiential_theology_as_a_model_for_faith-science_relationships.

25 James G. Moseley, Culture, Religion, and Theology."

26 In the opinion of Klaus Nurnberger "Theology challenges science to acknowledge the necessity of a transcendent frame of reference and moral accountability. Scientific insight challenges theology to reconceptualise its assumptions on God, creation, and eschatology to integrate best science." Available at: https://www.researchgate.net/publication/229865054_Martin_Luther's_experiential_theology_as_a_model_for_faith-science_relationships.

27 Stanley J. Grenz says, "While theology takes culture seriously it insists that its context becomes an authority with certain commitment to 'Scripture' which is theology's norming norm.'" Stanley J. Grenz, "Culture and Spirit: The Role of Cultural Context in Theological Reflection," *Asbury Theological Journal* 55/02 (Fall 2000): 45.

28 With reference *El-Shaddai* 'who grants "blessings of the womb and of the Breasts" Gen. 49:25, 'From the womb of God to creation' Job 38:29, 'Womb-love of God' in Jer. 31:20, *Abraham's Seed* in Gal. 3:29, *the imperishable seed* in 1 Pet. 1:23 and *God's Seed* in 1 John 3:9.

for life-sharing experiences in our world. As such, God created Nature as the cultural-bed for lives to flourish from within and without God-Self (Gen.1:1, 26-27; 3:8). God culturally cared for 'all flesh that are on the earth' and saved them through God's cultural covenant with Noah – a justful protection of TCAT (Gen. 9:1-17). God assured cultural blessings to all nations and all the families of the earth through the call and covenant with Abraham – a generational plan of TCAT (Gen. 12:1-3; 13:16; 15:5). God participated directly, culturally and actively to liberate Israel from all oppressive political crises – a liberative TCAT (Ex. 3:7-12; 13:17-22). God gave the 'Ten Commandments' as cultural ordinances to the people of Israel to practice certain theological ethics with moral and cultural values – A Socio-moral and ethical plan of TCAT (Gen 20:1-21). In all these, God, Nature and Humans interacted within a holistic TCAT formula of life.[29]

TCAT and Logos God

TCAT elucidates the *Logos-God's*[30] participatory interaction,[31] from below (Phil. 2:6-11). In that process, Jesus the God-Word subjectively and culturally incarnated in our scientifically perceivable world. He is, the theological 'Truth' being born into the cultural 'real.' Since the Creation, Jesus involved TCAT to establish the Reign of God in this world.

In the fullness of time (Gal. 4:5) God-Word became flesh and lived among us (John 1:1, 14), demonstrated God's Love (John 3:16) culturally fusioned theological values down to earth reality.[32] Jesus the Chief Shepherd offered himself as the *Lamb of God* – transformed the religious sacrifice

29 As mentioned in Isa. 11: 6-7: "The wolf shall live with the Lamb, the leopard shall lie down with the kid, the calf and the lion and the fatling together, and a little child shall lead them. The cow and the bear shall graze, their young shall lie down together; and the lion shall eat straw like the ox. The nursing child shall put its hand on the adder's den. They will not hurt or destroy on all my holy mountain; for the earth will be full of the the knowledge of the Lord as the waters cover the sea."

30 Referring to John 1:18, "No one has ever seen God; the only Son, who is in the bosom (*Kolpos*or pregnant) of God has made him known." For details see, Stramara and Daniel F. Jr, the Kolpos "Womb of God in the Greek Tradition," *Magistra*, 22/02 (2017). Available at: https://www.questia.com/library/journal/1P3-4317242101/the-kolpos-of-the-father-jn-1-18-as-the-womb-of (accessed, 17.10.2020).

31 "Long ago God spoke to our ancestors in many and various ways by the prophets, but in these last days (he) God has spoken to us by a Son ... through whom God also created the worlds." (Heb. 1:1-2). "Therefore we must pay greater attention to what we heard, so that we do not drift away from it" (Heb. 2:1).

32 As it is portrayed in the 'Seven I Am' sayings: "I am the bread of life" (John 6:35 & 41); "I am the light of the world" (8:12 & 9:5); "I am the door of the sheep" (10:7 & 9); "I am the good shepherd" (10:11); "I am the resurrection and the life" (11:25); "I am the way, the truth and the life" (14:6) and "I am the true vine"(15:1 & 5).

into a liberative process of TCAT - in our oppressive colonial world (Lk 4: 16-22). In fact, in his resurrection from the dead, he has entailed TCAT into *Eschatological* experience of a New Heaven and New Earth beyond this world (Isa. 65:17-25; 2 Pet. 3:13; Rev. 21:1-5).

TCAT and Ruach God

TCAT implores the proactive role of *Ruach* or *Pneuma* – the Holy Spirit in the overall life-generating culture; everywhere and always (Gen. 1:2; Ezek. 37:7-10). If YAWEH shares the Breath and the same Jesus lives in flesh and blood; the *Ruach* cultures them; the Breath being formed into Flesh and Blood. Indeed, "the pneumatology of the biblical faith communities arose out of the connection of the "spirit" with "Breath" and consequently with life."[33] In the biological sense, it is culturally the Umbilical Cord relationship; a conduit between the developing embryo and the placenta. This seems to be a common cultural experience of all individuals. Seemingly, this is a viable TCAT and the ground of *Ruach's* generative cultural activity that connects God, Nature and the Human beings. The Creator Spirit as the divine power creates[34] and sustains life.[35] Since the Creation, *Ruach* has been the ultimate culturati, in the formation of the whole cultural word from its formless void and darkness into the orderly world of Light and life (Gen. 1:2). Cause of the Jesus the *Logos* to be conceived and be born in the Womb of Virgin Mary (Lk.1:30-35). Indeed, all that is made and created do breathe *Ruach*, 'the Spirit' and 'the Wind.' *Ruach* was active in the origin of diverse cultures at the Tower of Babel (Gen 11:1-9).[36] It also, had been the Spirit of Pentecost (Acts 2:1-8) resolving the issue of different languages. Creating and sustaining the community of God culture with one Lord; into one faith one baptism (Eph. 4:5). In Jesus' discourse with Nicodemus the source of new cultural life/rebirth (Jn. 3:1-10. *Ruach* of God descended in the form of a dove on Jesus at his Baptism (Mt. 3:16-17). The 'advocate' and 'witnesses' from God (Jn.15:26).

The above discussions reveal that the Trinitarian Community God is active, interactive with the Nature and Humans, in the origin and process of TACT in our world.

---

33 Stanley J. Grenz, "Culture and Spirit: The Role of Cultural Context in Theological Reflection," *Asbury Theological Journal*, 55/02 (Fall 2000): 46.

34 As we read in Gen.1:2 & 2:7.

35 As we read in Ps. 104: 29-30; Isa. 32:15; Job 27:3; 34:14-15.

36 Theodore Hiebert, "The Tower of babel and the Origin of the World's Cultures," *Journal of Biblical Literature,* 126/01 (Spring, 2007): 29-58. Available at: https://www.jstor.org/stable/i27638414 (accessed, 17.11.2020).

TCAT and Nature

Indeed, all civilizations and cultures in the world are rooted in Nature. TCAT itself begins with the creation of Nature (Gen. 1) The Nature glory Creator (Ps. 19:1-6). As for humans the world is epistemologically 'observed' or ontologically existed.[37] Nevertheless, theologically God and Humans as inseparable entities together experience TCAT in the context of Nature. In that process, Nature as God's creation provides endless cycles of seasons for planting, harvesting, migrating and the overall living. Eventually, the norms of TCAT experience threat of existence and long for redemption (Rom. 8:19-23).

The Trinitarian God's love, life, culture preserves, controls and liberates Nature which is part of the whole creation. TCAT within the Nature, the following biblical references are made. First, in the creation process, humans were made of the dust of the ground (Gen. 2:7). Vegetation with fruits and seeds, the animals, birds and all creatures are given as food for biological survival of all living beings (Gen. 1:13). The Sun, Moon, Stars and Planets process seasons to favour all cultural events (Gen. 1:14). In the justful punishment as well as saving of all lives TCAT was demonstrated in the Ark of Noah (Gen. 7). In the liberative scheme, God cared for the people of Israel in the form of Pillar of Fire and Pillar of Cloud (Ex.13:22); making way for them through the Sea (Ex. 13:17 -14:29). Animals in the Old Testament were sacrificed as part of the worship culture. Jesus himself has been portrayed as the Lamb of the Passover (Ex.12: 1-4) and the very Lamb of God (Jn. 1:29-36; Rev. 5:5-14) and he rode on the Donkey to disclose his messiahship (Zech. 9:9 & Matt. 21-11). God challenges humans to learn TCAT from ants (Pro. 6:6-8) and animals (Job.12:7-10; Jer. 8:7; Matt. 6:26). Animals speak to humans and reveal God's will to the Humans (Num. 21:28-31).

Yet, Nature today is under great threat from the very humans. Some of the nature related problems of our times are 'global warming, ozone layer depletion, acid rain, natural resource depletion, waşte disposal, deforestation and so on. The teen age climate activist Greta Thunberg's anger upon the world leaders[38] is a justful cry for TCAT in our world today.

TCAT and Humans

Living the fullness of life together is one of the most pressing issues. People in our present world suffer revulsions and social divides. COVID-19 has brought the social divide as never before. 'Generation divide' based on 'impatience,

---

37 Hongbao Ma, "The Nature of Time and Space," *Nature and Science*, 1/1 (2003): 1-11.

38 Expressed at the Climate Action Summit, UN Headquarters, New York on 23rd September 2019. For details see: https://www.npr.org/tags/141229108/u-n.

over confidence, and materialistic'[39] and 'religious divide'- lives differently based on religious conviction like Hinduism, Islam, Christianity and etc., hamper the peace of the world. Human made 'Media and Technology' enforce 'Digital Divide' which is a major challenge to TCAT. Artificial Intelligence (AI) encounters the 'Image of God' and its cultural values.[40]

World Population Prospects of the United Nations reveal to us that "By 2050, one in four persons living in Europe and Northern America could be aged 65 or over. In 2018, for the first time in history, persons aged or above outnumbered children under five years globally. The number of persons aged 80 years or over is projected triple, from 143 million in 2019 to 426 million in 2050."[41] This report helps us to understand that Ageing is not an issue only for the aged but for the whole people; especially the children.

At this juncture, there seems to be two choices for human beings to live in this world. One is to live culturally responsible together with other human beings as well as God and the Nature in unity. The other is to live divided and to suffer natural, theological values. Even though this problem seems to exist since creation, the alarming socio-political, cultural and ethical, global and local, and natural and artificial adversities call us to realise the need for TCAT. Few role models from the Bible towards a participatory TCAT are: Abraham, an 'Individual Faith Model' (Gen 12); Joseph 'Familial Reconciliation Model' (Gen. 45:1-8); Samuel, a 'Prophet Model' (1 Sam. 3:5-9); Moses, a 'Liberation Model' (Ex. 3); Moabite Ruth, a 'Feminist' (Ruth 1:15-18); Jonah, a 'Universal Ecclesial Model' (Jonah 3); Mary the mother of Jesus, a 'Theological Cultural Model' (Lk. 2:38); and Jesus, a 'Shepherd Model' (John 10:11).

Taking the above facts into consideration, we cannot say any more let us be divided for any reason. The need for TCAT is from theoretical, theological and ageing points of view is felt highly indispensable and urgent need of the hour.

TCAT – Implications for Present Context

From the foregoing considerations and reflections, one could infer the following lessons for those who want to live in unity and peace, which

---

39 Ng Chia Wee, "Commentary: Regardless of Age, Here's How to Make Sense of Singapore's Generation Divide," *Channel News Asia*. https://www.channelnewsasia.com/news/commentary/millennials- (accessed, 20.11.2020).

40 *AI is going to change the world more than anything in the history of (hu)mankind: More than Electricity… In future, if you don't know coding, you don't know programming, it's only going to get more difficult*. Kai-Fu Lee quoted in Mike Thomas, "7 ways AI can change the World for Better … Worse," *Built-In*. Available at: https://builtin.com/artificial-intelligence/artificial-intelligence-future (accessed, 10.11.2020).

41 United Nations, *Ageing*. Available at: (accessed, 20.11.2020).

are primarily drawn from a theo-gerontological perspective as the current gerontological approaches do not involve theological values:

1. The Ageing, Ageism and Ageing Together are interconnected and their repercussions reach out far and wider than mere human concerns. Hence, new approaches are to be explored.
2. Both Community Life and Culture can only be effective, true and positive within the milieu of theological relationship. Theological experience in itself is to live and share the values of God[42] and the Reign of God, in a given context.
3. To aim at a culture specific, effective and meaningful continuity of 'goodness and blessings upon the Creation,'[43] certain God, Nature and Human communed Ageing Together is inevitable.
4. Changes in theological reflections with due importance to the contextual theoretical advancements. For example, TCAT is discussed with reference to the postmodern approach and beyond.
5. There is a need for new and appropriate theological methods to be formulated and employed in fields of cultural studies.
6. The ten suggestions given by Rossouw are suggested to be further researched and their findings may be implemented by the communities of faith in the Indian Context.
7. Nature to be a valid factor in every theological, social anthropological ontological study.
8. Theo-gerontology, to be part of the curricula of the Christian Education and Theological Education.
9. TCAT and its praxis form of GNHC to be widely practiced to maintain the holistic lives with values of the Reign of God.

Conclusion

This study started with a search for a viable Theological Culture of Ageing Together. In that process, a newly conceived theo-gerontology was employed as a viable methodology. It paved the ground to approach the problem of Ageing in a wider and holistic manner. The first section identified the cultural issues related to Ageing from postmodern perspective. It highlighted as many as ten

42 *Agape* – the unconditional love of God for people and vis-à-vis, Holiness – the divine nature of God, Justice – the socio-ethical values of God, Trinity Community Communion – God, Nature and Human Communion, Eternal Life – The Fullness of life: here and now and the otherworld (*eschatological*).

43 "And God saw that the light was good" (Gen. 1:4); 'the earth was good' (v. 10); 'the vegetation plants yielding seed … was good (vv. 11&12); 'the planets like Sun, Moon, Stars' were good (v. 18); 'living creatures were good' and God blessed them 'multiply' (vv. 21&22); 'wild animals, cattle and creeping things were good and God blessed them (v. 25b); God created 'humans in God's Image and blessed them (vv. 28&31).

contextually valid points to revisit theological reflection on cultural concerns. Section two of the study identified the cultural roles of Trinitarian Community God, Nature and Human beings - in the theological process of Ageing Together. This qualified the study theologically that God, Nature and humans are independent beings and yet fully dependants. They, always theologically interact in their social and culture related activities. However, in the process, it was identified that a fully scientific and technological approach to life severely challenges the possibilities of collective community and responsible ways of life today. Hence the study in the third section recommends TCAT as a God + Nature + Human Culture, to be implemented with due importance and equal participation in our world today.

17

Theo-critical Exploration of *Ageing* Towards a *Theo-gerontology*

Songram Basumatary

The long years of 969 was not too long for human life to live,
but surprisingly the short years of just 70 or perhaps 80 is
long enough for human life to get old and be gone!

Ageing[1] and issues around *Ageing* are not mere bio-physical processes or a social phenomenon, but a deep theological mystery and *theo-spiritual* reality. First and foremost, one of the tough theological questions is "If human beings are created in the image of God, why do they age and die?" Bringing this question into the dialectic with *bio-physiology*, "Is *Ageing* a natural process or God's design?" It is indeed mysterious as Strehler imagines and puts it this way: "*Ageing* and death do seem to be what Nature has planned for us. But what if we have other plans?"[2] "What this other plans could probably be?" Theologically, "Is there something like divine mystery behind and beyond *Ageing*?"

In fact, the answer to such questions, according to Biblical accounts is that it is God's design for humanity as human origin and destiny are determined

---

1 In various literatures, the spelling – *Ageing* and *Aging* are used. In fact, the former is British form and the later an American. As per the root word (Age) and English grammatical form are concerned, both are correct. As noun, both refer to the process of getting older, while as adjective it is description of people, animals or other elements that become old. Whatever may the English orientation and grammatical form be, the spelling *Ageing* is used consistently throughout the paper, which unless and otherwise indicated, means "getting old", "state of being old" and the "issues of old peoples."

2 Bernard L. Strehler, *Time, Cells, and Ageing* (New York: Academic Press, 1977). As cited in João Pedro de Magalhães, *Gerontology Information* (June 16, 2013). Available at: http://www.senescence.info. Also, Bruce Goldberg, *Reversing Aging: Add 25 to 50 years to Your Life Naturally* (Delhi: Pustak Mahal, 2001), 31. [Reprinted from *Look Younger Live Longer*, published by Llewellyn Publications, Minnesota, 1999].

by God. God gives life and God takes life. The *theo-anthropological* dynamic of creation and the relationship between God as Creator and human as created, show that human life and longevity are the gracious gifts of God within God's divine scheme. The Bible presents *Ageing* as blessed moments and a satisfying experience of life with dignified identity and honour attributed to and expected from young ones. However, as human society progressed, the Bible also presents the fact that such a blessed image of *Ageing* slowly and steadily regressed and even God had to cut the age down from 969 to 120 and much latter even to 70 or if strong enough, perhaps 80.[3] The reason for such shortening of life as well as pain, suffering and decay are all ascribed to sin and unrighteousness. It is because of sin and increasing wickedness in humans that God has done so.

Even much later in human history, *Ageing* appears to be conditioned by particular religio-cultural and socio-economic factors rather than divine design and gift of God, nor a consequence of sin. Instead of being a blessed moment and a satisfying experience of life, it is seen as a terrifying and burdensome stage of life. In the contemporary societies, the anthropocentric and mere economic counting on productivity of human life furthermore has led to a dreadful *Ageing* than graceful *Ageing*. One of the best simple examples is premium calculation insurance companies – "the older the costlier." Such socio-economic and culturally constructed binaries between young and old and negative image greatly challenged me to think and reflect theologically "what *Ageing* really is not" rather than what it is considered to be. Therefore, an attempt is made in this essay to construe the whole issues around *Ageing theo-critically* and construct a *theo-gerontology* that may help to see the issue with entirely different eyes.

As societies and the world around us witness the growing vulnerability and plight of the *Aged* people, despite various policies and agencies of care, it is perhaps of utmost necessity that the issue is addressed at its theological core. Not of mere sympathetic concern and care, but deliberate attempt towards recognising their human personhood and worth in the light of *theo-anthropological* understanding of *Ageing*. There may remain unanswered questions at the end, but a humble and yet an ambitious bold theological vision is taken towards liberating *Ageing* from de-humanizing and dreadful negative images with a conviction that "*Ageing* is a crucible – a point where communities can transcend the limits of *Ageing*" and provide not just a better space for *Aged* people to experience "Graceful *Ageing*" but to recognise their agency towards building a community of justice peace and harmony.

In order to arrive at this set objective, the essay is structured into four main sections – Conceptual Clarifications, Methodological Considerations,

3 Gen. 5:27; Gen. 6:3; Ex. 34:7; Ps. 90:10.

Gerontological Discourses on *Ageing*, and Towards a *Theo-gerontology* with introduction and conclusion.

Conceptual Clarifications

The terminologies used in the essay may appear over-loaded with biased subjective conceptual notion, theological jargons and impregnated dubious meanings. Therefore, for the sake of conceptual clarity it is felt necessary that two important, perhaps comparatively new terms, are defined and explained.[4] The first term is *Gerontology* which was coined by Ilya Ilyich Mechnikovz in 1903. He derived the term from two Greek root words: γέρων and λογία– *geron* and *logia* ("old person" and "word").[5] At present, the term is used by various gerontologists as a discipline that studies the social, cultural, psychological, cognitive, and biological aspects of *Ageing*. According to Erber, it is "the study of the biological, behavioural, and social phenomena that occur from the point of maturity to old age."[6] As a scientific academic discipline, *gerontology* examines the biological, economic, psychological, and social and health/ fitness aspects of the entire *Ageing* process. By nature, it is an interdisciplinary field where different disciplines seek to address the problems associated with *Ageing*.[7] For instance, biologists focus on the biological processes of *Ageing*; psychologists focus on aspects like mental abilities, personality and behaviour; and the sociologists study the social roles, group behaviour and status of older people. One of the important aspects of gerontological studies is that gerontologists do not focus only on the scientific study of the process of *Ageing*, but also on the improvement of the health and well-being of *Aged* people.

Secondly, in order to reflect and explore the issues in *Ageing* theologically, the term – *theo-gerontology* (*theos-geron-logia*) is coined just by adding *theos* as prefix to *gerontology* keeping its implied and used meanings intact. This coinage is done with a deliberate intention that the concept and issue of human biological '*Ageing*' cannot be separated from God and God's incompressible mystery of creating human in God's own image and the *telos* of human being and the entire creation. Perhaps, in strict sense of the term, "if God created human beings in particular, in God's own image, it implies that there is no question of *Ageing* in all aspects." It also implies that "if human beings age, God too must age." And if so, the very chilly theological question would be "Is God

4 Other technical terms are defined and explained along the content, either qualified in the text or in the footnote.

5 D. K. Harris, *Dictionary of Gerontology* (New York: Greenwood Press, 1988), 80.

6 J. T. Erber, *Ageing and older Adulthood*, 2nd edition (Chichester: Wiley-Blackwell, 2010), 394.

7 L. R. Aiken, *Ageing: An Introduction to Gerontology* (Thousand Oaks, CA.: Sage, 1995), 21.

subject to decay biologically as humans are?" In that case, even any children out of curiosity would ask, "How old is God?" In deeper *theo-ontological* and *anthropo-existential* sense, if birth, growth and decay are God's design in creation of human in God's own image, the young boy Gautama's question appears extremely a relevant theological question –"Why we get old? "Why we die?"

If we connect such complex theological questions on *Ageing* to the very heart of Christianity – the *Heilsgeschichte*, "*Ageing* is not the end, but a process towards living eternally unaged!" This suggests that the concept and issue of *Ageing* are inseparably related to the entire doctrinal and theological themes of Christian Faith. Therefore, the proposed theological construct – *theo-gerontology* is an attempt to connect theology *to gerontology* or vice versa, and explore possibilities of theological alternative means to address the socio-culturally created horrifying negative image of *Ageing*.

Methodological Considerations

To serve the purpose of reflecting and exploring '*Ageing*' and the underneath complex theological notions, "*theo-critical reading*" is used as a hermeneutical tool, and in order to engage in the stated theological issues objectively, a simplified "*geron-theo-praxis*" is adopted as a methodological approach with a deliberate intention that practical theology needs to take a lead in the *theo-professional* conversation with the field of *gerontology* and provide a theologically enlightened understanding of *Ageing*.[8] Though the concept is taken from the Practical Theology and Liberation Theologies, "*Geron-theo-praxis*" here does mean neither the exclusive concern for application of theology in the case of the former, nor the relevance of theology to the context in the case of the latter. Over and above these, it is engaging *theo-gerontology* in matters of public importance theologically with a goal towards shaping a public space and social reality for *Ageing* well. The objective her is to open up a space and agency where *theo-gerontology* not only meets the contemporary experiences and questions of *Aged* people, but also uses their agency for a wider public cause.

In other words, this approach, technically speaking, can be termed as "*reflective-praxis paradigm*" of theological engagement in the issues of public importance. To tune this into the concerned discourse at hand, *Ageing* is a matter of utmost public importance and a great challenge to the Church and societies worldwide. In the globalizing and even in a globalizing society, *Ageing* is a common issue that requires an effective praxis oriented theological response.

---

8 Cf. Davies, James. "A Practical Theology of *Ageing*: Biblical Perspectives for Individuals and the Church," *Christian Education Journal*, 5/2 (November, 2008): 274-293. Available at: https://link.gale.com/apps/doc/A187049931/AONE?u=tel_main&sid=AONE&xid=767d9c43. accessed August 17, 2020.

This approach in great extent may help the proposed *Theo-gerontology* push forward not only at serving the *Ageing*, alleviate their spiritual and emotional needs and fears, but also to position the *Ageing* in the right social space and proper theological personhood. Of course, practical theologians[9] have already identified certain *gerontological* issues and various aspects of needs of the *Ageing* such as experience of grief, reality of frailty, fear of death, search for new identity in old age, issue of sexuality, relationships with children, grandchildren and siblings, unresolved interpersonal conflicts, friendships, and the importance of religion and religious beliefs, self-esteem, desire for successful *Ageing* etc. However, my browsing through the recent researches show that *gerontology* is still much an uncultivated field in practical theology and the issues and concerns identified by the practical theologians are not addressed from an in-depth "*geron-theo-praxis*" perspective. Therefore, an attempt is made here to read and reflect the issue of *Ageing theo-critically* using the explored approach herein.

Gerontological Discourses on Factors of *Ageing*?

Ageing does not just mean the later life experience of a person, but the life-long process of growing older.[10] In a strict bio-anthropological sense, the term *Ageing* refers to the biological process of growing older in a deleterious sense.[11] It is one of the most complex biological processes which has been defined as the collection of changes that render human beings progressively more likely to die.[12] *Ageing* can also be defined as a progressive functional decline, or a gradual deterioration of physiological function with age, including a decrease

9 For example See, L. R. Aiken, *Ageing: An Introduction to Gerontology* (Thousand Oaks, CA.: Sage, 1995).; S. Pattison and J. Woodward, *A Reader in Practical Theology* (Oxford: Blackwell, 2000).; R. R. Osmer, *Practical Theology: An introduction* (Grand Rapids, MI: Eerdmans, 2008).; Dap Louw and A. E. Louw, *Adult Development and Ageing* (Bloemfontein, South Africa: Psychology Publications, 2009).; J. T. Erber, *Ageing and older Adulthood*, 2nd edn. (Chichester: Wiley-Blackwell, 2010).' Harold G. Koenig, *Ageing and God: Spiritual Pathways to Mental Health in Midlife and Later Years* (New York: Routledge, 2010).

10 James Birren, "Theories of *Ageing*," in *Handbook of Theories of Ageing*, ed. Vern L. Bengtson, et.al. (New York, NY: Springer Publishing Company, 1999), 467.

11 Some authors call it "senescence." See, G. C. Williams, "Pleiotropy, natural selection, and the evolution of senescence," *Evolution* 11 (1957): 398-411.; Alex Comfort, *Ageing: The Biology of Senescence* (London: Routledge & Kegan Paul, 1964).; Caleb E. Finch, *Senescence, Longevity, and the Genome* (Chicago and London: The University of Chicago Press, 1990).

12 P. B. Medawar, *An Unsolved Problem of Biology* (London: H. K. Lewis, 1952).

in fecundity[13] or the intrinsic, inevitable, and irreversible age-related process of loss of viability and increase in vulnerability.[14]

There are different dimensions of *Ageing* that are identified by the gerontologists and each dimension has its own definition and meaning. For example, according to bio-physiological dimension, as mentioned above, it is regressive by physical condition. And the psychological dimension[15] reveals that "when physical age go down, the psychological age also go down." This clearly suggests that human *Ageing* is associated with a wide range of physiological and psychological changes, which not only make *Ageing* more susceptible to physical regression and emotional anxieties in life but also reduces the normal functions of a person and renders him/her more susceptible to a number of other diseases.

With regard to the question – "Why Humans Age?" various theories suggest diverse factors behind human *Ageing*.[16] For example, the *Damage-based Theories*, as the name implies, defend that *Ageing* is a consequent result of a continuous process of damage accumulation originating from the processes of metabolism. The general idea is that there is a slow build-up of damage to the human body even starting from conception, which eventually leads to dysfunction or failure of critical organs like heart or the whole body system in latter stage of life.[17] In a nutshell, *Ageing* is a result of many forms of damage accumulation of defensive or protective genes. It is predominantly a result of interactions with the environment and damage from chemical reactions.

According to *Programmed Theories*, *Ageing* is programmed into the human body systems and it is an essential and innate part of the bio-physiology of humans.[18] If not, human beings would live forever. It is maintained that *Ageing* is predetermined and it occurs on a fixed schedule triggered by

13 See, L. Partridge and M. Mangel, "Messages from Mortality: The Evolution of Death rates in the Old," *Trends in Ecology and Evolution* 14/11 (1999): 438-442.; Lopez-Otin et al., "The Hallmarks of *Ageing*," *Cell* 153/6 (2013): 1194-1217.

14 Alex Comfort, *Ageing: The Biology of Senescence* (London: Routledge & Kegan Paul, 1964).

15 R. J. Havighurst, "Successful Ageing," in *Process of Ageing: Social and Psychological Perspectives*, vol. 1, eds. Richard H. Williams, Clark Tibbits, and Wilma Donohue (New Brunswick: Aldine Transaction, 1963).; J. K. Mcnulty and F. D. Fincham, "Beyond positive psychology? Toward a Contextual view of Psychological Processes and Well-being,"*American Psychologist* 67/2 (2012): 101-110.

16 T. B. L. Kirkwood and S. N. Austad, "Why do we age?" *Nature* 408 (2000): 233-238.

17 See Leonid A. Gavrilov and Natalia S. Gavrilova, "Evolutionary Theories of Aging and Longevity,"*The Scientific World Journal* 2 (2002): 339-356.; Leonid A. Gavrilov and Natalia S. Gavrilova, "The Reliability Theory of Aging and Longevity," *Journal of Theoretical Biology* 213/4 (2001): 527–545.

18 See Thomas B. Kirkwood, "Understanding the Odd Science of Aging," *Cell* 120/4 (Feb. 2005): 437-447.

genetic programmes of, particularly, the three inter-connected main systems – the endocrine or hormonal system, the immune system, and the genes. The changes that occur in these systems over time cause the symptoms and signs of *Ageing*.[19] However, there are also views that the environmental factors to a great degree influence the process and outcome of *Ageing*. Both, the intrinsic and extrinsic factors cited in various theories suggest that *Ageing* is perhaps a mysterious process, which in religious thought is conceptualised and believed that there is supernatural involvement in it.

Towards *Theo-gerontology*

While attempting to explore a *theo-gerontology*, a basic question I encountered is "What is *Ageing* theologically?" For various theories of *Ageing* do not clearly suggest something theological about it. Nevertheless, the common understandings and beliefs on *Ageing* in various societies suggest that it is a social and cultural construct rather than a mere bio-physiological process. This perhaps paves a way to reflect *Ageing* theologically. For the Biblical references and the theological inferences are answers to the questions arising out of the social realities. In order to understand this fact, it is in fact appropriate that "what the *Ageing* is not" is highlighted first before exploring it theologically.

What Ageing is NOT

The social realities show that there are numerous myths around *Ageing*. The mystery of *Ageing* and inevitable death of the human body have enthused more myths accumulated by passing days. Bruce Goldberg interestingly lists seven peculiar myths as follows:[20]

- Old people become Senile.
- Older people are no longer productive.
- Older people are always ill.
- Sex is either impossible or unenjoyable after 60.
- Older people are lonely and poor.
- Older people are sedentary.
- Creativity disappears in old age.

Such myths have created and still continue to create a negative image of *Ageing* across communities and cultures. Today, people in general know more of "What *Aged* people are not" than "what they are" due to such myths. With undue reasons *Ageing* has been seen in a negative light, though there are exceptional cases. When it comes to the human person and worth, it appears so paradoxical to the golden idea that "old is gold" and "Grey hair, a wisdom."

19 J. Campisi, "*Ageing*, Chromatin, and Food Restriction-Connecting the Dots," *Science* 289/5487 (2000): 2062-2063.

20 Goldberg, *Reversing Aging...*, 27 ff.

For such reasons, many *Aged* people face *Ageing* as terror; as frailty, anxiety, loss and loneliness haunts them day in and day out. Conditioned by religious, socio-cultural, economic and political factors, it appears to them terribly dreadful rather than what long life theologically is considered as a blessing. Perhaps, it is seen by many as the first step to death. Consider the following agonizing expression of a 95 years old Episcopalian and an unknown poet towards the terror of death in old age:

> *What does all that have to do with me now? They were young, all of them, and Jesus only thirty-three when he died. He suffered, yes, but only through one night and one day. Three hours on the cross, and I have been praying to die every day for ten years.*[21]

"Do not ask me to remember; don't try to make me understand,
Let me rest and know you're with me, Kiss my cheek and hold my hand.
I'm confused beyond your concept, I am sad and sick and lost.
All I know is that I need you, to be with me at all cost.
Do not lose your patience with me, Do not scold or curse or cry.
I cannot help the way I'm acting; can't (be) different though I try.
Just remember that I need you; that the best of me is gone,
Please don't fail to stand beside me; Love me 'til my life is done."

Is *Ageing* so terrifying theologically? Perhaps, if the above samples of expressions are read juxtapositorily, it appears that terror and agony of *Ageing* is seen even more than the Cross of Christ!

As it was expressed in the introduction, there are numerous tough theological questions around the issue of *Ageing*. First are the "What" questions: "What is *Ageing*?"; "What is behind and beyond *Ageing*? Death or life? "Do humans age out?" The second one is "Why" questions: "Why humans age?", "Do we age because of sin?"; "Do we age to die or do we age to live?" "Is *Ageing* a progression towards something like a greater end?" or "Is *Ageing* a movement towards life immortal?" The third is the "how" question: "How humans age?"; "What makes human age?"

From a *bio-gerontological* perspective, there are clear-cut scientific answers to the question of "How and Why humans age?" As it is already pointed out, *Ageing* in simple terms has been defined in *gerontological* studies as a biological process of growing older in the passage of time. For instance, Leonard Hayflick[22] the preeminent cell biologist presents the truth

21 Cited in Nancy J. Baxter, "Grey Theology: A Christian's Path to the Season of Wisdom," *Dilog: The Texas Episcopalian* 2/1 (March 2012), 10.

22 L. Hayflick, How and Why We Age (New York: Ballantine Books, 1995).; Leonard Hayflick, "*Ageing*: The Reality: "Anti-*Ageing*" Is an Oxymoron," *The Journals of Gerontology* 59/6

about human *Ageing* that not only the major biological systems change as a person grows older, but also the modes of thinking and feeling, moods and sexual desires, personality traits and memories get altered. This findings in fact dispels many of the most persistent myths on *Ageing*.

Theologically, it is more than a biological process. *Ageing* is presented in the Bible both positively and negatively – blessing as well as curse. Long life is considered a blessing of God and the short life the wrath of God. God blessed the years of human, but God also cursed the years of human…! God blessed people and they lived long or God gave long years to them and blessed their life? So, taken into consideration the multi-dimensional understandings discussed above, I instead realise that *Ageing* is not limited to a bio-physiological dimension alone and it can never be ugly, terrifying, dreadful, worrisome/burdensome, but *theo-spiritually* it is beautiful, inspiring, welcoming and hopeful!

Unfortunately, the existential reality of today exposes that *Ageing* persons enter into the space of identity delusion or "identity crisis" as Erikson puts it.[23] *Ageing* has become a threat to the very personhood of a person in which his/her identity, dignity and very meaning of life is challenged. The trend of '*Ageing*' and treatment to the Aged people raises numerous questions such as "Do *Ageing* people lose personhood?"; "Do *Ageing* people have worth of human beings?"; "Do *Ageing* people have social standing?"

These questions led me to think and conclude that there is a need for a "Counter Cultural Theology of *Ageing*"[24] which in my construction is *theo-gerontology* based on *Aged* people's own *geron-theo-spiritualis*.[25] I consider it as counter-cultural because it challenges the conditioned negative cultural notion that *Aged* people are not beautiful/handsome, non-energetic, non-productive, burdensome for family, too dependent, absent from the present etc. This theology would not just provide basis and open up avenues for advocacy and care for the *Aged*, but deconstruct the very negative notion of *Ageing*. It also would challenge the resultant common aspiration of everybody

---

(June 2004): B573–B578. Available at: https://doi.org/10.1093/gerona/59.6.B573; also see, Robert Arking, *The Biology of Ageing: Observations and Principles*" (Oxford: OUP, 2006).; Steven N. Austad, *Why We Age: What Science Is Discovering About the Body's Journey Through Life* (NY: John Wiley & Sons, Inc., 1997).

23 Erik Erikson, *Identity and the Life Cycle* (New York, London: Norton, 1980).

24 For further insights on the counter-cultural nature of "Theology of *Ageing*", see D. J. Maitland, *Ageing as Counter Culture* (New York: Pilgrim Press, 1991).; Stephen Ames, *Finding the Way: A Theology of Ageing* (Melbourne: Benetas, 2012).

25 The derived term "*geron-theo-spirituality*" (*geron* (old) +*theos* (god)+*spiritualis* (spirituality) here is used to mean not a mere supernatural oriented spirituality of *Aged* people, but the spirituality that transcends the religiosity or religionistic spirituality and encompasses both the explicit and implicit dimensions of spirituality.

wanting to be young or remain young, and also the market economy that takes advantage of the situation through various anti-*Ageing* beauty products such as cosmetics, anti-*Ageing* drug and laser treatments that unmask the signs of old. For Christian theology strongly affirms that human personhood is the irrevocable gift of God. Human worth does not rest in what one does or has but merely in whom he/she really is as created in the image of God irrespective of age.[26] It is counted on a person's being, not what he/she does or can do. As a gift of God, such human identity and worth is in every individual from womb to tomb. Therefore, there is an existential quest in every individual for living well and most importantly, *Ageing* well![27]

The well-being and *Ageing* well is determined jointly by the interplay between individual characteristics and qualities of people's social environments.[28] For a sense of well-being and *Ageing* well refer to an individual's feelings based on how older persons perceive the concept of well-being[29] and the state of well-being is a multifaceted phenomenon in the older population which generally involves happiness, self-contentment, satisfying social relationships, and autonomy.[30] All these perhaps depend on a positive outlook as it is conditioned by social, psychological and spiritual determinants.[31]*Ageing* well, therefore, needs certain social conditions and moral responsibility, mutuality and relationality which are the key to address the issue of *Ageing* particularly on negativity about it. In this regard, the following six specific social tasks or responsibility suggested by James Holly

26 Julie A. Gorman, "New Significance and Identity: A Practical Theological Perspective," in *Practical Theology for Ageing*, ed. Derrel R. Watkins (New York, London: Routledge, 2003), 185.

27 This concept is also expressed in various other construct like – "Healthy Ageing", "Positive Ageing", "Productive Ageing", "Active Ageing", and "Successful Ageing". See, L. Foster and A. Walker, "Active and successful *Ageing*: a European policy perspective," *Gerontologist* 55/1 (2015): 83-90.; L. Buys and E. Miller, *Active Ageing: Developing a Quantitative Multidimensional Measure, Active Ageing, Active Learning* (Berlin, Germany: Springer; 2012).

28 J. K. Mcnulty, F. D. Fincham, "Beyond Positive Psychology? Toward a Contextual View of Psychological Processes and Well-being," *American Psychologist* 67/2 (2012): 101-110.

29 W. W. Spirduso, K. L. Francis an P. G. Macrae, *Physical Dimensions of Ageing* (Champaign, IL, USA: Human Kinetics), 2005.

30 U. Kunzmann, T. D. Little and J. Smith, "Is age-related stability of subjective well-being a paradox?" *Psychology and Ageing* 15/3 (2000): 511-526.

31 John W. Rowe and Robert L. Kahn, "Successful *Ageing*," *The Gerontologist* 37/4 (1997): 433-434.; R. J. Havighurst, "Successful *Ageing*," in *Process of Ageing: Social and Psychological Perspectives,* vol. 1, eds. Richard H. Williams, Clark Tibbits, and Wilma Donohue (New Brunswick: Aldine Transaction, 1963).

are worth noting, which can create virtues and would provide conditions of *Ageing* well:[32]

1. Differentiated identity – independence;
2. Intimacy with another – selfless character;
3. Career consolidation – contribute to society;
4. Generativity – care for society;
5. Keeper of meaning – justice;
6. Integrity – wisdom.

If such agencies are imbibed into virtues, *Ageing* would never be a dreadful, worrisome or burden, but a gift, hope and wonder. This would embrace *Ageing* and the embracing *Ageing* would not only be an act of social responsibility of compassion and care, but also fulfilling the very Biblical and theological understanding of life as gift and *Ageing* as a blessing from God. In other words, it would theologically locate *Ageing* in their right place and help their agency of positive values to be recognised and considered as active participants in bringing the social fabric of community as a whole[33] rather than *Aged* people as mere recipients of younger one's compassion and care. This indeed would help go beyond carism and transform the social conditions from "*Ageing* to *Saging*."[34] This perhaps is an inescapable *theo-gerontological* task that would provide a strong impetus to enact the integrated understanding of *Ageing*. In order *geron-theology* make impact in breaking the myths of *Ageing* theologically, it is further necessary that a spirituality called – *Geron-theo-spirituality* is at hand as an important agency.

Geron-theo-spirituality

Geron-theo-spirituality here means not a mere supernatural oriented spirituality of *Aged* people, but the spirituality that transcends the religiosity or religionist spirituality. This encompasses both the explicit and implicit or supernatural and moral dimensions of spirituality. In order to make the concept clear perhaps it is important that the very terms "spirituality" and "spiritual theology" are first introduced and explained in brief.

Though it is difficult to make a sharp distinction between "spirituality" and "religion" or even "spirituality" and "spiritual", spirituality unlike religion

32 James L. Holly, "The Six Adult Life Tasks," *Southeast Texas Medical Associates*. Available at: http://www.setma.com/Your-Life-Your-Health/pdfs/the-six-adult-life-tasks.pdf. accessed January 3, 2017.

33 See, S. M. Golant, *Ageing in the right place* (New York: Health Profession Press, 2015).; A. E. Scharlach and K. Diaz Moore, "*Ageing in place*," in V. L. Bengtson & R. A. Settersten, eds., *Handbook of Theories of Ageing* (New York: Springer, 2016), 407–425.

34 Zalman Schachter-Shalomi and Ronald S. Miller, *From Age-ing to Sage-ing: A Revolutionary Approach to Growing Older* (New York, NY: Time Warner Books, 1997), 5.

refers to a more individual, personal, non-institutionalised search for the sacred. Taken originally from an ecclesiastical setting, spirituality refers to more than what happens in an institutional church. It is an abstract, sensitizing concept that points to a realm of human experience involving awareness of being and transcending purely personal, self-centered viewpoints.[35] It is "a belief in a power operating in the universe greater than oneself, a sense of interconnectedness with all living creatures, and an awareness of the purpose and meaning of life and the development of personal values."[36] But at the same time, it is also a "positive relationship with various measures of life satisfaction, psycho-social wellbeing, both physical and mental health, and is helpful in the quest for meaning and purpose in life."[37] Therefore, the common definition of Christian spirituality recognizes the frailty of human life while acknowledging humanity's ability to participate in God's work on earth that extends to life hereafter. "Spirituality", according to Alister McGrath, "thus refers to a lived experience of God, and the life of prayer and action which results from this; however, at the same time it cannot be conceived apart from the theological beliefs which undergird that life."[38] Perhaps, as per the dialectic Christian theological thought, spirituality holds the tension of life's paradoxes – the mystery and immanence of God, the evidence of evil and loss in the world with the transformational power of love, the hope of meaning while living with despair in suffering, and the beauty of what is commonly perceived as sacred and profane.

To be self-critical, too often theology is a mere means to an end – a search to find the right answer to a logical question.[39] It is often head knowledge of God rather than personal encounter with God. Contrarily, theology is all about life of love and relationships. It is rooted in one's purest experience of existence. It is a deep spiritual encounter and engagement with God in everyday practices and experiences of life.[40] It is therefore impossible to separate theology and

35 Atchley, *Spirituality and Ageing...,* 147.

36 Steven D. Ehrlich, "Spirituality," *University of Maryland Medical Center*, November 6, 2015. Available at: http://umm.edu/health/medical/altmed/treatment/spirituality.; Robert C. Atchley, *Spirituality and Ageing* (Baltimore, MD: John Hopkins University Press, 2009), 5. accessed June 10, 2020.

37 Helen Lavretsky, "Resilience and Ageing: From Conceptual Understandings to Opportunities for Enhancement," *The Gerontologist* 55, no. 4 (2015): 749.

38 Alister E. McGrath, *Christian Spirituality: An Introduction* (Oxford: Wiley-Blackwell 1999), 110.

39 Mary A. Pandiani, "*Ageing* Gracefully: The Art of Elegant Kenosis," *Doctor of Ministry*. 220, George Fox University (2017). Available at: http://digitalcommons.georgefox.edu/dmin/220 accessed, 29/08/2020 accessed, June 10, 2020.

40 Helen Lavretsky, "Spirituality and *Ageing*," *Ageing Health* 6, no. 6 (December 2010): 754. Available at: http://www.medscape.com/viewarticle/740654. accessed June 10, 2020.

spirituality. In fact, this is what the *theo-spirituality* is. Spirituality thus is best understood as a "concept that sensitizes... to a region of human experience and tells...generally what to look for in that region"[41] This understanding of spirituality indeed has closer affinity to gerontology than religion, as it matches the richness and complexity that it has in the everyday worlds of most of the *Aged* people.[42] As *Aged* people face more existentially oriented issues, they are more inclined to have interest in such spirituality than mere religion. What connects the *Aged* people is the consideration of what is sacred, which allows them recognition of a higher power, a transcendent reality, without adhering to the negative associations attached to religions.[43]

This may sound other-worldly, only concerned with what happens in spiritual realms, but its practices are closely related to daily affairs of life here and now – a*geron-theo-spirituality*, which bridges the relationship between not only God and the person *Ageing* but also the entire community. It begins with accepting of life as a gift from God, in which a person recognizes the wonder of life and believes in God with responsive spiritual practices within whatever context he/she encounters in. For theologically, human *Ageing* is inseparably connected with God, human person and faith of a person in God. It is towards realising the meaning of life in God.

From the spiritual dimension perhaps it is true that "when physical age goes down, the spiritual age goes up."[44] This can be understood through yet another concept called – *gero-transcendence* coined by Lars Tornstam.[45] The idea behind the concept is that the *Aged* people begin to see life from a decidedly positive angle through reflection on their experiences. On the one hand, they acknowledge and feel about their previous negative experiences, but on the other hand, appreciations for lessons they learn from them. Such acceptance of negative experience in life accompanied by review of life[46] leads a person to "... a shift in meta-perspective, from a material and rational vision to a more cosmic and transcendent one, normally followed by an increase in

41 Robert C. Atchley, *Spirituality and Ageing* (Baltimore, MD: John Hopkins University Press, 2009), 5.

42 Atchley, *Spirituality and Ageing...,* 149.

43 Brian J. Zinnbauer, Kenneth I. Pargament, and Allie B. Scott, "Emerging Meanings of Religiosity and Spirituality: Problems and Prospects," *Journal of Personality* 67, no. 6 (December 1999): 903-904.

44 MacKinlay, E. *The Spiritual Dimension of Ageing*. London: Jessica Kingsley Publishers, 2001.

45 Lars Tornstam, *Gerotranscendence: A Developmental Theory of Positive Ageing* (New York, NY: Springer Publishing Co., 2005), 3.

46 Constance McCloy, "Gerotranscendence Offer Reflection Acceptance for Elders," Indiana: University of Indianapolis, 2009. Available at: http://www.all-things-aging.com/2009/06/gerotranscendence-offers-refl ection.html. accessed December 12, 2019.

life satisfaction."[47] A conviction here is that *Aged* people are not mere passive receptors of spirituality, but active contributors. Their spirituality can open up a holistic spiritual atmosphere in the community. For various researches on the role of religion and spirituality on *Ageing* show that spirituality is not only part and parcel of "*Ageing* well", "Active *Ageing*", "Graceful *Ageing*", "Successful *Ageing,*"[48] but also wellbeing of community as a whole. For in such spirituality people find self-awareness and meaningful relationships and sense of belongingness. And in order to transcend the negative image of *Ageing*, there is therefore necessity that a deeper – *geron-theo-spirituality* becomes part of people's daily life, which will not only serve as a beacon of identity, but a dignity and human worth of *Aged* people. For spirituality in the true sense of the term is not only an agency to address the sacred matters of heart and soul, but are reservoirs of finding meaning and purpose in existential life which not only *Aged* people constantly crave and search for,[49] but every human person.

To justify farther the argument, it is well expressed by Mowat that "By the time one age, ego slowly goes off. When ego goes off, the power of spirituality emerges out of a natural desire for meaning in life."[50] The notion of "connectedness" with self, others, nature, and that which transcends all of these – is a widely accepted meaning of the term "spirituality"[51] that very well resonance with the heart cry of *Aged* people longing for relationships and connectedness. But more than these, *geron-theo-spirituality* serves as a foundation of the proposed *theo-gerontology* and provides not only means for *Ageing* well, but reservoir of spiritual resources for building inclusive and *geron*-embracive community where all have space to co-exist and live in peace and harmony.

---

47 L. Tornstam, "Gerotranscendence: A Reformulation of the Disengagement Theory," *Ageing: Clinical and Experimental Research*, 1/1 (1989): 60 [55 – 63].

48 Holly Nelson-Becker, "Research in Spirituality, Religion, and *Ageing*: An Emerging Area," *British Society of Gerontology* (July 2011): 1. Available at: http://www.britishgerontology.org/DB/gr-editions-2/generations-review/research-in-spirituality-religion-and-*Ageing*-an-eme.html. Accessed June 20, 2020.; S. B. Laditka et al., "Attitudes about *Ageing* well among a diverse group of older Americans: implications for promoting cognitive health," *Gerontologist* 49/1 (2009): S30-S39.; G. Y. Iwamasa and M. Iwasaki, "A New Multidimensional Model of Successful *Ageing*: Perceptions of Japanese American Older Adults," *Journal of Cross-Cultural Gerontology* 26/3 (2011): 261-278.

49 Neil Krause, "Deriving a Sense of Meaning in Late Life: An Overlooked Forum for the Development of Interdisciplinary Theory," in *Handbook of Theories of Ageing,* ed. Vern Bengtson, et al. (New York, NY: Springer Publishing Company, 2009), 101.

50 Harriet Mowat, "*Ageing*, Spirituality and Health," *Scottish Journal of Healthcare Chaplaincy* 8/1 (2005): 5.

51 Elizabeth MacKinlay, *Ageing, Disability and Spirituality: Addressing the Challenge of Disability in Later Life* (London/Philadelphia: Jessica Kingsley Publishers, 2008), 12.

Conclusion

The need of the hour in testing times such as ours today is an epistemic reversal in understanding the reality of *Ageing* by which creating a more *Ageing*-friendly family, community, society, and Church becomes possible. In this noble vision, theology cannot, but raise a dissent voice through counter-cultural theological postures, and challenge the forces that create de-meaning images and de-humanizing experiences of many vulnerable *Aged* people. Such theological challenges and postures surely would create a space where a graceful *Ageing* experience becomes a reality in society in general and the Church in particular.[52] Though the proposed *geron-theology* is not a concrete theological piece, it is anticipated that this would give direction towards such a vision. This possibly would pave a way for likeminded theologians and social scientists to think and reflect further to the deeper social realities and theological truths in *Ageing* so as to de-mythologize not only socially constructed myths, but also theological ones. This would possibly inspire to recognize the theologically rich agency of *Aged* people; and thereby the marginalised and excluded vulnerable *Aged* people are placed in their right place. The *geron-theology* seasoned with *geron-theo-spirituality* would in a small way help change not only the notion of *Ageing* as terror and dreadful and create a space for a blessed experience of *Ageing well*, but over and above, this would help understand *Ageing* as a divine design for humanity and human society. Indeed, the selfless *geron-transcendence*, the childlike harmless hearth and mind, and the self-transcendent spiritual qualities such as truthfulness, straightforwardness, innocence, honesty, sincerity, humility and decency of *Aged* people are truly the kingdom values that can create a community of love, justice, peace and harmony. In summing, using Jesus' words on the agency of children, let me conclude with a resilient affirmation that "unless one becomes old, he/she cannot become part of the kingdom of God!" and "without children and *Aged* people, it is impossible to have a peaceful community and human society as a whole!"

52 Cf. Robert Carlson, "A Theology of *Ageing* and a Vision for the Church," *Faith Formation and Spirituality of Ageing*: *Episcopal Church*, ESMA, April 1998, 61-62. Available at: http://www.episcopalchurch.org/files/2_faith_formation__spirituality_of_*Ageing*.pdf. accessed June 10, 2020.

Contributors

Rev. Dr. M. Peter Singh, an ordained minister of the Church of South India serves as Professor in the Department of Communication at Gurukul Lutheran Theological College & Research Institute, Chennai. Email: *mpetersingh@gmail.com*

Rev. Dr. John Samuel Ponnusamy, an ordained minister of the Church of South India serves as Professor of Old Testament and the Principal of Gurukul Lutheran Theological College & Research Institute, Chennai. Email: *johnsamuelgltc@gmail.com*

Dr. Aravind Jeyakumar Moniraj is a member of the Methodist Church in India and currently serves as Associate Professor and HOD of Old Testament at Gurukul Lutheran Theological College & Research Institute, Chennai. Email: *aravindjkl@gmail.com*

Rev. Nagayasamy N. S. Samuel is an ordained minister of TELC and currently serves as an Assistant Professor in the Department of Old Testament and Registrar of Gurukul Lutheran Theological College & Research Institute. Email: *nagaiya@gmail.com*

Rev. Dr. Shanthi S. Monica, an ordained minister of the Baptist Church, serves as Associate Professor in the Department of New Testament and the Dean of External Studies at Gurukul Lutheran Theological College & Research Institute, Chennai. Email: *monicashanthi@gmail.com*

Rev. Dr. Edwin Jebaraj is an ordained minister of the CSI Kanyakumari Diocese and currently serves as Associate Professor and HOD of New Testament at Gurukul Lutheran Theological College & Research Institute, Chennai. Email: *edwinjebaraj2013@gmail.com*

Rev. Dr. Babu C. is a member of CSI, Karnataka Central Diocese and currently serves as Associate Professor and HOD of History of Christianity at Gurukul Lutheran Theological College and Research Institute, Chennai. Email: *babucnaik47@gmail.com*

Rev. Dr. S. David Joseph Raj is an ordained minister of the CSI Kanyakumari Diocese, currently serves as Assistant Professor in the Department of History of Christianity at Gurukul Lutheran Theological College & Research Institute, Chennai. Email: *davidsjr1976@gmail.com*

Ms Rebeca Azariah is a member of CSI, Madras Diocese and serves as Assistant Professor in the Department of Missiology at Gurukul Lutheran Theological College & Research Institute, Chennai. Email: *rebecca_azariah20@yahoo.com*

Rev. Dr. K. Vijayan is an ordained minister of Evangelical Church of India and currently serves at Gurukul Lutheran Theological College & Research Institute, Chennai as Associate Professor and HOD of the Department of Missiology. Email: *revvijayan@gmail.com*

Rev. Dr. Giri K. is an ordained minister of the Assemblies of God in India currently serves as Associate Professor and HOD of Religion at Gurukul Lutheran Theological College & Research Institute, Chennai Assemblies of God in India. Email: *girikjohn@rediffmail.com*

Rev. Dr. Wilson Paluri, an ordained minister of the Church of North India, Durgapur Diocese serves as Associate Professor in the Department of Religion at Gurukul Lutheran Theological College & Research Institute, Chennai. Email: *wilsonpaluri@gmail.com*

Dr. D. Samuel Sounderaraj Singh is a member of Church of South India, Madras Diocese and currently serves as Assistant Professor in the Department of Communication at Gurukul Lutheran Theological College & Research Institute. Email: *dsamuels4@gmail.com*

Rev. Dr. Mervin Shinoj Boas is an ordained minister of the CSI Cochin Diocese and currently serves as Associate Professor in the Department of Christian Theology & Ethics at Gurukul Lutheran Theological College & Research Institute, Chennai. Email: *molyboas@gmail.com*

Rev. Dr. Nelavala Gnana Prasuna is an ordained minister of South Andhra Lutheran Church currently serves as Associate Professor in the Department of Christian Theology and Women Studies at Gurukul Lutheran Theological College & Research Institute, Chennai. Email: *ngpsalc@gmail.com*

Rev. Dr. J. Daniel Kirubaraj, is an ordained minister of Arcot Lutheran Church, currently serving in Gurukul Lutheran Theological College & Research Institute, Chennai as Professor and HOD of Communication. Email: *daniel4uin@yahoo.co.in*

Rev. Dr. Songram Basumatary is an ordained minister of Northern Evangelical Lutheran Church currently serving as Professor and HOD of Christian Theology & Ethics at Gurukul Lutheran Theological College & Research Institute. Email: *songramb@yahoo.co.in*

List of Books by Gurukul Publications & Faculty

1. *Embracing Childhood-Embodying Childness: Re-locating Children in Church and Society* -Songram Basumaary & -Gladson Jathanna (eds.)
2. *Migration in Perspectives* (2018) -Songram Basumatary (ed.).
3. *Transforming Reformation* (2017) -Songram Basumatary (ed.)
4. *Child Rights: A Theological Exploration* (2011) -Samuel W. Meshack (ed.)
5. *Critical Pedagogy & Theological Education* (2010) -Samuel W. Meshack (ed.)
6. *Communication of the Gospel: in the Context of Globalisation, Religious Pluralism & Nationalism* (2002) -Samuel W. Meshack & -Evon de Heyde (eds.)
7. *Communication in Voluntary Action* (2000) -Samuel W. Meshack
8. *Women, Church and Society* (1999) -Prasanna Kumari (ed.)
9. *Women in Indian Culture* (1999) -Katti Padma Rao
10. *Dalit Women's Experience: A Theological Imperative for Indian Feminist Theology* -Prasanna Kumari (ed.)
11. *Building God's Kingdom on Earth: Writings in Honour of D. W. Jesudoss* (1999) -Samuel W. Meshack (ed.)
12. *Gender in Contemporary India* (1998) -Prasanna Kumari
13. *Christian Gurus: A Study on the Life and Work of Christian Charismatic Leaders in South India* (1998) -Werner Hoerschlelman
14. *Frontiers of Dalit Theology* (1997) -V. Devasahayam (ed.)
15. *Prejudice: Issues in Third World Theologies* (1996) -Andreas Nehring (ed.)
16. *Contemporary Reflections of the Faith of Our Mothers & Fathers: Personal Witness*-Vol. 2 (1995) -P. Victor Premasagar (ed.)

17. *Communication: A Discipline in Distress* (1995) -K. E. Eapen
18. *Caste and Alternative Culture* (1995) -Katti Padma Rao
19. *Contemporary Reflections of the Faith of Our Mothers & Fathers: Personal Witness*-Vol. 1 (1994) -M. Mani Chacko (ed.)
20. *Ecology: A Theological Response* (1994) -Andreas Nehring (ed.)
21. *A Reader in Feminist Theology* (1993) -Prasanna Kumari (ed.)
22. *Abortion: The Agony & the Aftermath* (1992) -Prasanna Kumari
23. *Churchless Christianity* (1991) -Herbert E. Hoefer
24. *Ecology & Development: Theological Perspective* (1994) -Daniel D. Chetti (ed.)
25. *A Reader in Dalit Theology* (1990) -Arvind P. Nirmal (ed.)
26. *Heuristic Explorations* (1990) -Arvind P. Nirmal
27. *Towards a Common Ideology* (1989) -Arvind P. Nirmal & -V. Devasahayam (eds.)
28. *Violence and Non-violence* (1989) -D. W. Jesudoss
29. *Dalits and Women: Quest for Humanity* -V. Devasahayam (ed.)
30. *Christian Fredrick Schwartz* -Daniel Jeyaraj (ed.)
31. *Fundamentalism and Secularism: The Indian Predicament* -Andreas Nehring (ed.)
32. *Curriculum for Communication Studies in Theological Education* -Samuel W. Meshack (ed.)
33. *Challenges to Media on Poverty Reporting* - Samuel W. Meshack (ed.)
34. *Empowering Society* -Prasanna Kumari (ed.)
35. *Feminist Theology: Perspective and Praxis* -Prasanna Kumari (ed.)
36. *Gender in Contemporary India* -Prassana Kumari (ed.)
37. *Liberating Witness* -Prasanna Kumari (ed.)
38. *A Missionary Congregation* -K. Rajaratnam (ed.)
39. *Ten Commandments and Today's Challenges* -K. Rajaratnam & -V. Devasahayam (eds.)